# JEWISH EXPLORATIONS OF SEXUALITY

EUROPEAN JUDAISM

*General Editor:* Jonathan Magonet
We are pleased to announce a multidisciplinary series of monographs
and essay collections, to be published in conjunction with Leo Baeck
College, exploring contemporary issues in Jewish life and thought.
As with the complementary journal *European Judaism,* it reflects the
wide range of academic, social, historical and theological areas that
are studied at Leo Baeck College with its multinational staff and student body and its unique position as the only progressive Jewish seminary operating in Europe.

Vol. 1: **Jewish Explorations of Sexuality**
*Edited by* Jonathan Magonet

Vol. 2: **Jewish Identity in Modern Times.**
*Leo Baeck and German Protestantism*
Walter Homolka

# JEWISH EXPLORATIONS OF SEXUALITY

*edited by*
Jonathan Magonet

***Berghahn Books***
Providence • Oxford

First published in 1995 by
**Berghahn Books**

Editorial offices:
165 Taber Avenue, Providence, RI 02906, USA
Bush House, Merewood Avenue, Oxford, OX3
8EF, UK

© Jonathan Magonet 1995

**Library of Congress Cataloging-in-Publication Data**
Jewish explorations of sexuality / edited by Jonathan Magonet.
        p.    cm. -- (European Judaism (Providence, R.I.) ; v. 1)
    Includes bibliographical references.
    ISBN 1-57181-868-5            -- ISBN 1-57181-029-3  pbk

    1. Sex--Religious aspects --Judaism. 2. Homosexuality--Religious
aspects--Judaism. I. Magonet, Jonathan, 1942-    . II. Series.
BM720.S4J48    1995                                    95-17237
296.3'8566--dc20                                          CIP


**British Library Cataloguing in Publication Data**
A catalogue record for this book is available from the British Library.

# Contents

# GLOSSARY

| | |
|---|---|
| *Aggadah* | Literally 'narrating' – early rabbinic Bible exegesis other than of a legal kind – including stories, ethics, folklore etc. |
| *Ashkenazi* | Jews originating from Central and Eastern Europe as distinct from 'Sephardi' Jews originating in Spain before the expulsion in 1492. |
| *Daven* | 'Praying' with full mental and physical involvement. |
| *Devekut* | A term from the Jewish mystical tradition, 'cleaving to God'. |
| *Get* | A Jewish divorce document. |
| *Goyim* | Literally 'nations', referring to non-Jewish people. |
| *Halakhah* | Jewish law. |
| *Hasidism* | Popular pietist and mystical movement that developed in Eastern Europe in the eighteenth century. An adherent is a *Hasid*, and his spiritual master is a *Tzaddik*, 'righteous one'. |
| *Havurot* | Gatherings of 'friends', the term was adopted for informal, egalitarian, religious communities, outside, or as independent units within, the formal synagogue. |
| *Hesed* | Hebrew term, variously translated as 'loving-kindness', 'love' or 'mercy' -signifying the binding loyalty between the partners in a covenantal relationship. |
| *Ketubah* | Jewish marriage document. |

| | |
|---|---|
| *Kiddush* | Literally 'sanctification', it refers particularly to the blessings recited over wine at the inauguration of the Sabbath. The term *Kiddush HaShem*, 'the sanctification of the divine name' refers to martyrdom. |
| Lubavitch | The town of origin and hence name of the largest *Hasidic* group. |
| *Mamzer* | Biblical term of uncertain meaning, used to refer to the child of a forbidden sexual union such as adultery or incest. (Often mistakenly translated as 'bastard'.) |
| *Mechitzah* | An artificial barrier in an Orthodox synagogue to separate men and women. |
| *Midrash* | 'Explanation' – rabbinic interpretation of the Bible of either legal (*Midrash Halakhah*) or homiletical (*Midrash Aggadah*) character, sometimes expressed in parables. |
| *Mikveh* | Jewish ritual bath. |
| *Mitzvah* | 'Commandment'. A divine command derived from the Hebrew Bible, though the term has a looser usage implying the doing of any good deed. |
| *Nachas* | Hebrew term meaning 'rest', used in Yiddish to mean 'pleasure', emotional ease. |
| *Nashim* | Hebrew term meaning 'women', also the title of a tractate of the Talmud. |
| *Niddah* | Hebrew term for 'menstruation'. |
| *P'ru u-r'vu* | 'Be fruitful and multiply', Genesis 1:28, God's command to all creatures, including human beings, to increase in numbers and fill the earth. |
| *Pesach* | The Passover festival. |
| *Shaatnez* | The mixing of animal and plant fibres in a single garment which is forbidden under Jewish law. |
| *Shalom Bayit* | Hebrew for 'peace in the house'. |
| *Shekhinah* | 'The indwelling presence of God', sometimes seen as the feminine aspect of the deity. |
| *Shidduch* | A 'match', an arranged marriage. |
| *Shul* | 'Synagogue'. |
| *Siddur* | The 'order' of prayer, hence the term for the prayerbook that contains it. |

| | |
|---|---|
| *Simchah* | 'Joy', hence the term for a celebration with a party. |
| Talmud | (Teaching) compilation of the commentaries of the rabbis on the Mishnah, the 'Oral law', from the second to the fifth century, covering both religious and civil matters. |
| *Tephilin* | Phylacteries – two boxes containing biblical verses worn on the head and arm during morning prayers. |
| Torah | (Teaching) The Five Books of Moses (Pentateuch). The term is also used to mean the whole of the Bible and subsequent Jewish teaching. |
| *Tzaddik* | See *Hasidism.* |
| *Tzedakah* | Literally 'righteousness', it is the term for 'charity' i.e. that which is someone's right to receive. |
| *Tzitzit* | Fringes to be worn on the edge of garments. |
| *Yeshivah* | Traditional Jewish 'academy' where Talmud is studied. |
| *Yom Tov* | Literally 'a good day', a day containing a religious festival. |
| *Yom Kippur* | The Day of Atonement, the most solemn day of the Jewish festival calendar, a twenty-four hour fast in which Jews pray for the forgiveness of their sins. |
| *Zohar* | 'Splendour' – the central document of Jewish mysticism, an esoteric commentary on the Pentateuch. Compiled in the thirteenth century it contains earlier material. |

# INTRODUCTION

*Rabbi Dr Jonathan Magonet*

This book is based on a series of lectures held at the Leo Baeck College in the autumn of 1993. The model for the series was a regular summer lecture programme at the College under the general title 'Judaism and Psychotherapy'. This had been conceived as a kind of dialogue opportunity for Jews engaged in classical Rabbinic studies and those who worked in the areas of psychotherapy and counselling. For over twenty years the College had pioneered a course in Pastoral Care and Counselling Skills for its Rabbinic students that spanned the whole of their five-year study programme to Ordination. Some graduates had gone on to obtain qualifications as psychotherapists and were either practising in this field or utilising their skills and insights in the counselling area of their congregational work.

From the same group that started the Pastoral Care and Counselling Skills programme had emerged the Raphael Centre, a Jewish counselling service. However in its early days, whenever Raphael advertised for clients, it tended instead to receive applications from psychotherapists, who 'just happened' to be Jewish, who wished to offer a voluntary session to the Centre. Many had felt quite remote from their Jewish roots for much of their lives, had made a contribution to the 'non-Jewish world' through their professional work, but now felt the need to offer some kind of 'service' to the Jewish community, as a possible first step towards re-entering a relationship with it. In some cases it was a kind of late-in-life spiritual quest that could hardly even be expressed. It soon became evident that there was an audience for a dialogue with Judaism, provided that the 'official' Jewish partners respected the skills and breadth of knowledge brought by the therapists and were open to a mutual learning experience. In such a context it became possible to present materials from Jewish tradition, contemporary Jewish life and the range of psychotherapeutic disciplines, and explore overlapping insights, shared or conflicting values.

The College set up the series jointly with the Raphael Centre and over several years fostered a lively debate which led also to the publication of a number of special editions of the College's journal *European Judaism*, the book *Soul Searching*, edited by Rabbi Howard Cooper, and innumerable personal encounters and journeys for those who took part. The model was successful precisely because those representing 'Judaism' were open to learn from the 'non-Jewish Jews' who provided both the lectures and, to a large extent the audience. Together we gained a fund of insights into contemporary Jewish issues: the long-term experiences of Holocaust survivors and the impact on the second generation; the reality and nature of problems within the Jewish community, such as child abuse and wife beating, that had for so long been concealed; an introduction to a vast array of techniques from art-therapy to re-birthing currently available for the exploration of the human mind; and new dimensions for Jewish studies through, for example, the psychological analysis of Biblical stories.

With this model in mind it seemed that there were many other areas of contemporarary Jewish existence that would benefit from such a dialogue framework. From there it was a short step to considering the subject of sexuality because of its obvious significance. Moreover, two particular contemporary issues demanded a major reassessment of Jewish thought and practice: the feminist movement whose insights require a re-examination of all pre-suppositions and structures of Jewish tradition and the 'coming out' of Jewish gays because of their challenge to fundamental assumptions about who belongs within Judaism and on what basis. So much of the Jewish debate in these and related areas seemed limited or frustrating, being polarised between attempts to manipulate classical texts that were often unsuited to the nature or complexity of the issues, and a straight humanistic approach that saw little value, if any, in Jewish tradition. A lot of information needed to be gathered and exchanged before any significant dialogue could take place. The series produced a number of excellent papers and generated a lot of interest. Publication became an obvious next step.

At this point I should probably note my own credentials in taking on this task. As a medical student I had certainly been made aware of the 'biology' and 'pathology' of human sexuality, though little was taught us in those days about the psychology of human relations or indeed very much about the variations in human behaviour. (I recall only one lecture about infertility where the lecturer advocated considerable precision in taking the case history. It seems that in about six per cent of cases of apparent infertility within marriage, sexual intercourse has never actually taken place because of ignorance on the part of the couple.) From my father, who was a medical hypnotherapist, working in the area of psychiatry and psychosomatic medicine, I learnt something about the variety of cases that came to his practice. I recall in particular his talking about homosexuals who would come to him asking to be 'cured', because of so much guilt and shame, not to mention the fear of legal action or blackmail, being associated with their life-style. He had experimented with some kind of hypnosis-based re-conditioning but recognised that in many cases it was useless. So his policy was to help the homosexual accept the reality of his situation and gain the self-confidence to live with it. I am sure that this openness to the varieties of human nature and experience had an important impact on my own views and affected my approach to Jewish teachings when I began my Rabbinic studies at Leo Baeck College.

I soon discovered the disjunction between much of what I learned of 'official' Jewish values and the range of contemporary human experience and reality. The gap was well expressed by a colleague who pointed to the difference between the generalisations that might be given from the pulpit about, for example, Jewish family life, and the often very different advice that was given in the privacy of the Rabbi's study. This 'splitting' has never been acceptable – human realities continue to be more interesting and urgent than either theological formulations or Jewish legal pronouncements. A new meeting ground, with a different kind of basis, seemed essential.

Perhaps, in the case of Jewish law, I was still influenced by the experience as a child of glancing through the *Code of Jewish Law,* given to me as a Barmitzvah present. Inevitably I turned to Volume 4, chapter 151: 'The Crime of Causing the Effusion of Semen in Vain and Remedies for those Who were Caught in this Trap'.

> It is forbidden to cause in vain the effusion of semen, and this crime is severer than any of the violations mentioned in the Torah. Those who commit fornication with their hands and cause the vain effusion of semen, not only do they violate a grave prohibition, but they are also to be banned; and concerning them it is said: 'Your hands are full with blood' (Isaiah 1:15); and is analogous to the killing of a person ... Occasionally as a punishment for this children die while young, God forbid, or they become wicked, while he himself becomes poverty-stricken.

This must have had an effect on me at the time because I remember my father taking me aside to discuss masturbation and reassuring me that it was perfectly harmless and a normal part of growing up. The conflict between the text and my experience reinforced my feelings that the Orthodox Judaism I had grown up in was a long way from my own life, though I was in no position at the time to place such Jewish laws into an historical or other context. It was the influence of people whom I came to recognise as my 'teachers' that brought me back to recognising my own religious commitment and the need to express this through Judaism, but Judaism viewed with highly critical eyes.

From my days in the Reform youth movement in the UK, I remember two incidents that awoke an interest in the difficulty of reconciling Jewish attitudes to sexuality and contemporary reality. The first was an invitation to speak to a youth group in the early 1960s about Jewish sexual values. What little I had read at the time did not seem very helpful. Classical Jewish teaching assumed a society where marriages were arranged from childhood and there was virtually no gap between reaching adolescence and marrying (a subject touched upon in David Biale's paper in relation to the Hasidic court). The reality of our own open society, of relatively late marriage and that after much experimentation, seemed remote from the traditional view, with little guidance available. Driving up to the conference in Manchester, I stopped at a service station. In the toilet someone had scribbled on the newly installed condom machine, itself a sign of the changing times: 'Buy me and stop one!' It was a great line with which to begin my talk, something, I suppose, about the need to establish a 'caring relationship', but symptomatic of the conflict between traditional assumptions and those of today.

(Some thirty years later, while preparing this introduction, I was intrigued to come across the following passage by Chief Rabbi Jonathan Sacks quoted in the *Jewish Chronicle* (May 13, 1994, p 24):

> We have abdicated the teaching of clear and shared moral rules. We have given our children freedom but not guidance, condoms instead of sexual restraint. When they most need us, we are not there. It sometimes seems as if we care more about threatened wildlife and rain forests than about our own children, whose own human environment has been systematically degraded since the Sixties.)

The other moment that radically altered my experience came early in the 1960s when I was driving a friend, a recently ordained Rabbi, to conduct a service. He casually mentioned something about being homosexual and the difficulties that he was currently experiencing. Why he chose that particular moment to tell me I do not know – possibly some kind of death wish given my extreme difficulty in keeping control of the car!

My immediate thought was of my father's reactions to some of the more bizarre experiences told to him in his consulting room: a straight-faced calm acceptance before the patient, following which

he would excuse himself briefly, and come out and unload his astonishment and disbelief to my mother who acted as his secretary. He
would then return and continue the session with appropriate objec-
tivity. So I suppose I nodded as if such a revelation was old hat and
invited him to tell me more.

What emerged in various discussions over a period of time as I
listened to his stories was an awareness of the appalling suffering he
had experienced because of his homosexuality. The confusion and
uncertainty in his earlier years, the loneliness, isolation and lack of
anyone to talk it over with, the fear of disgrace, let alone the law, the
first tentative explorations of an underground gay world which, at
the time, was itself distorted and sometimes highly dangerous
because of the need for secrecy, and the first experience of a kind of
liberation in Amsterdam. I learned, too, that the pragmatic Amsterdam municipality had created a licensed society for homosexuals as
a way of tackling the high suicide rate within that population. I think
that this sealed for me the distinction between the supposed morality of Jewish, and for that matter Christian and British attitudes, and
the utter immorality of the treatment of gays. It ceased to be a theoretical matter and became an individual story of suffering and
pain, together with a realisation that this same person was a significant spiritual teacher, perhaps the more so because of the suffering
he had experienced.[1]

Some years later I was introduced to the story of Jacob Israel De
Haan (1881–1924), the Dutch poet and journalist. Though ultra-
orthodox, he suffered throughout his life from attempting to square
this with his homosexuality. He emigrated to Palestine in 1913 where
he was assassinated in mysterious circumstances. He is the subject of
Arnold Zweig's novel, *De Vriendt Goes Home*. In his poems he
expresses the anguish of his situation:

*All Is God's*
Man has separated lust and sorrow.
But God holds them together like day and night.
I know lust. I know intense suffering.
I praise God's one name.

*God's Gifts*
My most pious songs have I written
On rising from my sinful bed.
God has given me a wealth of sins,
And God alone has saved me from my sins.[2]

---

1. An excellent description of the experience of a Rabbi coming to recognize the difficult situation of gays in the Jewish community can be found in Rabbi Janet
Marder's ground-breaking article 'Getting to Know the Gay and Lesbian Shul' *(The
Reconstructionist* October; November 1985, 20–25).
2. Translated by David Soetendorp in *European Judaism* Vol. 5,2 p. 10.

My original intention on graduating from medical school and completing my 'house jobs' (internship) had been to enter Leo Baeck College to study for the Rabbinate, and then combine it with Psychiatry, the 'family business' in which I had long taken an interest. In the event Rabbinic studies led to the Bible and a slightly different career, though some therapists have pointed to the similarities between the 'close-reading' of a text and 'reading' the 'story' of a client in therapy. The 'Judaism and Psychotherapy' series at the College was my own way of keeping up some sort of link between these two disciplines and, as already indicated, a logical extension of the dialogue process was to apply it to a subject like sexuality.

Even a superficial examination of the field indicates that there are innumerable disciplines that need to be introduced and a vast area of materials to be mastered.[3] I began preparing this volume aware of my limited qualifications to do so, a view reinforced as the search for topics and writers has continued. So this is the book of an inquisitive individual pleased to be able to assemble a number of significant contributions to some aspects of the topic and aware of much else that needs to be pursued in exploring the particular Jewish contribution to our thinking about sexuality this century.

## Jewish Explorers of Sexuality

Before looking at the actual contents of the book I would like to point to a phenomenon that has intrigued me since first thinking about this subject matter during my Rabbinic studies, namely the astonishing contribution made to our knowledge of sexuality this century by certain pioneers in this area of Jewish origin. This section is simply a way of noting three in particular whose insights or biography deserve more attention. To what extent their Jewish origin, or in some cases, their Jewish situation in society or fate, were impor-

3. Among the more obvious topics that could be covered are child sexual abuse and its aftermath in adult life; abortion and the debate about the 'right to life'; circumcision; different forms of 'intersexuality'; the nature of marriage and its breakdown, including phenomena like partner swapping, mistresses/lovers, the whole range of 'adjustments' between married couples to each other's sexual habits, etc; prostitution. A curious sidelight on the development of popular attitudes to sexuality in the UK in recent years has been the emergence of a number of Jewish women as 'Agony Aunts' in newspaper columns – in particular, for many years, Marjorie Proops, but also Wendy Greengross, Anna Raeburn and Claire Rayner. Clearly the most successful exponent of popular sex education through the media is the phenomenal Dr Ruth Westheimer (1991). But the turn of the century had already seen a number of Jewish women whose struggle to improve social conditions for women included new attitudes towards sexuality – particularly Bertha Pappenheim and Emma Goldman. A section of the original lecture series focused on sexuality in contemporary Jewish literature and remains open for major exploration.

tant in their work is open to speculation, indeed reflects precisely the problematic nature of a book like this. Nevertheless no examination of the Jewish role in examining attitudes to sexuality in the twentieth century can ignore them.

Freud and his followers are clearly central and it would need several separate studies to present their insights and to try locate them, wherever relevant, within some kind of Jewish context.[4] However, Freud's Vienna was also the home of Otto Weininger (1880–1903), whose book *Sex and Character* and whose death by suicide at the age of twenty-three, had an extraordinary impact on Viennese Jewry. I first came across his name from Rabbi Dr Ignaz Maybaum who taught Jewish theology at Leo Baeck College from its inception and felt the need to examine the phenomenon of Weininger. In his book, *Creation and Guilt. A Theological Assessment of Freud's Father-Son Conflict,* he places Weininger very firmly in his Austrian environment.

> Otto Weininger committed suicide because he hated his human existence as a Jew with the fierceness of an anti-semite. He saw the two worlds, the Jewish world and the world which he admired, the ideal world created by artists and great politicians. The approaching end of the decaying Austrian Empire was not visible to Weininger. In the Vienna Opera he revelled in the works of Wagner, he revered Beethoven. The works of Goethe and Shakespeare were his Holy Scripture. The officers of the Hapsburgs in their impressive uniforms appeared to be heroes. An ideal world was not an illusion, it was there in contemporary history. Reality, as far as it was not affected by the ideal superstructure, was contemptible. Reality could be called, in the vein of Schopenhauer's idealism, 'Jewish', the attribute used with the venom of the anti-semite ...
>
> Weininger, although an expert in modern science, was a medievalist. In medieval society there was no place for two kinds of human beings: women and Jews. They were regarded as contemptible. Weininger wrote a book called Sex and Character in which he accepted the medieval scale of values. He proves 'scientifically' the inferiority of women, and as to the Jewish case he drew the same conclusion. He went to an exhibition of Beethoven manuscripts, and in this place, exalted in his eyes through the relics of the great master, he shot himself ... (Maybaum pp. 50–51)

In her book *The Feminine character: History of an Ideology,* Viola Klein similarly examines Weininger's world:

> It was a period of decline in which sensitive minds could anticipate the future fall and become aware of facts which to people in general still remained indistinct and inarticulate. They belonged to a group which by its very structure and mobility made them responsive to the slightest disturbances. All the authors mentioned [Freud, Weininger, Arthur Schnitzler, Karl Kraus] – and other representative writers of the decaying Austrian Empire, too – have in common that they are Jewish intellectuals with a bourgeois background. They were detached in a twofold sense.

---

4. Sander Gilman's exploration of Freud's views on race and gender provides a fascinating survey and invaluable bibliography of aspects of this theme.

As intellectuals they were detached to a considerable extent from their class, as Jews, who only a few generations ago were emancipated from the Ghetto, they were not completely absorbed or assimilated by the society of which they were a part ... (p. 67)

In spite of their revolutionary attitude against a world of taboos Weininger and Freud are still children of the passing age in so far as they accept the relation between the sexes, as it prevailed in their special bourgeois social milieu, as eternally valid. The type of masculine superiority and feminine passivity which they have in mind is linked up with experiences they were bound to have in the world in which they lived ... (p. 67)

The picture we thus gain is that of a woman who has but two possible social functions: that of mother and that of prostitute. She is in her spiritual no less than in her material standards entirely dependent on men. Her attitudes and judgments are formed by the men of her surroundings. She is not the master of her own will, and if she wants to obtain something she has to resort to indirect means. Her status is not acquired by virtue of her own individuality, but is conferred upon her by the man on whom she depends for her living. Her field of interests is limited, according to the social functions which she is called upon to perform. Convinced of her inferiority she feels uncertain and self-conscious in all other spheres outside her 'own'. But the very sphere which alone is assigned to her is, by Christian standards, considered to be vicious. She lacks the sense of her own value, the dignity which only personal achievements are able to confer ...

The analogy between many of her characteristic attitudes and those of Jews, which Weininger extensively elaborates, really exists, though in a different sense from the one he has in mind: it is the effect of a similar social position. Those attitudes are not, as Weininger would have it, innate characteristics, but the result of subordination. Any subject group which for generations has lived in close contact with the dominant class would develop – with variations, of course, according to circumstances and dispositions – similar psychological traits. (pp. 68–69)

No survey of Jewish contributions to the understanding of sexuality this century, and indeed the struggle for tolerance of the varieties of human sexual expression, would be complete without consideration of the work of Magnus Hirschfeld (1868–1935). Again I came first came across his name during the early years of my Rabbinic studies when a gay colleague referred affectionately to 'Tante Magnolia'. Hirschfeld was born in 1868 in Kolberg in Pomerania, his father was a doctor who had made a major contribution to the development of the town as a health resort. In his early years he was torn between his interests in medicine and in literature. He did pioneering work on alcoholism but early on began to explore the nature of homosexuality (being himself homosexual), transvestism and other sexual variants. As a founder member of the 'Scientific-Humanitarian Committee', he fought for reform of anti-homosexual legislation and this led him to collaborate with the Feminist movement to fight attempts to introduce anti-lesbian legislation. But his interests also included far wider areas of social reform. In 1919 he founded the

Institute for Sexual Science in Berlin, the first such centre in the world. As well as research into all aspects of human sexuality it provided psychological and medical therapy and marriage guidance. One of the first acts of the Nazis on coming to power in 1933, was to close the Institute down, his books, and even a bronze bust of him, were burnt. Hirschfeld went into exile in Paris and subsequently Nice where he died in 1935. During the 1920s Hirschfeld had been subject to anti-semitic attacks, including physical assault, particularly because of his part in promoting the first documentary film sympathetic to homosexuality, *Anders als die Andern*. In exile he compiled a book, based on his previous writings on Eugenics, condemning Racism:

> There is no difference between races, only between individuals. I can appeal to an experience which must be almost, if not quite, unrivalled, so numerous are the men and women from every part of the world who have consulted me about sexual matters. (quoted in Wolff, pp. 404–405)

He left a huge literary output and during his lifetime had a considerable influence world-wide on the study of sexuality and the broadening of attitudes. His life and work are explored by Charlotte Wolff (1986).

Equally significant, though tragically best remembered for the controversial nature of the theories of his later years of paranoia and persecution, is Wilhelm Reich (1897–1957). Yet again I came across his name during my student years at Leo Baeck College through the influence of the Vedantist, folklorist and Reichian analyst Leslie Shepard. Apart from major contributions to psychoanalysis in his earlier years, Reich's exploration of the relationship between sexuality and politics remains of fundamental importance. In 1931 in Berlin he started his Verlag fur Sexualpolitik (SexPol) which published practical and theoretical pamphlets. The psychoanalyst Marie Langer, herself of Viennese Jewish origins, writes about the impact of Reich's work:

> Sexpol was very important, although in the long run it was before its time ... Reich devoted himself to his work with a lot of zeal. Later, in Berlin, when he tried to create a movement within the Communist youth based on the demand for sexual freedom, at the same time as Nazism was on a dizzying ascent and Communism was experiencing very violent and direct confrontations, he obviously clashed with the Party and, finally, he broke with it. In practice he was mistaken in doing that.
> But in his analysis of the German family and the consequences of the sexual repression of women, he shows himself to be a pioneer of great brilliance. Today it is almost a platitude to say that the family, as an ideological tool, reproduces the subjects the state needs. At the time nobody except Reich would have said that. But a sexually repressed and frustrated mother is easily converted into being conservative, submissive to men, and dominating and repressive with children. These are the mothers who reproduced the subjects prone to obedience, and to a more or less sublimated homosexuality, which led them to submission to, and admiration for, a Fuhrer. (Langer, 1989, p.156)

Reich's ideas come nearer to home, in terms of the Jewish experience this century, when he writes in 1942 on the nature of German fascism:

> In Europe, the 'preservation of the family' had always been an abstract slogan behind which were hidden the most reactionary mentality and behavior ... The typical authoritarian German family, particularly in the country and small town, bred Fascist mentality by the million. This family created in the children a structure characterized by compulsive duty, renunciation and absolute obedience to authority which Hitler knew so splendidly how to exploit. By advocating the 'preservation of the family' and at the same time taking youth out of the family and putting them in its own youth groups, Fascism took into account *the fixation to the family as well as the rebellion against the family*. Because Fascism emphatically impressed on the people the emotional identity of 'family', 'state', and 'nation', the familial structure of the people could easily be continued in the Fascist, national one ...
>
> Hand in hand with the longing for 'purity of blood', i.e., liberation from sin, goes the persecution of the Jews. The Jews tried to explain or prove that *they too* were moral, that *they too* belonged to the nation, or that *they too* were 'German'. Anti-Fascist anthropologists attempted by way of skull measurements to prove that the Jews were *not* an inferior race. Christians and historians tried to point out that Jesus was of Jewish origin. But – it was not a matter of rational problems at all; that is, it was not a question of whether the Jews *too* were decent people, whether they were *not* inferior or whether they had *proper* skull sizes. The problem lay somewhere else entirely.
>
> When the Fascist says 'Jew', he means a certain irrational feeling. As one can convince oneself in every treatment, of Jews and Non-Jews, which penetrates deeply enough, the 'Jew' has the irrational significance of the 'money-maker', the 'usurer', the 'capitalist'. On a deeper level, 'Jew' means 'filthy', 'sensual', 'brutally lustful', but also 'Shylock', 'castrator', 'slaughterer'. The fear of natural sexuality is as deeply rooted in all humans as is the horror of perverse sexuality. Thus we can easily understand that the persecution of the Jews, so cleverly executed, stirred up the deepest antisexual defense functions of the antisexually brought up individual. Thus, the ideology of the 'Jews' made it possible to harness the *anticapitalist* as well as the *antisexual* attitudes of the masses and put them completely at the service of the Fascist machinery.
>
> *Unconscious longing for sexual happiness and sexual purity, plus simultaneous fear of normal sexuality and abhorrence of perverse sexuality, results in Fascist sadistic anti-semitism* ... (Reich, 1942, pp. 213–215)

In naming these figures I am indicating that there are major questions, from a Jewish perspective, about what led them to explore the theme of sexuality, the degree to which each of them related in some way, positively or negatively to Jews and Judaism, and the implications of at least some of their teachings for a contemporary Jewish sexual ethic. This last point leads us into an overview of what has been included in the book and some elements of the dialogue between Jewish tradition and modernity that need to be addressed.

## The Scope of the Book

The Rabbis of the Talmudic period were open to consulting with their contemporary 'experts' on any subject when formulating their debates and decisions. The greatest available knowledge was sought so that their decisions could be true reflections of the human reality created by God. Nor were they squeamish in asking questions about sexual practices or acknowledging the complexity of our sexual nature. From today's perspective we recognise the degree to which classical Rabbinic views were coloured by and indeed constrained by the patriarchal nature of their society. The record they left was self-evidently written 'by the boys for the boys'. Nevertheless within their own terms of reference they displayed an openness and curiosity, as well as a sense of justice, that led them to struggle as far as they could against the imbalance of power in Jewish law between men and women, that was presupposed in the earlier society out of which the Torah emerged. Today, as the inheritors of the vast range of Jewish law and lore, the options for change for a contemporary Orthodox Judaism are greatly restricted. Surprisingly, however, this limitation affects even some of the more 'progressive' branches of Judaism. The *Halakhic* (Jewish legal) categories of thought tend to dominate the debate among traditionalists and liberals alike, so it seems important to broaden the arena of discourse and bring in the kind of outside voices that would have been invited to teach the Rabbis in a previous age.

This was the general brief I gave to Micky Yudkin who set about organising the College's lecture/discussion series, and much of the subject matter of this book and a number of the articles arose out of the range of her contacts and the accident of availability of speakers on any particular topic.

Inevitably the question arises as to what a particular topic or speaker has to do with 'Judaism'. Does the accident of being Jewish make any difference to what the speaker has to say on some general topic like 'the myths of male or female sexuality'? My own answer is yes, insofar as we need partners for the dialogue and have to start the exploration somewhere. As part of the pattern of the lecture series, we tried to pair each speaker who came from the 'humanistic' tradition with a Rabbi to introduce the 'Jewish input', insofar as it was possible or relevant. But I must stress that this was meant to be a shared learning experience, for myself as much as for the audience, and this book is intended as a continuation of that process, a resource and reader to open up further debate. This also accounts for the variety of materials – ranging from academic papers to more popular accounts and clarifications to advocacy of certain ideas.

As the lecture series developed a number of themes and approaches began to emerge which are reflected in the sections of this book. Given this somewhat arbitrary initial framework I sought to fill gaps in areas that I felt needed at least an exploratory paper. The result has been the four sections that make up this book:

## In the Tradition

This section is particularly rich through having articles by five leading authorities on specialist areas of classical Jewish studies. The impact of feminism on the re-reading of Biblical materials is evident in the papers by Tikva Frymer-Kensky and Francis Landy respectively, as they explore the way in which the threatening 'anarchy' of sexuality is addressed within Biblical law and the use of misogynist imagery in prophetic literature. Daniel Boyarin introduces us to the Rabbinic concept of the two 'desires' within human beings, often expressed in terms of the sexual drive, which make up the basis of Rabbinic psychology. Sara Sviri shows how the biblical *Song of Songs* was viewed in Jewish mystical tradition, and David Biale explores the paradoxical tension in Hasidism between the commandment to be 'fruitful and multiply' and the equally strong pull towards asceticism.

## Homosexuality and Lesbianism

This is the area which most challenges traditional Jewish understandings of what is 'normal' and 'appropriate' Jewish sexual orientation and activity. It is also the point where traditional Jewish morality is tested against contemporary views. Some of the pieces reflect a personal witnessing, but all are rooted in the knowledge of Jewish tradition and the struggle to find ways of making it address this question in a fresh way.[5] One paper speaks from within the limitations imposed by a strictly Orthodox position (Alan Unterman) while others introduce broader categories to the debate (Mark Solomon, Rodney Mariner, Elizabeth Sarah, Sheila Shulman). Lionel Blue's paper was originally given as a lecture to the Gay Christian Movement in the UK and reverses conventional assumptions by asking what religious insights and values gays can offer to 'straight' society.

---

5. In this context tribute should be paid to the pioneering pamphlet *Jewish and Homosexual* by Dr Wendy Greengross published in 1982 by the Reform Synagogues of Great Britain, based on work begun in 1976 by Dr Greengross and a group of Rabbis and lay people.

   For a survey of the full range of the debate on homosexuality, particularly within the American Jewish movements, and a valuable bibliography, see Yoel H. Kahn 'Judaism and Homosexuality: The Traditionalist/Progressive Debate' in *The Journal of Homosexuality* Vol. 18 (3/4), pp. 47–82.

## Therapeutic Views on Sexuality

So much of our contemporary understanding of sexuality is derived directly or indirectly from the work of Sigmund Freud that this entire book could be made up with articles from the therapeutic perspective. It was the wish to broaden the boundaries of the subject and not restrict it to such an approach that led us in the original series to limit the contribution in this area. Much of the material in this field is highly technical and reflects a multiplicity of theoretical models. The more I looked for appropriate materials the more I recognized that a far more specialised book would be needed to do them justice. Instead I intended to restrict the papers to those originally delivered in the lecture series, (Sara Cooper and Sheila Ernst writing on ideas of female sexuality) however, during the course of my research I constantly came across the writings of Sander Gilman and was delighted at his readiness to contribute to the book.

## Tradition and Modernity

The closing section focuses on the way in which traditional Jewish views and modern issues live in uneasy relationship with each other.[6] John Cooper's article charts the period of transition using first-hand accounts of Jewish social life prior to the First World War. Hannah Rockman's paper was designed to give non-Jewish social workers an insight into the sexual behaviour of traditional Jews, and is complemented by the work of Eduardo Pitchon as a psychiatrist working with the Hasidic community in North London. New areas for exploration are being opened up daily through scientific advances in genetic engineering and Julia Neuberger addresses these issues. But what about 'normal' sexual relationships today? What values should underly them? Does Jewish tradition have something specific to offer? The papers by Arthur Waskow and Daniel Landes originated in the magazine *Tikkun*. Dr Waskow was initially unaware that his paper had been offered for comment to Rabbi Landes, as his response indicates. I am grateful to both of them and the editor of *Tikkun* for allowing their valuable exchange to be included. Finally Howard Cooper's imaginative re-reading of the Genesis story of Adam, Eve and the snake, offers a creative, witty and profound approach to the interface between sexuality and spirituality.

6. Among the few materials that offer some help in seeking a contemporary Jewish sexual ethic are Eugene Borowitz' *Choosing a Sex Ethic* (Schocken, New York 1969), three short articles under the general title 'Sex and Sexuality' by Hershel Matt, David Feldman and Arthur Green in *The Second Jewish Catalogue– Sources and Resources*, Compiled and Edited by Sharon Strassfeld and Michael Strassfeld (Jewish Publication Society of America, Philadelphia 1976, pp. 91–99) and Harold M. Schulweis' 'Sex and the Single God' in *The Reconstructionist* Vol. 47, 7, November 1981, pp. 17–26.

## Conclusion

This book is offered as a contribution to a variety of debates that need to be conducted within the Jewish world about our contemporary understanding of sexuality. If it offers any surprises it is in the extent to which, alongside the more conventional views of a positive attitude towards sexuality within the Jewish tradition, such a strong ascetic streak can be found. Howver, many of the articles reflect a contemporary 'paradigm shift' that we are still trying to cope with, from sexuality being subsumed within the framework of marriage and 'ownership', fertility and physical continuity, to sexuality freed from reproduction that is but one expression of a human relationship. Moreover a contemporary awareness of the variety of sexual relationships, the complexity of gender identity, the politics of sexuality and the subtle interrelationship between sexuality and spirituality, all bring insights and challenges to traditional Jewish attitudes and values. But the first sexual act in the Hebrew Bible, between Adam and Eve, is described using a verb meaning 'to know', which itself contains a multiplicity of dimensions; intellectual, experiential, emotional and spiritual. The essays in this book are reflections on all these dimensions and are a tribute to a Jewish curiosity about all aspects, and a respect for all the rich varieties, of human life.

## Bibliography

Solomon Ganzfried, *Code of Jewish Law (Kitzur Schulchan Aruch)* (Hebrew Publishing Company, New York, 1927)

Viola Klein, *The Feminine character: History of an Ideology* (Reprinted with an Introduction by Janet Sayer. Routledge, London, 1989 [1946])

Marie Langer, *From Vienna to Managua: Journey of a Psychoanalyst* (Free Association Books, London, 1989)

Ignaz Maybaum, *Creation and Guilt: A Theological Assessment of Freud's Father-Son Conflict* (Valentine, Mitchell. London, 1969)

Wihelm Reich, *The Discovery of the Orgone: The Function of the Orgasm*. Tr. by Theodore P. Wolfe (The Noonday Press, New York, 1961 [1942])

Ruth Westheimer (with Ben Yagoda) *All in a Lifetime* (Futura Publications, London, 1991).

Charlotte Wolff, *Magnus Hirschfeld: A Portrait of a Pioneer in Sexology* (Quartet Books, London, 1986)

# IN THE TRADITION

# LAW AND PHILOSOPHY
## The Case of Sex in the Bible*

*Tikva Frymer-Kensky*

For the modern scholar, ancient law offers many challenges and types of inquiry.[1] First and foremost, of course, it demands to be studied for itself, as a legal system of a society: how are problems adjudicated, what is to be done in the case of theft, what are the nature of property rights, and so forth? Second, it is a record of the socio-economic system of that society: what are the social classes, who holds the property and how, what are the economic concerns addressed by the laws? Third, it presents questions of intellectual history: where did a given law come from, what is its relationship to other legal systems, what if any is the inner development within that society itself? And above all, it is an intellectual mirror of the philosophical principles of a given society. Through a culture's laws, we can see its values and some of its basic ideas about the world. Sometimes, our only access into the mind-set of a culture is through its laws. This is the case with sex in the Bible.

Sex is inherently problematic. At once cultural and physical, it defies categorization. In pagan religions there is a mystique, expressed through the sacred marriage ritual, in which sex has an important role in the bringing of fertility. The sacred marriage also gave rise to songs and poems that provided for the expression and celebration of sexual desire in a religious setting. Furthermore, the goddess of sexual attraction imparts a divine aspect to erotic im-

---

\* This chapter is based on an article published in *Semeia* 45, 1989, 89–102.
1. For previous studies see Cosby (1985), Dubarle (1967), Larue (1983), and Perry (1982). This essay is based on my book *In the Wake of the Goddesses* (The Free Press: Macmillan, 1989).

pulse and a vocabulary to celebrate it and to mediate and diffuse the anxieties it may engender.

## Sex and the Biblical God

But what about the Bible? Whatever may have been the case in empirical Israel, all the pagan sexual trappings disappear in the Hebrew Scriptures. The God of the Bible is male, which would make it difficult for him to represent the sex drive to a male. Even more, the God of Israel is only male by gender, not by sex. He is not at all phallic, and cannot represent male virility and sexual potency. Anthropomorphic biblical language uses body imagery of the arm, right hand, back, face and mouth, but God is not imagined below the waist. In Moses' vision at Mount Sinai, God covered Moses with his hand until he had passed by, and Moses saw only his back (Exodus 33:23). In Elijah's vision, he saw nothing, and experienced only a 'small still voice' (1 Kings 19:12). In Isaiah's vision (chapter 6), two seraphim hid God's (or the seraphim's) 'feet' (normally taken as a euphemism), and in Ezekiel's vision (chapters 1–2), there is only fire below the loins. God is asexual, or transsexual, or metasexual (depending on how we view this phenomenon); but he is never sexed.

Nor does God behave in sexual ways. God is the 'husband' of Israel in the powerful marital metaphor. But there are no physical descriptions: God does not kiss, embrace, fondle, or otherwise express physical affection for Israel. By contrast, in the erotic metaphor that describes the attachment of Israel to Lady Wisdom, there is no hesitation to use a physical image, 'hug her to you and she will exalt you, she will bring you honour if you embrace her' (Proverbs 4:8). Wisdom is clearly a woman-figure, and can be metaphorically embraced as a woman. But God is not a sexual male, and so there can be no physicality.

God could not model sexuality, hence it could not be a part of the sacred order. In order to underscore this, God also does not grant sexuality, erotic attraction or potency. These are taken as matter-of-fact components of the universe and are not singled out as part of God's beneficence.

There is a concern to separate the sexual and the sacred. Before the initial revelation of God at Mount Sinai, Moses commanded Israel to abstain from sexual activity for three days (Exodus 19:15).[2]

---

2. The point of this command is to separate the sexual from the sacred experience. This purpose is often obscured by the unfortunate male-centred wording of the passage. God is reported as having commanded that the people wash and sanctify themselves and was their clothes, making preparations for the third day (Exodus

This temporal separation between the sexual and the sacred also underlies the story of David's request for food during his days of fleeing from King Saul, in which he assures Ahimelech that his men can eat hallowed bread because they have been away from women for three days (1 Samuel 21:4–5).

The priests, guardians of Israel's ongoing contact with the Holy, were to be conscientious in preserving a separation between Israel's priestly functions and attributes and any kind of sexuality. They were not celibate, a totally foreign idea, but their sexual activity had to be a model of controlled proper behaviour. The unatonable wrong of Eli's sons was sleeping with the women who came to worship; for this they lost forever their own and their family's right to be priests (1 Samuel 2:22–25). The priest's family also had to be chaste. His wife had to be a virgin, for he was not allowed to marry a divorcee. His daughters had a particular charge to be chaste while under their father's jurisdiction: he could not deliver his daughter into prostitution, and, should a priest's daughter be improperly sexually active, she was considered to have profaned *her father* and was to be burned.

Any sexuality was to be kept so far from temple service that even the wages of a prostitute were not to be given to a temple as a gift.[3] All hints of sexuality were kept far away from cultic life and religious experience.

The separation of sexuality and cult is also embedded in the impurity provisions of the sacral laws. Israel's impurity rules were intended to keep intact the essential divisions of human existence: holy and profane, life and death. They conveyed no moral valuation, and even doing a virtuous and societally necessary act, like burying the dead, would result in entering the impure state. There was also no danger involved in such 'impurity'; the impure individual was not expected to die or to become ill. Such impurities were characterised by two major features: the major impurities (which last a week) were contagious, in that all who come in contact with someone impure in this way will themselves become impure for a day. And all those who are

---

19:10–11). When Moses relayed this to the people, he added his own command, 'do not approach your wives' (Exodus 19:15). By this addition Moses explains how the people are to prepare for the third day, but he adds his own perspective, suddenly erasing half of the people, addressing only the men. It is interesting that the Bible records this as Moses' invention rather than God's; it sheds new light on the Deuteronomic injunction to the people not to add to the laws.

3. On the basis of the interpretation of the term *q'deshah*, 'holy one', as a cult prostitute, scholars have long argued the existence of sacred prostitution in Israel, which the Bible was trying to stamp out. More recent work has indicated that there is absolutely no evidence that a *q'deshah* was a prostitute, nor that any sexual rites ever existed in ancient Israel. In any event, the wages not to be vowed to the temple are those of a *zonah* which everyone agrees is an ordinary prostitute-for-hire, not attached to the temple.

impure are isolated ritually: they cannot come to the temple or participate in sacred rites for the duration of their impurity.[4] Under these
regulations, any man who has had a sexual emission, or anybody
who has engaged in sexual intercourse must wash and will nevertheless be ritually impure until that evening (Leviticus 15:16–18). In this
way, there was a marked temporal division between engaging in sexual activity and coming into the domain of the sacred.[5]

## Control of Sexual Action by Law

Sexuality has been desacralised. It has not been demonised or condemned. On the contrary, it is not given sufficient status and importance to accord it a conscious valuation, even a negative one. It is
talked about (or, most often, not talked about) as part of the social
realm, as a question of societal regulation. The proper sphere for
considering or mentioning sexuality was the law. The ideal state of
existence envisioned by the Bible is marriage.[6] The monogamous
nuclear family was established by God at the very beginning of
human existence: 'therefore a man leaves his father and mother and
cleaves to his wife and they become one flesh' (Genesis 2:24). Furthermore, 'he who finds a wife, he finds a good thing and gets favour
from the Lord' (Proverbs 18:22).[7] Within this marital structure, sexuality is not only permitted: it is encouraged. In God's description of
life in the real world, he tells Eve, 'your desire is for your husband,
and he shall rule you' (Genesis 3:16). Deuteronomy includes a pro-
vision for the exemption of a new bridegroom from campaigns for a

4. For a detailed discussion of these issues, see Frymer-Kensky (1983), Douglas (1966).
   My analysis is somewhat different from that of Mary Douglas' classic study in that
   she does not distinguish between the 'impurity' beliefs, which deal with a contagious state which is neither morally deserved nor dangerous to the individual and
   Israel's separate set of dangerous pollutions, a non-contagious state caused by mis-
   deeds which bring the perpetrator into the danger of divine sanction.
5. Menstrual taboos are also to some extent sexual taboos. In Israel, a woman was
   impure for seven days after the beginning of her menses. During this period, her
   impurity (as all impurity) was contagious, and could be contracted by anyone who
   touched her, or even sat in her seat. Intercourse with a menstruating woman was
   considered absolutely forbidden, and was sanctioned by the *karet* penalty, which
   means the belief that one's lineage would be extirpated. The reminder in menstruation of a sexual dimension of existence would not by itself account for the seven-
   day duration of the impurity, however. Another element is at play, the blood and
   its association with death, for contact with death also results in a week-long impurity. It is noteworthy that only intercourse with a menstruant results both in temporary impurity and in the divine sanction of *karet.*
6. That marriage was evaluated positively throughout the ancient Near East, see
   Lambert (1963).
7. For Proverbs, see Snell (1987). Snell notes the structural parallel to 8:33, in which
   Dame Wisdom says 'he who finds me finds life and gets favour from the Lord.'

year so that he may be free to cause his wife to rejoice (Deuteronomy 20:7, 24:5). The enjoyment of marriage is sexual as well as social:

> let your fountain be blessed;
> find joy in the wife of your youth –
> a loving doe, a graceful mountain goat,
> let her breasts satisfy you at all times;
> be infatuated with love of her always. (Proverbs 5:17–18)

And the wise man is encouraged to enjoy his marital sexuality.

Sexuality has a place in the social order in that it bonds and creates the family. The sex laws seek to control sexual behaviour by delineating the proper parameters of sexual activity – those relationships and time in which it is permissible. Sexual behaviour was not free. Despite the indubitable double standard in which adultery means sex with a married woman, men were also limited by the sex laws. In the case of homosexuality, men were more bound than women, since homosexuality was considered a major threat requiring the death penalty (whether real or threatened) and lesbian sex was not a matter of concern. The unequal definition of adultery results from the fact that for a man to sleep with a woman who belonged to some other household threatened the definition of 'household' and 'family'; for a married man to sleep with an unattached woman is not mentioned as an item of concern, and the very existence of prostitutes indicates that there were women with whom a man (married or unmarried) could have sexual experiences. This was not an unusual definition of adultery, and it has been suggested that this unevenness is the essence of male control over female sexuality, and that possibly it demonstrates a desire to be certain of paternity. Within Israel this treatment of adultery is not examined; it is part of Israel's inheritance from the ancient Near East and, like slavery and other elements of social structure, it is never questioned in the Bible.

The Pentateuchal laws also rule on sexual intercourse with a girl still living in her father's house, at which time she is expected to be chaste. According to Exodus 22:15–16, if a man seduced an unbetrothed girl he had to marry her; he has engendered an obligation that he cannot refuse, and must, moreover, offer the customary bride-price. Her father had the option to refuse her to him, in which case the seducer must pay a full virgin's bride-price. The assumption in this rule is that the father has the full determination of his daughter's sexuality, a situation also assumed in the two horrible tales of the abuse of this right, Lot's offering of his daughters to the men of Sodom (Genesis 18–19) and the man of Gibeah's offering of his daughter and the Levite's concubine to the men of Gibeah (Judges 19). These men were attempting to cope with an emergency situation in which they felt their lives at risk, but the narrative considers them within their rights to offer their daughters, and Lot, in particular, is considered the one righteous man in Sodom.

The obligation of a girl to remain chaste while in her father's house is underscored in Deuteronomy 22:20ff, which prescribes that a bride whose new husband finds her not to be a virgin is to be stoned, because 'she did a shameful thing in Israel, committing fornication while under her father's authority'. There is good reason to suspect that this law was not expected to be followed. According to the procedure laid out in Deuteronomy 22:13–14, after the accusation, the case was brought before the elders at the gate, and the parents of the girl produced the sheet to prove that she was a virgin; once they did this, the man was flogged, fined, and lost his rights to divorce her in the future. Since the parents had plenty of time to find blood for the sheets, it is unlikely that a bridegroom would make such a charge; if he disliked the girl he could divorce her. If he nevertheless made such a charge, she and her family would have to be very ignorant not to fake the blood. But the law certainly lays down a theoretical principle very important to Israel, viz., that a girl was expected to be chaste while in her father's house. Stoning, moreover, is a very special penalty, reserved for those offences which completely upset the hierarchical arrangements of the cosmos. In these cases, the entire community is threatened and endangered, and the entire community serves as the executioner.[8]

Stoning is also prescribed when a man comes upon a betrothed woman in town; in this case both are stoned; the girl because she did not cry for help (which would have been heard, since they were in town) and the man because he illicitly had sex with his neighbour's wife (Deuteronomy 22:23–24). The law assumes that the act was consensual: even though the word *'innah'* is often translated 'rape', it rarely corresponds to forcible rape, but rather implies the abusive treatment of someone else. In sexual contexts, it means illicit sex, sex with someone with whom one has no right to have sex.[9] The sense of the law about sex with a betrothed woman is that a girl, although

8. On stoning, see Finkelstein (1981). In addition to the two cases discussed here, stoning is used for the ox that gores a man to death (Exodus 21:12–14), one who lures others into idolatry (Deuteronomy 13:7–8), the disobedient son (Deuteronomy 21:18–21), the practitioner of child sacrifice (Leviticus 20:3d), a sorcerer or necromancer (Leviticus 20:27), blasphemer (Leviticus 24:10–11), violator of the Sabbath (Numbers 15:32–35), and, by inference, the seditionist (1 Kings 21).

9. In the sexual uses of this root, there are instances where it means rape: in Judges 19–20, where the concubine in Gibeah was raped to death, and in the story of Amnon and Tamar, in which he is said to have overpowered her (2 Samuel 13:12–13), and in Lamentations, in which the women of Zion are said to have been raped (Lamentations 5:11). But forcible rape is not always the issue. Some cases are ambiguous. In Deuteronomy 22:28–29, a man has grabbed an unbetrothed girl; he

still a virgin, is legally considered married to the man to whom she has been betrothed; hence the two are guilty of adultery and are deserving of death. Moreover, death by stoning is prescribed, whereas in regular adultery the penalty is death, but not by stoning. Sex with a betrothed girl is compound adultery: the rights of the future husband have been violated, and the girl has offended against her obligations to her father.[10]

There is a question as to who properly exercises control over sexuality. In Exodus, the father can refuse to grant his daughter to her seducer; and this kind of paternal control is also implied in Lot's offering his daughters and the man of Gibeah offering his. But Deuteronomy indicates that the father's rights were not all that absolute (at least by the time of Deuteronomy). In Deuteronomy 22:28–29, if a man grabs an unbetrothed girl and they are found, the man is to give the father fifty shekels, and he must marry her without the right to divorce her in the future. Unlike the comparable law in Exodus, there is no mention of the father's right to refuse to give his daughter to this marriage. The laws have superseded his discretion and now require what had once been the father's discretionary act.

Husbands also do not have limitless control over their wives' sexuality. According to Assyrian laws, a husband has a right to determine the penalty for his adulterous wife, or even to pardon her outright; his freedom is limited only by the fact that whatever he chooses to do to

---

must marry her and not divorce her, because he has illicitly had sex with her. The same scenario is involved in the story of Dinah and Shechem (Genesis 34). There is no indication in the story that Shechem overpowered her. The issue is that she was not free to consent, and he should have approached her father first. Similarly, the man who sleeps with a menstruant (Ezekiel 22:10) or with his paternal sister (Ezekiel 22:11) is said to have 'raped' her only in the sense of 'statutory rape', i.e. that he had no right to have sex with her even if she consented. In Deuteronomy 21:10–13, the verb paradoxically seems to imply a failure to offer a sexual relationship. This is the case of a man who takes a captive woman as a wife. She must first spend a month in his house mourning her past; after which the man can have sex with her. If, however, he does not want her, he must emancipate rather than sell her, for he has 'violated' her. He has put her in a position in which she expected to become his wife, and then has not carried through. The verb does not always have sexual connotations; in non-sexual contexts it means to treat harshly, exploitatively, and/or abusively. Sarah treated Hagar oppressively (Genesis 16:6,9); Laban warns Jacob not to treat his daughters badly (Genesis 31:50). The most common subject is God, who is said to treat Israel badly (Deuteronomy 8:2,3,16; 2 Kings 17:20; Isaiah 64:11, Nahum 1:12), David and his seed (1 Kings 11), the suffering servant (Isaiah 53:4), and individual sufferers (Psalms 88:8, 89:23, 119:71, 75; Job 30:11). The most common victim is Israel, which is treated badly by God, by Egypt (Genesis 15:13; Exodus 1:11–13) and by enemies (2 Samuel 7:10, Isaiah 60:14, Zephaniah 3:10, Psalm 94:4, Lamentations 3:33).

10. In the case of actual rape, as when a man grabs the betrothed girl, the offence is capital, but only the man is culpable. Forcible rape is explicitly likened to murder, a realization that rape is a crime of aggression and violence rather than sex, and that the girl is a victim (Deuteronomy 22:25–27).

his wife, the same will be done to her adulterous partner. Israel also may have known of such husbandly determination, for the book of Proverbs, in warning the young man against adultery, warns him: 'the fury of the husband will be passionate; he will show no pity on his day of vengeance. He will not have regard for any ransom; he will refuse your bribe, however great' (Proverbs 6:34–35). In the formal, scholastic formulation of the laws, however, the penalty for adultery is officially death, with no option of clemency.

Deuteronomy vests some of the control over these matters in the hands of the elders of Israel. It is their responsibility to uphold the social order and eliminate dangers to it. They try the recalcitrant son (21:18–21); they investigate the question of the bride's virginity (22:13–19); they oversee the release of a *levir* (25:7); and they perform the decapitated heifer ceremony (21:1–9).

But above all, the laws place the locus of control outside the discretion of individuals, by prescribing mandatory sentencing for certain offences and leaving others for divine sanction. In the prohibited relationships of Leviticus 20, adultery, homosexuality, bestiality, and sex with step-mother, mother-in-law, and daughter-in-law are all to be punished by death; sex with a sister, sister-in-law, aunt, uncle's wife, and menstruant are also prohibited, but they are outside social sanctions and are to be punished by God.

The Bible defines the parameters of permissible sexuality by forbidding intolerable relationships. One may not have a sexual relationship that infringes on another family (adultery or sex with a girl still in her father's household), but within one's own family there are strong incest prohibitions, detailed in Leviticus 18 and 20, and Deuteronomy 27. One cannot have sex with father and mother, step-mother, paternal uncle[11] and his wife, and both maternal and paternal aunts.[12] In one's own generation, both sister and brother's wife are prohibited.[13] In the next generation, one's daughter-in-law, and,

11. Occasionally in these laws, a male is mentioned, which seems to indicate that the law also considers women and their permissible relations, but does not consistently list all of a female ego's choices.
12. It is hard to know whether the omission of mother's brother means that mother's brother and his wife were permitted as being of a different family, or whether they would have been prohibited. A similar question arises with father's brother's children (first cousins) and with brother's and sister's daughters. In this case it would seem that since father's brother is prohibited, brother's daughter must also be, even though it is not mentioned.
13. This was not always so in Israel. In Genesis 20:16, Sarah and Abraham are described as having the same father by different mothers. A similar situation lies behind Tamar's entreaty to her would-be rapist paternal brother Amnon: 'Speak unto the king, for he will not withhold me from thee' (2 Samuel 13:13). This is not the only instance in which the patriarchal and Davidic narratives differ from later biblical law. Jacob is married to two sisters, which is not allowed in Leviticus. Jacob's and David's sons vie for inheritance position while, according to

we presume, one's daughter[14] are prohibited, as are one's children's daughters. Furthermore, once one marries, one's wife's lineage is off limits: mother-in-law, wife's sister (while wife is alive), wife's daughters and granddaughters.

These incest laws seem particularly complex, and it has been suggested that the laws sought to include all those women who might be found in the same household in an extended family. However, mothers-in-law would not have been expected in these households and prohibitions on father's daughters is explicitly said to include those daughters born outside the household. Moreover, these laws took their final form when Israel already had nuclear households. The laws are defining and clarifying family lines. There is a sense, expressed in Genesis, that the marital bond creates a family even though there are no blood ties, and so father's wife, father's brother's wife, and brother's wife are said to be prohibited because the 'nakedness' (the conventional translation of Hebrew *ervah*) of the woman is tantamount to the nakedness of her husband. So too, since one's wife is also bonded to him, her bloodlines (*sh'ar*) are parallel to his own and thereby prohibited. Sex within the family would blur family lines and relations and cause a collapse of family relations, and sex with a daughter-in-law is explicitly called *tevel*, 'mixing', in Leviticus 20:12.[15]

## Sexuality As Danger To Boundaries

The power of sex to cross over the lines between households or blur distinctions between units of a family is an example of sex's power to dissolve categories. This is problematic on a national scale. This issue is clearly highlighted in Genesis 34, a chapter often called the 'rape of Dinah', even though it is probably not about a forcible rape, and really is not a story about Dinah at all. Dinah had 'gone out to see the daughters of the land'.[16] Shechem saw her and lay with her, thus treating her improperly. In this way, he treated her as a whore (v. 31), a woman whose consent is sufficient because her sexuality is not part of

---

Deuteronomy, the first to be born is considered the first-born, whatever the wishes of the father.

14. The omission of daughter in the prohibited relations is another glaring omission. One might argue that since grandchildren are prohibited, children must also be, but one might equally argue that the idea of paterfamilias was still strong enough that the laws could not absolutely prohibit a father's access to his daughter. From the expectation of virginity in unmarried daughters, however, it is clear the father-daughter incest was neither expected nor encouraged.

15. It is also called *zimmah* in Leviticus 20:14, a term reserved in these laws for incest outside blood kin, applied to mother-in-law, wife's sister, wife's daughter and granddaughter.

16. Probably a snide remark in the order of 'she asked for it'.

a family structure. Even though Dinah may have consented to the act, the fact that he had not spoken to her parents in advance constituted an impropriety. The integrity of the family has been threatened, and Dinah's own wishes are incidental. Shechem, who loved her, asked his father Hamor to acquire her for him as his wife. But there are further implications in this, made explicit by Hamor, who not only tendered the offer, but extended it, saying to Jacob, 'Intermarry with us; give your daughters to us and take our daughters for yourselves; you will dwell among us, and the land will be open before you' (34:9–10); he further says to his own fellow townsmen, 'the men agree with us to dwell among us and be as one kindred', even intermingling 'their cattle, substance and all their beasts'. This intermixing was the great threat to Jacob's family. Even though the generation of Jacob's sons was the first to intermarry with the local inhabitants, they had to do so under controlled conditions in which they could remain a distinct unit. The free exercise of erotic love by Shechem threatened that type of control. There is, of course, also a concern that intermarriage with non-Israelite women would make it possible for them to influence their husbands to worship other gods (Deuteronomy 7:1–5), as reportedly happened to King Solomon. Ultimately, after the return from Babylon, when the community of Israel was small and in danger of being overwhelmed by the other people in the land, these dual concerns resulted in a ban on foreign wives during the time of Ezra.

The desire to maintain categories is also a cosmic issue. The Primeval History of Genesis, which underscores the basic features of human existence, is concerned to divide humanity from the divine realm, on the one hand, and the animal realm on the other. As humans become cultured creatures, they become more god-like, not resembling the great monotheist conception of God, but certainly like the divine beings to whom God speaks in Genesis 1–11, the *b'nei elohim*. To preserve the difference between humans and divine, God takes steps to insure the ultimate mortality of humans. This difference is threatened when the *b'nei elohim* find human women fair (they were, after all, created in the physical likeness of the divine beings) and begin to mate with them. To further reinforce the difference, God limited the human life-span (Genesis 6:1–4).

As a practical matter, one did not have to be overly concerned with human-divine matings. No divine beings were observed in the post-flood era seducing human women; presumably women were not successfully attributing unexpected babies to angelic intervention; and there is no record in the Bible of divine females coming to seduce the men of Israel, even in their sleep.

However, the animal-human boundary was more problematic. The primeval history acknowledges a kinship between humans and animals: Genesis 1 understands God to have created the land animals on the same day as humans, and Genesis 2 records that the animals were first created as companions to Adam. After the flood, action was taken to establish a clear and hierarchical boundary between the human and animal world; humans could kill animals for food (sparing the blood), whereas no animal could kill a human without forfeiting its own life. In reality, this uncrossable boundary of human existence could be easily crossed by mating with animals. Such mating could threaten the very existence of humanity, for the blurring of borders would be a return to chaos.[17] Every legal collection strongly forbids bestiality (Exodus 22:28, Leviticus 18:23, 20:15–16, Deuteronomy 17:21); Leviticus 18:23 explains that bestiality is *tevel*, '(improper) mixing'.

The maintaining of categories is particularly important in the priestly writings, for one of the essential priestly functions was the maintenance of the categories of existence (pure and impure, holy and profane, permissible and impermissible foods, family lines, sacred time, sacred space). But preoccupation with neatness is not limited to Leviticus; Deuteronomy also manifests this concern, prohibiting even the wearing of linsey-woolsey cloth, which combines wool from animals and linen from plants (Deuteronomy 22:9–11, cf. Leviticus 19:19).

Deviations from these neat categories are dangerous, and Leviticus proscribes male homosexuality under penalty of death (Leviticus 20:13, cf. 18:22). This extreme aversion to homosexuality is not inherited from other Near Eastern laws,[18] and must make sense in the light of biblical thought. It does not really disturb family lines, but it does blur the distinction between male and female, and this cannot be tolerated in the biblical system. Anything that smacks of homosexual blurring is similarly prohibited, such as cross-dressing (Deuteronomy 22:5).[19]

It has long been noted that lesbianism is not mentioned. This is not because these Levitical laws concern only male behaviour: bestiality is explicitly specified to include both male and female interaction with beasts. But lesbianism was probably considered a trivial matter: it involved only women, with no risk of pregnancy; and, most important, it did not result in true physical 'union' (by the male entering the female).

17. On the importance of categories in Israel, see Douglas (1966), Frymer-Kensky (1983), and Finkelstein (1981).
18. Though the Sumerian laws consider an accusation of catamy as parallel to an accusation that one's wife is fornicating.
19. Having eunuchs is not considered the same kind of blurring. A eunuch, like people with visible physical defects, could not serve in the temple. But eunuchs were found in Israel, particularly in the royal court (2 Kings 20:17–18, Isaiah 56:3–4; Jeremiah 29:2, 34:19, 38:7, 41:16).

## Public Interest in Control of Sex

Issues such as adultery, incest, homosexuality, and bestiality are not simply the private concerns of families. Like murder, they are treated as a national issue for, like murder, sexual abominations are thought to pollute the land. The very survival of Israel was at stake. Leviticus 18 relates that the inhabitants of the land before Israel indulged in the incestuous relations listed there, in bestiality and homosexuality and *molech*-worship, and that as a result the land became defiled and vomited out its inhabitants. Israel is warned against doing these same abominations: 'Let not the land spew you out for defiling it, as it spewed out the nation that came before you' (Leviticus 18:28). Israel's right of occupation is contingent upon its care not to pollute the land with murder, illicit sex and idolatry. The people must not only refrain from murder, they must not pollute the land by letting murderers go free or allowing accidental murderers to leave the city of refuge (Numbers 35:31–34) or by leaving the corpses of the executed unburied (Deuteronomy 21:22–23). So too, they must not only refrain from such illicit sex as adultery and incest, but must be careful to observe even such technical regulations as not allowing a man to remarry his divorced and since remarried wife (Deuteronomy 24:1–3, Jeremiah 3:1–4).

The danger to the nation that ensues from murder and adultery explains the mandatory death sentence; it also clarifies two very odd biblical rituals. In the ceremony of the decapitated heifer, when a corpse is found but no one can identify the murderer, the elders of the city nearest the corpse go to a wadi and decapitate a heifer, declaring their lack of culpability and seeking to avert the blood-pollution of the land (Deuteronomy 21:1–9, see also Patai and Zevit). The second ritual is the trial of the suspected adulteress (Numbers 5:11–21; Frymer-Kensky 1984), which provides that whenever a husband suspects his wife he is to take her to the temple, where she is to drink a potion made from holy water, dust from the floor of the sanctuary, and the dissolved curse words while answering 'amen' to a priestly adjuration that should she be guilty the water will enter into her and cause her 'belly to swell and her thigh to drop' (probably a prolapsed uterus). After this oath she returns to her husband. This ritual allowed a husband to resume marital relations after he suspected adultery. Otherwise, intercourse with a wife who had slept with another man could be expected to pollute the land in the same way as remarriage to a divorced wife who had been married in the interim.

Improper sexual activity had even greater danger than the threat to Israel's right to the land (which was certainly a serious consideration). The blurring of the categories of human existence through sexual activity was a danger to creation, for in biblical cosmology the universe is seen rather like a house of cards; if the lines are not kept neat, the whole edifice will collapse, 'the foundations of the earth totter'. Wrongful sexual activity can bring disaster to the world.

## Conclusion

This is the great problematic of sex. The ideal of the bonded, monog-amous nuclear family conveys a positive place for sexuality within the social order. But at the same time, that same sexual attraction which serves to reinforce society if it is controlled and confined within the marital system can destroy social order if allowed free rein. Sexuality itself is good, but the free exercise of sexuality is a prime example of wrongful activity. The exercise of free sexuality (particularly by the woman, who owes sexual exclusivity to the man) is a prime example of a lack of fidelity and a failure of allegiance. In time, all wrongful behaviour was seen through the metaphor of sexual activity, with the result that in the prophets, particularly Hosea, Jeremiah, and Ezekiel, there is so much sexual imagery that it is hard to sort out what might be a literal depiction of too much sexual license, from a metaphorical depiction of allegiance to foreign powers and other gods.

There is no coherent biblical treatment of sexuality. On the surface, sexuality is treated as a question of social control: who with whom, and when. There is only one explicit statement that sexuality is a cosmic force: 'For love is fierce as death, passion is mighty as *Sheol*, its darts are darts of fire, a blazing flame; vast floods cannot quench love, nor rivers drown it' (*Song of Songs* 8:6–7). The stories of Pharaoh and Sarah, David and Bathsheba, and Amnon and Tamar show a sense that erotic attrac-tion can cause men to abuse their superior position and strength.[20]

But all of this is inchoate and essentially inarticulate. There is no vocabulary in the Bible in which to discuss such matters, no divine image or symbolic system by which to mediate it. God does not model sex, is not the patron of sexual behaviour, and is not even recorded as the guarantor of potency; and there is no other divine fig-ure who can serve to control or mediate sex. Our only indication that the Bible considers sex as a volatile, creative, and potentially chaotic force is from the laws themselves. These laws of control reveal a sense that sexuality is not really matter-of-fact, that it is a two-edged sword:

20. John van Seters believes this is a particular motif in the Sucession History and the Yahwist corpus. He also considers the concubine tales of Abner and Rizpah, and Adonijah and Abishag to be instances of this, but he does not sufficiently consider the political rather than sexual motivations of these acts. See further Blenkinsopp (1966). I cannot agree that the emphasis is on love leading to death, though I agree with van Seters that in none of these stories is the woman blameworthy.

a force for bonding and a threat to the maintenance of boundaries. They cut through the silence on this topic, which we consider so important, but about which there is little explicit mention in the Bible. Through the laws we can find an inkling of biblical Israel's appreciation and anxiety about the topic of such vital concern.

The laws also reveal a great danger: when a society has such legitimate concerns about an important aspect of life, it needs a way to discuss and channel anxieties productively. This the Bible does not provide. We can see the concerns about sex expressed in the laws, but we cannot see how they were mediated, detoxified, expressed and understood. The result is a core emptiness in the Bible's discussion of sex. This vacuum was possibly filled by folk traditions not recorded in the Bible. Ultimately, in Hellenistic times, it was displaced by the complex of anti-woman, anti-carnal ideas that had such a large impact on the development of Western religion and civilization.

## BIBLIOGRAPHY

Blenkinsopp, J.J. 1966, 'Theme and Motif in the Succession History (2 Samuel 11:2f.) and the Yahwist Corpus.', *Vetus Testamentum Sup.* (VT) 15:44–57.

Cosby, M. R. 1985, *Sex in the Bible*, Prentice Hall, Englewood Cliffs.

Douglas, M. 1966, *Purity and Danger: Analysis of Concepts of Pollution and Taboo*, New York, Praeger.

Dubarle, A.M. 1967, *Amour et fecondité dans le bible*, Privat, Toulouse.

Finkelstein, J.J. 1981, 'The Ox That Gored' *Transactions of the American Philosophical Society*, 71:26–29.

Frymer-Kensky, T. 1983, 'Purity, Pollution and Purgation in Biblical Israel.' pp. 399–414 in Meyers, C. and O'Connor, M. eds., *The Word of the Lord Shall Go Forth. Essays in Honour of David Noel Freedman.*, Philadelphia Free Press.

Frymer-Kemsky,T. 1984, 'The Strange Case of the Suspected Sotah (Numbers 5:11–31)', *VT* 34:11–26.

Lambert, W.G. 1963, 'Celibacy in the World's Old Proverbs', *Bulletin of the American Schools of Oriental Resaerch* (BASOR) 169:63–64.

Larue, G. 1983, *Sex and the Bible*, Prometheus, Buffalo.

Perry, F. L. 1982, *Sex and the Bible*, Atlanta, Christian Education Research Institute.

Patai, R. 1939, 'The "Egla" Arufa or the Expiation of the Polluted Land', *Jewish Quarterly Review* (JQR) 30:59–69.

Snell, D. C. 1987, 'Notes on Love and Death in Proverbs' In Marks, J. and Good, R. eds., *Love and Death in the Ancient Near East. Essays in Honor of Marvin H. Pope*, Guilford, CT, Four Quarters Publishing Co.

Van Seters, J. 1987, 'Love and Death in the Court History of David' pp. 121–124 in Marks J. and Good R., *Love and Death in the Ancient Near East.*

Zevit, Z. 1976, 'The 'Egla Ritual of Deuteronomy 21:1–9', *Journal of Biblical Literature* 95:377–390.

# SEX AND SADISM IN HOSEA*

*Francis Landy*

v.4.   Strive with your mother, strive,
       For she is not my wife, and I am not her husband,
       That she may remove her harlotries from her face,
       And her signs of adultery from between her breasts.

v.5.   Lest I strip her naked,
       And display her as on the day she was born,
       And set her like a wilderness
       And render her like a land of drought,
       And make her die of thirst.

v.6.   And for her children I will have no compassion,
       For they are children of harlotry.

v.7.   For their mother has played the whore,
       Their conceiver has acted shamefully,
       For she said, 'I will go after my lovers,
       Givers of my bread and my water,
       My wool and my flax, my oil and my strong drink.'

v.8.   Therefore, behold I hedge your way with thorns,
       And I will fence her about,
       And her paths she will not find.

v.9.   And she will pursue her lovers, and will not catch them,
       And she will seek them, and will not find,
       And she will say, 'I will go and will return
       To my first husband, for it was better for me then than now.'

v.10.  And she did not know that I gave her
       The corn, the new wine and the clear oil,
       And silver and multiplied for her, and gold –
       They used for Baal.

v.11.  Therefore I will return, and I will take back
       My corn in its time, and the new wine in its season,
       And I will reclaim my wool and her flax,
       For covering her nakedness.

---

*The following is an excerpt from a commentary in progress on Hosea. The passage in question is Chapter 2.4-15.

v.12.  And now, I will expose her shame to the eyes of her lovers,
       And no man shall deliver her from my hand.
v.13.  And I will cause to cease all her joy,
       Her festivals, her new moons, her sabbaths,
       And all her festive seasons.
v.14.  And I will lay waste her vine and her fig tree,
       Of which she said, 'They are my hire,
       Which my lovers gave me.'
       And I will turn them into a forest,
       And the beasts of the field shall devour them.
v.15.  And I will visit upon her the days of the Baalim,
       To which she would offer incense,
       And she would deck herself with her earrings and jewels,
       And go after her lovers –
       And me she forgot, says the Lord.[1]

The principal problems in chapter 2 of Hosea are: i) how to reconcile
– if one may – the violence and obsessiveness of the first part of the
chapter with the blissful tour-de-force of the second; ii) how it inter-
acts with the framing parable in chapters 1 and 3; iii) how it functions
as a microcosm, a *mise-en-abime*, of the book as a whole. The feminist
critique of the chapter is by now well-established: that it robs the
woman of her voice and her point of view, that it objectifies and
degrades her. We can build on this critique, not only by a detailed
reading of the text, but by asking, where does the author stand, is 'he'[2]
the speaker or the addressee, what is the relationship in it of mystification and discovery, desire and knowledge; to see beneath the male
control, undercut by uncertainty, revisions, and impossibility, a desire
for surrender of power, knowledge and discourse. This will not
breach the exclusivity of the male fantasy, but note that, as repeatedly
in Hosea, it is also a fantasy of the transfer of gender, of slippage
between male and female personae. This can be illustrated at the end
of the chapter where the male child, Jezreel, is suddenly feminised;
since Jezreel is etymologically correlated with the divine seed, God's
insemination of the earth is also 'his' surrender to it.

  The first part of the chapter (4–15)[3] is a repeated fantasy of desolation and sexual exposure. The distancing parable frames the inner
dynamic of God's jealousy, rage and cruelty. But it is also framed by
visions of reconciliation, marked by the transformation of the children's names in verses 1–3 and verses 24–25. The continuity
between God's speeches in verses 3 and 4, with their matching

1. The translation is mostly my own, with a little help from the New Jewish Publication Society of America (NJPS) and the New Revised Standard Versions (NRSV).
2. I have put 'he' in inverted commas to distinguish, at least this once, the biological
   gender of the presumably male author from his symbolic gender.
3. Many English-language versions have a slightly different verse numbering from the
   Hebrew text. In these, 2.4 = 2.2, 2.5 = 2.3 etc. I have retained the Hebrew verse
   numbering, however, since there are translations, such as the NJPS, which follow it.

imperatives, 'Say ...', 'Strive ...', suggests that from the far future he turns to present alienation, that his acknowledgement of kinship and love for his children, reflected in their words to each other, is undercut by their immediate predicament, as agents of familial strife, and by doubts about their legitimacy. Inciting the children is, however, a displacement of his own quarrel. That it is transparently a delaying tactic, a mirror for his own contention, is evident from their silence; the only words we hear are his. Another form of displacement is that which renders the fantasy hypothetical, by introducing it with 'lest' (v.5); only if the children's strife does not succeed, will it come into effect. Both are rationalizations that distance the fantasy from himself; the children are screens or ventriloquists, whose intercession will avert punishment. In the next section (vs.7–9), children and hypothesis disappear; instead God proposes to bring about the woman's return through preventive measures. Blocking her path with thorns may parallel the fantasy of exposure or preempt it; at any rate, it is justified as a means of rehabilitation. This line of thought is abandoned; in the last section (10–15) the fantasy is unmediated by preventive measures or postponement.

Repetition is characteristic of obsession; the same scenario recurs, with greater or lesser aesthetic or ethical revision. In the above section, the masks are progressively stripped away; this may either be a Freudian 'working through', or typical of a sadistic process, in which the expenditure of violence leads to an access of love. Symptomatic of obsessiveness is its hypertrophic language: the long lists, the extended verses, the insistence of the repeated imperative 'Strive', the punning focus on particular phonemes, whose elaboration suggests either a single underlying thought or the baroque pressure to generate as many permutations as possible.[4]

The fantasy is complex, overdetermined, and pornographic, in that, as Setel says,[5] it depicts women's sexual shame. The infusion of violence into sexuality is not, however, primarily or only a means of excitation. Chapter 2 belongs to the literature of sexual disgust, in which desire appears only spectrally, as a revenant, and in reverse. Exposing the woman's nakedness to the gaze of her lovers is doubly voyeuristic; the viewer sees her through the eyes of others, and participates vicariously in their pleasure. Except that the sight renders

---

4. *Te'enata*, 'her fig tree,' in v.14 is compressed into *'etna*, 'a (harlot's) hire', three words later; another example is the extraordinary concatenation of 'n's and 'p's in *wetaser zeNuNeha miPPaNeha weNa'aPuPeha mibben shadeha, PeN 'aPshiteNNa* ('that she should remove her harlotries from her face, and her adulteries from between her breasts, lest I strip her bare') in vs.4–5.
5. T. Drorah Setel, 'Prophets and Pornography: Female Sexual Imagery in Hosea' *Feminist Interpretations of the Bible*, ed. L.M. Russell (Philadelphia, Westminster, 1986) pp. 86–95.

the lovers impotent: 'no man shall deliver her from my hand' (v.12). The object of desire becomes undesirable, *nablut,* both 'contemptible' and 'foolish.' The jealous husband paradoxically acts as pander, but only to nullify the sexual transaction, to divest the woman of cultural and social significance. She becomes a sign of the libidinal body; the word *nablut,* 'folly' or 'shame', at least metonymically refers to her genitalia, and associates them with folly, contempt, and cosmic disorder.[6] The body, imagined as anarchic and subversive, is nevertheless passive, subject to the look of the surrounding males. Vision is a means of appropriation, of immense symbolic resonance, as the rhetoric of striptease, advertising and so on, shows. The underlying fantasy, then, is of gang-rape, the woman encircled by predators. The fantasy, however, is reversed; the sight turns back on the seers, and taunts them with their incapacity to claim her. The husband, in exhibiting his wife, simultaneously discards her and asserts his prerogative over her.

The exposure of the woman is the prelude to her devastation, related in vs.5 and 14. Predation is climactically embodied in the wild beasts, that consume 'them' – vine and fig tree, but also Israel – at the end of v.14. The wild beasts are displaced figures for God, as executioners of his will; the identification becomes closer later in the book, when God adopts feral imagery for himself (5.14, 13.7–8). In 5.14, God, a metaphorical lion, boasts that 'none can deliver' from him, as does the husband in v.12. Their rapacity converges with the desolation God brings in the first part of the verse . Verse 5 combines imagery of exposure with dessication. There is a reversal both from adulthood to infancy, since the woman is as naked 'as on the day of her birth' and from life to death. Death by thirst and drought negate her role as the source of life and sustenance, perceived through the prism of her breasts in v.4. One may note a similar fantasy in the case of the woman suspected of adultery in Numbers 5, whose womb and thigh will wither if she is guilty. Verses 5 and 14 somewhat schematically match and oppose each other; in v.5, God's threat to make Israel 'like a wilderness' is coupled in v.14 with his intention to make it 'as a forest',[7] two antithetical margins of culture. The vision in v.5 is passive, the woman abandoned and parched, while that in v.14 is active, ravaging by wild beasts. In v.5, moreover, there is a

6. The word *nablut* only occurs here in the Hebrew Bible, and is subject to extensive discussion. For *nablut* as a metonymy for the genitalia see H.W. Wolff, *Hosea: A Commentary on the Book of the Prophet Hosea,* tr. G. Stansell (Philadelphia, Fortress, 1974) p. 31 and D. Stuart, *Hosea-Jonah* (Word Biblical Commentary 31; Waco, Texas, Word, 1987) p. 51. For the proposal that it is a term for cosmic disorder, see R. Murray, *The Cosmic Covenant* (London, Sheed and Ward, 1992) p.47.

7. The parallel is perhaps clearer in Hebrew than in Engliah, since the verbal forms used are identical: *wesamtiha kammidbar* and *wesamtim leya'ar.*

fantasy of infancy, immediately succeeded in v.6 by YHWH's rejection of his children. The baby is not merely helpless, but a precultural being; reducing her to its condition ejects the woman from the symbolic – social and linguistic – order to pure animality, as does the exposure of her body in v.12. But it also infuses the fantasy of sexual exposure with the far more terrible one of the exposure of children. Lasciviousness and sexual disgust supervene on infanticide.

The husband is motivated by jealousy, which turns love into anti-love, rendered more intolerable by the memory of the love that has been defiled. Jealousy extenuates his vindictiveness; he is not intrinsically hateful, the common wisdom goes, but driven to it by circumstances. Circumstances, however, license a pre-existing reservoir of repressed thoughts. Of these the most important is the belief that women, archetypally the mother, will always let one down and the present betrayal merely confirms this inherent unreliability, and that aggression, impelled by greed, hatred and envy, is therefore justified. That the woman, from being a source of succour, becomes a desert is the germinal fantasy in v.5; that she is torn to pieces is that of v.14. The transfer from breasts, in v.4, to infant, in v.5, suggests a projection, an exchange of identity between mother and child. This is amplified in v.5, in which the abandoned child turns the mother into a figure of abandonment. One is reminded of those children who, according to Donald Winnicott, are deprived of their mothers' presence for too long and, in despair, inwardly abandon them.[8]

The two fantasies, of abandonment and aggression, are mutually dependent, in that the rage is provoked by frustration, and in turn results in rejection. At the same time, they are incompatible, since the woman is both absent, dying of neglect, and available for laceration. For that reason, perhaps, they are separated by the span of the passage. Contradictory and complementary, they enact the metaphorical play of likeness and difference, the resistance of the imagination to a single construction. The satisfactions of violence breach, yet leave intact the narcissistic space outlined by the presence/absence of the mourned mother/lover, in which the child fears death by exposure, reflected in the sexual sphere by the cross-currents of sadism, isolation, and sterility.

Another element is introduced by the metaphor of blocking the woman's path with thorns in v.8. This is a prelude to her subjection to her lovers' gaze in v.12; as O'Connor shows,[9] a non-sequitur intervenes between prevention of access to them and humiliation before them. The logical obstacle is not only a sign of resistance to and ratio-

8. D.W. Winnicott, *Playing and Reality* (London, RKP, 1991) pp. 112–113
9. M.O'Connor, 'Pseudo-sorites in Hebrew Verse' in *Perspectives on Language and Text* ed. E.W. Conrad and E.G. Newring (Winona Lake, Eisenbrauns, 1987) p. 243.

nalization of the underlying fantasy, but contributes an additional
scenario of the woman's suffering. At this point the passage comes
closest to pornography, in the sense of the inscription of women's
shame for the sake of male pleasure. It feeds off the woman's desper-
ation and frustration, gratifying the man both with the vision of
female desire and the assertion of his power; this may be combined,
voyeuristically, with hatred and envy that the desire is not for himself.
The thorns, in particular, suggest cruelty, and presage entrapment by
the gaze of the lovers in v.12. The sadistic fantasy relies on the pain of
the woman, on imagining her consciousness; one notes the care with
which God puts words in her mouth, projects himself into her speaking and acting. For this reason, it can never culminate in her destruction; it ritualistically exorcises the hatred on which it draws, to which
it alludes. The erotic cover is evoked only to be displaced; under-
neath the hint of perversion (or diversion), toying with the woman,
tormented by the memory of desire and the wish to punish, are the
nullification of the sexual transaction through exposure and the complex metamorphoses suggested by the superimposed images of rape
and bestial voracity. If the one scene conceives of the woman,
stripped of her humanity, surrounded by hunters, the other turns the
hunters into animals. They become, symbolically clothe themselves
in, their victim; nothing suggests more clearly the contagion of
destruction, that making the woman into a wilderness, consuming
her, reflects their desolation and fear of dissolution.

The erotic substratum of the text, its reversal of the language of
love, is more poignant because of its echoes of the *Song of Songs;*
these are particularly evident in vs. 8–9 and contribute to the sexual
suggestiveness of those verses. In *Song of Songs* 3.1–4, the woman
seeks her lover through the city at night, encountering watchmen
before she eventually finds him; the phrase 'I sought him and did not
find him' is repeated at the end of 3.1 and 2. In vs.8–9, we find the
same pair, 'seeking' and 'finding'; the phrase 'she will not find' likewise recurs at the end of clauses. In *Song of Songs* 5.2–7, a variant of
the same passage, the phrase 'I sought him and did not find him'
reappears (5.6); here, however, the watchmen beat and strip the
woman. In both texts, the woman's search for her lover, contraven-
ing social propriety, is invested with erotic anticipation, intensified
by frustration; she represents the amorous body. In both, she suffers
humiliation. However, they are from opposite perspectives. Whereas
in Hosea the voice is male and articulates a fantasy that passes from
the sadistic game to voyeuristic exposure, in the *Song* it is female and
expresses her outrage; we do not know what the watchmen feel, and
the ordeal permits the celebration of her lover's beauty and thus of
her own eros in 5.10–16.

Another difference is that in Hosea the woman's speech contradicts appearances; the pornographic gratification of witnessing her love-sickness is undercut by her confessedly economic motives. She will go after her lovers, because they provide her with sustenance, according to v.7; she determines, in v.9, to return to YHWH because he was a better investment. As Fokkelien van Dijk-Hemmes shows,[10] economic dependence is a powerful instrument of male control and rhetoric; women do not have libidos, or at least they do not count, but merely know where their interest lies. Since they are not genuinely sexual beings, they can be subsumed by male fantasy. The woman then corroborates her whorishness by being mercenary, and is subject both to the man's resentment and his will. More important, however, necessity provides a potential counter-argument against the passage's polemic: that the woman is compelled by ignorance and destitution, not by lust. If she genuinely does not know that YHWH is her benefactor (v.10), and suffers from amnesia (v.15), her guilt is extenuated. The counter-argument is developed in chapter 4, where the people perish 'without knowledge' (4.5), because the priests have been negligent of their duty; on the other hand, daughters and brides are granted immunity, in a curious inversion of the double standard, because their sexual liaisons follow men's bad example.

The *Song of Songs* is a much more pervasive presence in this passage than has been previously recognised,[11] not so much on the surface of the text as in its basic imagery. Whether one is dealing with the genre of love poetry, an early forerunner of the *Song,* or simple serendipity is impossible to determine, since the *Song* itself was probably composed much later. In any case, the invective in Hosea is directed against a valorisation of love and the world represented most comprehensively by the *Song*. In the *Song* 1.13, the woman's lover lies between her breasts like a sachet of myrrh; in Hosea (v.4) this is replaced by the signs of her adultery. In the *Song,* the birth of the lovers is an epiphany; the woman was 'splendid to the one who gave her birth' (6.9), the man is awakened to love and to life in a birth scene under an apple tree, full of cosmic significance (8.5). In Hosea, being reduced to one's birth state is evidence of utter dehumanisation; nakedness is the subject of shame instead of celebration, as in the *Song*. The wilderness, in Hosea, is a sign of the woman's desolation and death by thirst; in the *Song,* it is the place of the lovers' tryst, associated with exotic spices and sights (1.14, 3.6,

---

10. F. van Dijk-Hemmes, 'The Imagination of Power and the Power of Imagination: An Intertextual Analysis of Two Biblical Love Songs: The Song of Songs and Hosea 2', *JSOT* 44 (1989), p. 82.
11. The two previous studies are those of van Dijk-Hemmes and A. van Selms 'Hosea and Canticles' *OTSWA* 7/8 (1964–5) pp.85–89.

8.5). In the *Song* 4.8, the woman is invited to come down from Lebanon, the home of wild beasts; here they threaten devastation.

Like Hosea, the *Song of Songs* exposes the woman to the sight of others, the 'lovers' and 'friends'[12] who are urged to 'eat' and 'drink' in the garden of love in 5.1, and in particular the spectators who elicit her return in 7.1,[13] that they may 'gaze' at her. In contrast to Hosea, however, their vision is positive; the voices must at least concur with that of the male lover in the descriptive catalogue of her beauty in 7.2–7. Like the woman in Hosea, she is metaphorically correlated with the land of Israel;[14] the description fragments the body into part-objects, each one of which develops a life of its own and is complexly interconnected with the others. The metaphorical process simultaneously splits and recombines, resulting in a total vision of the world, integrated and transformed through love. In Hosea, the sexual metaphor provides similar opportunities for the vision of recreation; fragmentation and integration are, however, projected successively into the text, rendering problematic their logical cohesion: are they simply juxtaposed, is the transformation an act of will? The denial of the sexual relationship at the beginning of the passage ('For she is not my wife and I am not her husband') implicitly cancels out all of its associated couplings, the entire interaction of God and Israel. It thus becomes a metaphor for the failure of the metaphorical process, just as, in the *Song of Songs,* the union of lovers is the sign of its success; the work of the poem corresponds to their discourse. The failure of metaphor, however, can only be communicated through metaphor, which thus subverts itself. Further, the denial is countermanded by the YHWH's assumption of marital authority over the woman, by the woman's acknowledgement in v.9, as well as by the framing narrative.

There is another contrast, another way in which the metaphor in Hosea is suspect. We know that the *Song of Songs* has its literal meaning, actually refers to the love of lovers. The reference of the metaphor in Hosea is quite opaque. It may refer to the exclusiveness of the cult, sacrificial communion as analogous to sexual communion, or to the transfer of moral qualities – loyalty, compassion etc. – as an equivalent to seminal fluids, as v.22 might suggest, or to fertilisation of the earth, corresponding to the imagery of 'sowing' and 'answering' in vs.23–25 . Betrothal may or may not mean consummation. If the passage accuses Israel of a category mistake – YHWH is its husband, not Baal – it propagates the Baalisation of YHWH it

---

12. This may be obscured in translations, e.g. NRSV substitutes 'with love' for 'lovers'.
13. 6.13 in English-language translations.
14. This metaphorical dimension is too pervasive to require illustration; it is particularly evident in 7.2–7.

denounces.[15] The 'wife' may be land or people; the identification is alternatively assumed by the text and abandoned by it.[16] The metaphor may accordingly be interpreted in various ways, none of which is decisive.

If the 'wife' is Israel, then it comprises both genders. The literal negation of the bond between 'my people' and 'I am' in 1.9 is transposed to the metaphorical one between 'husband' and 'wife' in v.4. But this is hardly innocent. The supplementation, or mystification, is also a displacement: the male-dominated Israelite society is characterized as female. God is the supreme patriarch, before whom all men are women; the relation of male to female is that of God to humanity. Except that the metaphor is meaningless; the shift in gender of the men corresponds to no social or sacred reality. Their classification as 'women' is not reflected in their behaviour or in their self-perception; its sole function, indeed, is to activate the contrast between wife and whore as a metaphor for their faithlessness, to compound their vilification with misogyny, even if only in drag. However, the transfer from male to female serves also to foreground, to render visible, women as social actors. We catch glimpses of women's normal life, especially cultic life, in the indictment that fuels YHWH's fantasy, in prospective nostalgia for the complacent present. It may be, as Phyllis Bird suggests,[17] that women are especially implicated in the accusation of sacred and sexual perfidy, that while the polemic is ostensibly against Israel, male and female, and lacks overt sexual content on the level of denotation, in fact it connotes women as preeminent vehicles of estrangement, that a polemic against Israel easily becomes one against women.

In that case, the identification of her lovers is also in question. In v.15, the lovers are parallel to the Baalim, whose days YHWH will visit, and in v.10, YHWH's gifts of silver and gold are dedicated to Baal's image. The lovers whom she credits with her sustenance are likewise easily decoded as the indigenous gods, who are responsible for its fertility. There may be some reference to foreign powers, as elsewhere in the book. But the transfer from metaphorical to real women, the focus on women as exemplars of Israel's cultic perversity, will also direct our attention to their real lovers, whose licentiousness at festivals is condemned in 4.12–14. If the lovers are not

15. For this interpretation, see, e.g. H. Fisch *Poetry with a Purpose* (Bloomington/Indianapolis, Indiana U.P., 1988) pp.147–148, Wolff, *Hosea* (p.34), and H. Balz-Cochois' monograph *Gomer* (Frankfurt/Bern, Peter Lang, 1982).
16. For an accurate account of this, see J. Jeremias, *Der Prophet Hosea* (Das Alte Testament Deutsch; Göttingen, Vandenhoeck and Ruprecht, 1983) p.41–42.
17. 'To Play the Harlot: An Inquiry into an Old Testament Metaphor' in P. Day ed. *Gender and Difference in Ancient Israel* (Fortress, Philadelphia, 1989) pp.75–94, esp. p.83.

only Baalim but Israelite men, they participate in the scapegoating of the woman who, as Israel, represents themselves. The men are then ambiguous; as literally male and figuratively feminine, they are invited by YHWH to a parody of male bonding whose victims they are. Literal and metaphorical domains mutually interact, in that the actual affairs of Israelite men and women give rise to, and are encouraged by, their metaphorical promiscuity. At the same time, the collapse of the metaphorical into the literal threatens the distinctions on which metaphor is based. The intensity and detail with which the passage is elaborated is proportionate to its tendency to fragment. The repetition of the argument is not only a sign of obsessiveness, but of a wish to integrate discordance, to achieve reconciliation.

# DIALECTICS OF DESIRE
## 'The Evil Instinct is Very Good'*

*Daniel Boyarin*

The second implication which R. Hanina bar Papa found (in the verse, *Many ... are Thy wonderful works ... and Thy thoughts which are towards us* [Ps. 40.5]), was this: Many are all the wonderful works and thoughts which Thou, O God, dost employ to have a man feel desire for his wife. Of this feeling it is written *Adam knew his wife yet more* (Gen. 4.25). What is implied by Scripture's saying *yet more?* That his desire had been increased by so much more desire than formerly: formerly he had not felt desire when he did not see his wife, but now he felt desire for her whether he saw her or did not see her.

It is such strong desire which compels travelling merchants and sea-farers – so said R. Abba bar Yudan in the name of R. Aha – to be reminded of their wives and return to them.

William G. Braude and Israel J. Kapstein, trans., *Pesikta de-Rab Kahana: R. Kahana's Compilation of Discourses for Sabbaths and Festal Days,* Routledge and Keegan Paul, 1975.

In the above passage, from one of the 'classical' homiletic midrashim, the essential attitudes of rabbinic Judaism toward licit, married sexuality are made as clear as could possibly be. Notwithstanding certain anxieties and peripheral ambivalences, the role of desire within rabbinic culture was understood as positive, as a great gesture of beneficence that God had made towards human beings, binding men with women and women with men in bonds of *charis, hibbah,* fond and loving kindness.

Far from being a simple legacy of its cultural heritage, the rabbinic insistence on the positive valence of sexuality itself seems to

* This essay is reprinted, slightly abridged and slightly revised, from Daniel Boyarin, *Carnal Israel: Reading Sex in Talmudic Culture* (Berkeley and Los Angeles, 1993), by permission of the University of California Press.

have been hard won and contested (Boyarin forthcoming). The Talmud relates the following strange history of the returnees from the exile in Babylonia:

[1] 'And they cried out unto God in a loud voice' [Nehemiah 9.4]. What did they say? Rav (and some say Rabbi Yohanan) says: 'Woe, Woe: This is the one who destroyed the temple, and burned the Holy Place, and killed all of the righteous ones, and exiled Israel from their land, and still he dances among us. What is the reason You gave him to us? Is it not to receive reward [for resisting him]? We don't want him or his reward!' A sherd fell from heaven with the word,'truth' written on it. *Said Rav Hanina: Learn from this that the seal of the Holy Blessed One is truth!* They sat in fast for three days and three nights, and he was given over to them. A figure like a lion of fire went out from the Holy of Holies. A prophet said unto Israel; 'that was the Desire for worship of strange gods, as it is said, *This is the evil'* [Zachariah 5.7]. While they were capturing him, a hair was pulled from his head. He cried out, and his voice carried four hundred parasangs [The entire distance from heaven to earth is five hundred!]. They said: What shall we do? Perhaps, God forbid, they will have pity on him in heaven. A prophet said to them: Throw him into a leaden pot and stop up his mouth with lead, for lead absorbs sound, for it says, *This is the evil, and he threw the leaden stone into its mouth.*

[2] They said, 'Since this is a time of [God's] favour, let us pray regarding Desire for sexual sin.' They prayed and he was committed into their hands. He said to them, 'Be careful, for if you kill that one, the world will end.' They imprisoned him for three days, and then they looked for a fresh egg in all of the Land of Israel, and they did not find one. They said, 'What shall we do? If we kill him, the world will end. If we pray for half [i.e. that people will only desire licit sex; Rashi], in heaven they do not answer halfway prayers. Blind him and let him go.' At least, a man does not become aroused by his female relatives. (Babylonian Talmud, *Yoma* 69b.)

This dark and strange tale is the way that the Rabbis of the Talmud communicate their deepest thoughts on human psychology and especially the complex notion of the *Yetser Hara'*, with which this essay will be concerned. The concept of the *Yetser Hara'*, usually translated as the 'Evil Inclination' is one of the most intriguing formations in talmudic culture and one, I think, that is easily misunderstood. Close reading of this story will help us to clarify it.

The first half of the story is an etiological myth which explains why the Jews of rabbinic times are no longer attracted to the worship of idols. Upon returning from the Babylonian exile, the Jews prayed to God to have the desire for such worship removed from them, and their prayers were answered favourably. They were able to capture the Desire for idolatry and to execute him. In the second half of the story, the suggestion is made that the same be done for the personified Desire for sexual transgression, i.e. adultery and incest. Upon capture, Desire himself warns them that he is necessary to the continuation of the world. Prudently they heed his words and do not execute him, but imprison him for three days, only to discover that there are no eggs in the world. Eggs are, of course, the ultimate symbol of generation and regeneration. Realizing that nothing can be done about the situation, for halfway prayers are not answered, they blind him and let him go. The blinding avails to reduce the desire for incest with one's closest relatives – no more.[1]

The crucial sentence in the story is that halfway prayers are not answered. It is this which gives us the central clue to the rabbinic psychology and their concept of Evil Desire. In order for there to be desire and thus sexuality at all, they are saying, there must also be the possibility of illicit desire. Desire is one, and by killing off desire for illicit sex, you will also kill of the desire for licit sex, which is necessary for the continuation of life. Unlike the desire for idolatry which serves no useful purpose other than testing resistance, the desire for sex itself is productive and vital – but it has destructive and negative concomitants. It is these which need to be controlled, and can be but only with difficulty. Desire itself is referred to as the 'Evil Desire', because of this admixture of destructiveness and lawlessness which it necessarily carries, not because licit sexual desire and expression are evil in any way according to the Rabbis. This interpretation gives us important clues for the understanding of several rabbinic dicta which have been until now quite mysterious.

Several rabbinic sayings seem paradoxically to identify the 'Evil Desire' with good. The most explicit is perhaps the following:

Nahman in the name of Shmuel [said]: *Behold it was good* [Genesis 1.31]. This is the Good Desire. *Behold it was very good* [ibid.]. This is the Evil Desire! Is the Evil Desire indeed good? Incredible!
Rather, without the Evil Desire a man would not build a house or marry a woman or beget children. (Theodor & Albeck 1965:73)

This is an unambiguous rejection of ethical dualism, that is the doctrine that there are two forces contending within a human being, one for evil and one for good. In contrast to other religious formations around and among the Rabbis (including Jewish ones), which held that there were opposing forces of good and evil in the world, the Rabbis insisted that everything came from God, and since everything came from God, then everything was good. This interpretation of the passage is supported from parallel texts in its context, in which suffering, punishment and even Hell are identified as 'very good'. We must then interpret the Evil Desire in these Rabbis dialectically, as itself composed of constructive and destructive forces within its own singular existence and essence. Sexuality is not identified as itself evil

---

1. My brother the anthropologist reminds me that for Levi-Strauss (as for Freud) this 'blinding' is absolutely foundational.

because it is a desire, nor is it left as an uncomplicated good because it leads to building houses, marrying and procreation. It is called the Evil Desire solely because of this destructive side, from which it cannot escape, but at the same time there is full recognition not only of the necessity for desire but of its very positive overtones. This interpretation is supported as well from the following text: 'Rabbi Meir said: *You shall worship God with all of your heart* [Deuteronomy 11.13]. The word "heart" is written with an extra letter, to teach that one should worship God with both of his Desires, with the Good Desire and the Evil Desire' (Mishna *Berakot* 9.5). Both of these midrashim have about them a touch of the provocative and the paradoxical. In both of them, the term 'evil' in 'evil desire' is turned on its head, from that which is condemned to that which is praised above all. These paradoxical texts can also only be understood on the basis of the interpretation that I have given above, namely that the Evil Desire is called thus because desire itself has within itself the necessary potential for evil, not because desire is essentially evil, for it would be impossible to worship God with that which is essentially evil or for God to have referred to it as 'very good'. In other words, just as the term 'Evil Desire' is turned on its head by midrashic manipulations, so can its very evil be turned to good by psychological-spiritual manipulations. One text resists the unambiguous evil of the evil desire because God is its source, and the other insists that this very force can be turned for worship.

Questions, however, remain. If that is the role and the possibility of the Evil Desire, then, what is the Good Desire? And more: since the Rabbis obviously consider Desire itself to be positive and important, why do they refer to it as the 'Evil Desire' and not as something neutral which can be turned to good or to evil? To answer these questions, I am would like to take a closer look at some more texts that treat the question of the 'Evil Desire'.

## Two Views of the Evil Desire

I wish to suggest that there were two partially conflicting psychologies within rabbinic culture. One was more simply dualistic.[2] It considered the human will to be composed of good and evil instincts which were at war with each other, while the other, the one to which I have been relating up until now regards the human being as having a singly monistic nature, which is, however, dialectical in

2. Porter (1901:115 and especially 120) already perceived that there were two different ideologies on the *yeçer*.

structure.[3] The very force within the human being that causes him or her to create; this is the very same force that causes human beings to do evil and destroy. They are inseparable from each other, because they are one and the same force. When one is strengthened, the other is necessarily strengthened as well:

> *And the Northern [or 'hidden'] one, I will remove from among you:* [Joel 2.21]: This is the Evil Desire which is hidden and present in the heart of man . . . *For it has performed mightily* [ibid]: Said Abbaye: among the Torah scholars more than anyone. As in the story of Abbaye who heard a certain man saying to a woman. 'Let us get up early and go together on the way.' He [Abbaye] said: 'I will go and separate them from doing that which is forbidden.' He went behind them for three parasangs in a meadow. When they separated from each other, he heard them saying 'Our way is long, and our company is sweet.' Said Abbaye, 'If that had been me, I would not have been able to control myself.' He went and swung on the door-hinge [a sign of depression] and was miserable. A certain old man came by and taught him, 'Everyone who is greater than his fellow, his Desire is greater also.' (Babylonian Talmud *Sukkah* 52a)

Abbaye heard that an unmarried man and woman were to travel together and was certain that this would lead to illicit sex. How surprised and depressed he is when he discovers that they travel easily in each other's company, enjoy it and then part when they arrive at the crossroads that leads to their respective villages. Abbaye's depression is generated by his self-understanding that he would not have been able to part from her without having sex (or at least trying to), and he a great Rabbi while they are only simple villagers. The tension is resolved (and the depression lifted) by the explanation which the story gives in the guise of an anonymous old man – along with children a frequent purveyor of truths in talmudic texts. The very passion that drives Abbaye to study Torah and become a 'great man', which for the Rabbis always means one learned in and devoted to Torah, is the very same passion that would have prevented him from simply saying goodbye to the woman and parting from her without sex. The desire is one, and the only way for the one of great desire to keep himself out of sin is to simply stay out of its way. The same drive that in the Studyhouse will lead one to study Torah or in bed with one's wife to have intercourse with her, is the very same drive that will lead into sin when alone with a woman to whom one is not married. The passion is one.[4]

3. Note that by 'dualist' here I do not mean the dualism of body and soul or matter and spirit. Porter (1901:98–105 and especially 133) already demonstrated very elegantly that the good and evil desires are not to be located in the soul and body respectively, against earlier interpretations which had held that they are. Gammie 1974 is especially useful in distinguishing different modes of dualism, a multi-variate phenomenon, which I am using here for taxonomic convenience.

4. Another reading of this story, complementary with the first, would have it fit the Foucauldian paradigm perfectly. What Abbaye is saying is that the 'naive', who

However, other sayings on the very same page of the Talmud (and in many other places [Porter 1901:128]) indicate that Torah is the cure for the Evil Desire, suggesting a dualistic notion in which Desire is not the driving force of Torah but its enemy. My hypothesis is that the anthropology more generally held among Jews of this period was the dualist one, and that the dialectic alone is an antithesis to that widespread construction (Porter 1901:125). The use of the term 'Evil Desire', then, to refer to this dialectically composed force of Good and Evil would be partly a relic of the other structure and partly a purposefully paradoxical way of undermining that structure.[5] What could be more dramatic than the declaration that the Evil Desire was declared by God to be 'very good'? Indeed, there are many rabbinic texts which reflect the dualist psychology, whereby the human being possesses two opposed inclinations, one good and one evil which are at war in his or her breast. Typical of such a psychology is the following quotation, 'Let a man always incite his Good Desire against his Evil Desire' (*Berakot* 5a). It is on this version of rabbinic psychology that the Talmud could declare as well that 'There are four things that God is sorry that he created: exile, Chaldeans, Ishmaelim, and the Evil Desire' (Babylonian Talmud *Sukkah* 52b; Palestinian Talmud *Ta'anith* 66a without 'exile' and attributed to the very early R. Pinhas ben Yair), whereas according to the tradition which I have explored above, such a statement would be impossible (Porter 1901:120–1), for according to this tradition not only does God not regret having created this Desire, but the world cannot exist without it.

---

have not studied Torah and therefore do not know of the terrible power of Desire are also not so plagued by precisely that power. The study of Torah with its system of controls on sexuality arouses and strengthens desire as effectively (or even more effectively) than it restrains and constrains it. Therefore, one who is greater in Torah than his fellow has greater sexual desire as well. This is a perfect example of Foucault's 'effects that may be those of refusal, blockage, and invalidation, but also incitement and intensification: in short, the "polymorphous techniques of power".' (Foucault 1980:11).

5. I do not attempt to place the two concepts in a chronological order. On the one hand the monistic, dialectical view may be a survival of an earlier biblical conception. On the other hand, it may be a reaction against Hellenistic or Persian dualist anthropologies, or it may be both at one and the same time! Compare the view of Porter:

The good impulse is rarely spoken of, and probably can not be traced so far back, and *yeçer* frequently stands unmodified and always in the evil sense. This in itself suggests the error of connecting the evil *yeçer* with the body, the good with the soul, making them expressions of the character of two equally essential parts of man. Rather it is the nature of man as a whole that is in mind, and in it the evil tendency, or disposition, dominates. (Porter 1901:109)

I am inclined to think that a good monographic study would be able to introduce more precise chronology here, but that lies beyond the scope of the present work. My only dissent from Porter here would be in his assumption that for the 'dialectical' or monistic position it is clear that the evil tendency dominates. Porter's work remains excellent, and it is a shame that it is not more often referred to.

Once again, my hypothesis here is that those rabbinic texts which speak of the 'Evil Desire' as being necessary and even good represent a dialectical anthropological tradition which stands in opposition to an alternative dualist one, and that this oppositional tradition holds that good and evil are inextricably bound up in the human being and especially in sexuality. There is a strong tendency in the dialectical tradition to give up the usage of the term 'Evil Desire' entirely, and refer to that entity simply as 'Desire'. Notice that in the legend from the Babylonian Talmud with which this section was begun, we do not have a reference to the 'Evil Desire' at all but only to 'Desire'. Since this text is perhaps the most openly thematised representation of the impossibility of separating the evil from the good in sexuality, this provides confirmation of my suggestion that texts which refer only to Desire hold to the dialectical and not the dualistic ideology.

## Sex as Food: The Body of Desire is the Body of Procreation

> Modern societies tend more and more to separate the body that reproduces, a link in an immemorial genealogical adventure, from the body that desires, a lonely object, a consumer of briefly gratifying encounters. Thus, modern man has two distinct bodies, using one or the other as he pleases. This caesura is perhaps merely the persistence of a split opened two millennia ago by the ideological victory over one part of the inhabited world of the Christian conception of carnal relation – and of carnal filiation – as separate from spiritual life and devalued in relation to it. (Mopsik 1989:49)

Perhaps the most arresting fact about the discourse of sexuality which we encounter throughout the talmudic literature is that desire is nearly always concatenated with having children. When 'improper' sexual activity is considered it is related to the production of improper children, and proper sexual behaviour and intimacy produce children beautiful in body and spirit. Indeed, 'procreation' (Hebrew *piriya uriviya*) is often used as a synonym for sexuality itself. We, in 'our' culture[6] are quick to read this concatenation as a contamination, as a devaluing of sexuality, as if it were a purely instrumental approach to the body and one that is repressive vis-à-vis Eros itself, partly because we easily associate it with the medieval church doctrine that essentially sinful sex is only redeemed by procreation (Gardella 1985:10). In fact, I suggest, our reading of this connection

---

6. I am using 'our culture' here in a sense very similar to that of Mauss (Mauss 1979) throughout his work, to refer to that generic European (Western European) formation. See also, 'But there may be another reason that it is so gratifying for *us* to define the relationship between sex and power in terms of repression' (Foucault 1980:6 [emphasis added]).

needs to be studied anthropologically, denaturalized and accounted for. I agree with Mopsik that we reinscribe on the desiring body the very split between the carnal and the spiritual that determines our sense of the body. In this section I wish to deepen and specify Mopsik's brilliant insight. Mopsik makes here two points. The first is that in modern culture, we separate the functions of sexual pleasure and procreation, conceiving them as, in effect, two bodies. The second point is more complex. It is that the split that we make between desire and procreation is the continuance of the split between flesh and spirit for which Christianity was the vehicle of achieving hegemony in the West.[7] Now this equation is not obvious at all, for our dualism of the two bodies is ostensibly produced as the agency of a sexual liberation, as a valorization of pleasure as opposed to its utilitarian aims, while the 'Christian' split is precisely both the result and cause of a denigration of sexuality. We would wish, then, to see them as antitheses and not discursive allies. By exploring here the figuration of sexuality in the rabbinic culture, I hope to show why Mopsik's analysis is powerfully revealing of what the cultural stakes are in our dissociation of desire from reproduction.[8]

One of the most pervasive metaphors for sex in talmudic literature associates it with food.[9] I will turn now to an exploration of this metaphorical field, because I think that reading it closely will provide important clues to the rabbinic discourse of sexuality in general. Once more, in contrast to other cultural formations that conceived of sexuality as being in the semantic field of elimination, for the Rabbis the most pervasive and common metaphors and analogies all have to do with food. Thus, to cite just one example, wives in the talmudic texts describe their and their husbands sexual practice as 'setting the table' and 'turning it over', and the Talmud itself produces a comparison between sexuality and food – both of which one may 'cook' however one pleases, provided only that it is kosher to begin with (Boyarin 1993:116–120). This metaphorical association is very productive in the culture, producing (or supporting) normative determinations of various types. Reading it will, I think, help us to see the connection between the two splits that Mopsik connects genetically.

Let us think about the functions of eating in our culture. I think that we all assume that its primary purpose has to do with the continuation of the vitality of the body. We recognize nevertheless other very

---

7. The reader will note that consistently with my thesis in the whole book, I have not attributed the origin of the split to Christianity, merely its propagation.
8. This becomes, then, another moment in the discrediting of the 'repressive hypothesis', carried out so brilliantly in Foucault 1980.
9. This is actually a frequently attested phenomenon in many cultures. See Levi-Strauss 1970: 1, 269–70.

important functions and values for eating, including pleasure in good food, social binding from sharing food and eating together and even ritual purposes in many groups from particular acts of eating. All of these are understood, however, as being subordinated to and generated by the primary function of eating, which is the continuation of life in the body. We consider absurd if not repelling such practices as those of the Romans who reportedly caused themselves to vomit so that they could eat again.[10] I think that for the Rabbis, sexuality was conceived of in an analogous fashion. It was clear to them that the primary purpose for the existence of sexuality was the continuation of creation – in many senses: first and foremost procreation, but also the existence of food in the world was a product of sexuality and the desire that humans have to create and build was also a fruit of the sexual drive. However, there were also well understood and valorized secondary purposes for sexuality as well: pleasure, intimacy and corporeal well-being. When the Rabbis speak of pleasure and intimacy as leading to the conception of desirable children, then, this reflects simply an integration for them of erotic life into one harmonious whole. When sex could not be procreative for whatever reason its other purposes remained valid and valorized, for in this culture's normative determinations, sex was permitted and indeed encouraged with pregnant and sterile wives.[11] And when pregnancy was contra-indicated for medical reasons contraception was permitted also for the pleasure and health of the body.[12] Sexuality was primarily oriented towards the needs of the body, and the central need of the body was to continue its life, through eating and ultimately through reproducing.

Interpreting Mopsik's remark then, I would suggest that what occasions our discomfort with both the indissociable connection of sex with procreation and the pervasive metaphors of sex as eating is our desire to spiritualize sexuality itself. Still inhabiting the Platonic universe of dualism, in which the body is devalued vis-à-vis the spirit, and yet desiring to valorize sexuality, we have discovered a powerful strategy. We have spiritualized desire, removing it from the realm of such bodily processes as becoming pregnant: the body of desire is almost not a body at all but an adjunct of the spirit. The effect is a reinscrip-

10. In the Middle Ages some rabbinic thinkers would actualize this aspect of the metaphor in a way that the talmudic Rabbis never envisioned, regarding all non-procreative sex as equivalent to eating and then vomiting (Biale 1992).
11. See *Carnal Israel*, p. 56.
12. Interestingly enough, in the early modern period when technologies of contraception became readily available, the condom was rejected as a mode of contraception by rabbinic authorities, while such devices as the pessary were acceptable. The rationale advanced by at least one leading seventeenth-century Rabbi was that the condom interfered with the 'pleasure of one body with another', which *was the natural purpose of sex.*

tion within desire of that spiritualizing impulse of which Judith Butler speaks as transcending desire: 'That sexuality now embodies this religious impulse in the form of the demand for love (considered to be an "absolute" demand) that is distinct from both need and desire (a kind of ecstatic transcendence that eclipses sexuality altogether) lends further credibility to the Symbolic as that which operates for human subjects as the inaccessible but all-determining deity' (Butler 1990:56). In the split of the two bodies, sexuality itself eclipses sexuality altogether by disembodying it. This is part and parcel – if a sort of reversal – of that very moralizing process regarding sexuality that Foucault has documented so powerfully in his works. Peter Gardella has documented this process in American culture, 'Finally, experts on sex inherited their faith in liberation through orgasm from Christians who had found freedom from sin in moments of religious ecstasy. The quest for ecstasy in orgasm then led people to neglect sensuality. Western mystical tradition has always known that in ecstasy the action of the senses is suspended. In America the pursuit of orgasm as the equivalent of religious ecstasy quickly became an ascetic practice ...' (Gardella 1985:7 and 117). According to Gardella, then, that very Christian impulse which had produced the doctrine of sensuality as sin was continued in the doctrine of a paradoxically disembodied sex.

For the Rabbis in general, sexuality was a powerful drive with very destructive possibilities but essentially a creative force in the world's life. Its proper deployment was as unproblematic as proper eating, and violation of its proper practice was similar to the eating of food that is non-kosher, a violation of the laws of the Torah, no more or less.[13] The hidden workings of desire have not become yet – as they would in the Middle Ages for many Jewish thinkers – the object of an intense activity of personal scrutiny and the marker of the state of the soul. Foucault could have supported his claim that 'sexuality' in the modern sense, that is in the sense that someone *has* a sexuality, is culturally specific to our modern formation by referring to Late Antique Jewish culture as well as to the Greeks and Romans.

In fine, then, what I am suggesting is that rabbinic Judaism was marked by a double discourse on human good and evil.[14] The first

13. Ironically, the Gardella quotation continues, 'Marabel Morgan, evangelical author of *The Total Woman*, urged wives to seduce their husbands every day for a week. But she also illustrated the gulf that innocent ecstasy set between sex and sensuality when she wrote that "sex is as clean and pure as eating cottage cheese"' (Gardella 1985:7). The desensualization of sex here is not in the metaphor of food but in the choice of menu. One could write as well, 'sex is as meaty and bloody as eating rare steak', a suggestion which I imagine some of my readers will find crude, thus helping me make my point.

14. I do not find any way of sorting these two discourses out chronologically or geographically between authorities or between documents. This entire topic of the

was one in which there was a fully formed Evil Instinct which contested with a Good Instinct within the breast of each human being. The goal was, of course, on this moral psychology for the Good Instinct to defeat the Evil Instinct. There is a tendency – but only that – for the Evil Instinct to be identified with sexuality in this anthropology, although some texts seem only to identify illicit sexuality with the Evil Instinct. In contrast to this, there is another ideology which has humans made of only one kind of Desire. Although sometimes this tradition uses the term Evil Desire, it uses it in paradoxical ways that subvert its association with evil per se and make it refer to the destructive aspects which are inseparable from sexuality along with its creative aspects. At times, in this tradition, we find even the disappearance of the modifier 'evil', and we are left with Desire alone, Desire which leads human beings both to enormous feats of creativity and love and to enormous deeds of destruction and violence as well. 'To the extent that a person is superior to his or her fellows, to that extent will his or her Desire be greater also.' Although the second (dialectical) tradition uses the language of the dualist tradition, it does so only to subvert it. For this tradition, the use of the term *yetser hara'* does not by any means mark desire as evil but only a recognition of the potential for evil which resides within all sexuality and desire.

Procreation is then not the 'purpose' or the justification or excuse for sexuality but its very essence in rabbinic thought. Just as, for them, the very essence of eating is to continue the life of the body, so the very essence of sexuality is to continue the life of the collective body. In neither case, however, are other values and purposes excluded or even marginalized. There is, however, a strong construction of desire as problematic and ineluctably dangerous as well. In this reading of desire, then, rabbinic culture fits neither with medieval Christian theological notions of the sinfulness of all concupiscence, nor with modern conceptions of the innocence of all desire, but somewhere else, all its own.

The 'carnality' of rabbinic Judaism did not enable the faithful simply to bypass the sexual anxieties whose spiritual and social dimensions Peter Brown explores in his great work (Brown 1988). Rather the solutions that Christianity came up with to deal with these anxieties were not available; the body – and, specifically the sexualized body – could not be renounced, for the rabbis believed as a religious principle in the generation of offspring and hence in intercourse sanctioned by marriage. This belief had the effect of binding men to

---

*yetser hara* could be the subject of an entire monograph, and I have barely scratched its surface here. Cf. Leaney (1966:42).

women, making impossible the various modes of separation chronicled by Brown for Christianity and found also in various Hellenistic Judaisms. The commitment to coupling did not, however, imply any reduction of the radically unequal distribution of power that characterized virtually all of the societies of late antiquity. Indeed, such inequality is implied (rather as self-understood) in the very quotation with which this essay was opened. Such inequality not only remained a fact of life for rabbinic Judaism but was confirmed in a whole conceptual apparatus, along with a complex tangle of emblematic stories, articulated in the talmudic literature. The early rabbinic conception and treatment of women, however, in contrast to the Roman culture described by Amy Richlin (1992), did not rest on a culturally based loathing of the female body nor on a disregard for female desire.

# Bibliography

Biale, D. 1992. *Eros and the Jews: From Biblical Israel to Contemporary America.* New York, Basic Books.

Boyarin, D. forthcoming. 'Brides of Christ: Paul and the Origins of Christian Sexual renunciation.' In *The Ascetic Dimension in Religious Life and Culture,* ed. V. Wimbush. New York, Oxford University Press.

_____, 1993. *Carnal Israel: Reading Sex in Talmudic Culture. The New Historicism: studies in cultural poetics.* Berkeley and Los Angeles, University of California Press.

Brown, P. 1988. 'The Body and Society: Men, Women and Sexual Renunciation in Early Christianity'. *Lectures on the History of Religions,* vol. 13. New York, Columbia University Press.

Butler, J. 1990. 'Gender trouble: Feminism and the subversion of identity.' *Thinking Gender.* London, Routledge.

Foucault, M. 1980. *The History of Sexuality. Vol. 1. An introduction.* Trans. Robert Hurley. New York, Random House, Vintage.

Gammie, J. G. 1974. 'Spacial and Ethical Dualism in Jewish Wisdom and Apocalyptic Literature'. *Journal of Biblical Literature* 93:365–85.

Gardella, P. 1985. *Innocent Ecstasy: How Christianity gave America an Ethic of Sexual Pleasure.* Oxford, Oxford University Press.

Lévi-Strauss, C. 1970. *Introduction to a Science of Mythology. Vol. 1. The Raw and the Cooked.* Trans. John Weightman and Doreen Weightman. New York, Harper and Row, Harper Torchbooks.

Mauss, M. 1979 (1950). 'Body techniques.' In *Sociology and Psychology: Essays.* Trans. Ben Brewster, 95–123. London, Routledge & Kegan Paul.

Mopsik, C. 1989. 'The Body of Engenderment in the Hebrew Bible, the Rabbinic Tradition and the Kabbalah.' In *Fragments for a History of the Human Body* vol. 1, ed. Michel Feher and et al., 48–73. New York, Zone Books.

Porter, F. C. 1901. 'The Yeçer Hara: A study in the Jewish doctrine of sin.' In *Yale Historical and Critical Contributions to Biblical Science: Biblical and Semitic studies*. In Yale Centennial Publications, 93–156. New York, Charles Scribner's Sons.

Richlin, A. 1992. *The Garden of Priapus: Sexuality & Aggression in Roman Humor*. New York, Oxford University Press.

Theodor, J. & H. Albeck, eds, 1965. *Genesis Rabbah*. Jerusalem, Wahrmann.

# THE SONG OF SONGS
## Eros and the Mystical Quest*

*Sara Sviri*

In order to get a taste of the erotic and poetic quality of the ancient biblical love poem known as the *Song of Songs* or as the *Song of Solomon*, let me start by quoting a few verses from it. The opening verse of this love poem, which has become traditionally sacred, is probably the best known and the most commented upon line in Hebrew love poetry:[1]

> Let him kiss me with the kisses of his mouth
> For thy love is better than wine                                    1:2

> Draw me, we will run after thee.
> The king hath brought me into his chambers
> We will be glad and rejoice in thee,
> We will remember thy love more than wine ...                        1:4

> While the king sitteth at his table
> my spikenard sendeth forth the smell thereof.
> a bundle of myrrh is my wellbeloved unto me
> he shall lie all night betwixt my breasts ...                       1:12–13

> As the apple tree among the trees of the wood
> So is my beloved among the sons.
> I sat down under his shade with great delight
> And his fruit was sweet to my taste ...                             2:3

> Support me with flagons, comfort me with apples
> For I am sick of love ...                                           2:5

> A garden inclosed is my sister, my spouse;
> A spring shut up, a fountain sealed ...                             4:12

---

* This paper is based on lecture delieverd at the Leo Baeck College, 24 November 1993.
1. All passages quoted from the Authorized English Version.

I sleep, but my heart waketh:
It is the voice of my beloved that knocketh, saying,
Open to me, my sister, my love, my dove, my undefiled ...                    5:2

How fair and how pleasant art thou, O love ...
This thy stature is like to a palm tree,
And thy breasts to cluster of grapes ...
And the roof of thy mouth like the best wine
For my beloved, that goes down sweetly,
Causing the lips of those that are asleep to speak.                    7:6–9

I am my beloved's
And his desire is toward me ...                    7:10

O that thou wert as my brother,
That sucked the breasts of my mother!
When I should find thee without, I would kiss thee;
Yea, I should not be despised.
I would lead thee and bring thee into my mother's house
Who would instruct me.
I would cause thee to drink of spiced wine
Of the juice of my pomegranate ...                    8:1–2

Make haste, my beloved,
And be thou like to a roe or to a young hart
Upon the mountains of spices.                    8:14

As we listen to these evocative, ancient verses we too may become emotionally involved, touched by the direct and unabashed passion which speaks with such strong erotic images. It speaks in a language which is extremely sensual about familiar areas hidden within our own selves. It expresses the well-known inner emotional drama, as well as the outer frustrations and gratifications, which love between two people is all about. A poem such as this, with its universal erotic sets of metaphors, may stir within us dormant emotions and sensations. In our daily routines, these emotions may have become veiled from us for a time, but we can only truly relate to them from our own experiences of love: of the ecstatic fulfillment as well as of the bottomless despair in the wretched state of separation from the beloved. We have become accustomed to protect this pitiless multi-faceted experience of love by means of defences, or – to use a more antique and more suggestive image, borrowed from the vocabulary of mystics – by means of 'veils'. But when we allow these anguished, erotic words of yearning and desire to filter through these veils, they may reach our hearts and awaken in us too the dormant lover. Then, the words of warning spoken by the heartbroken female lover of the *Song of Songs* may reverberate in the ears of our hearts:

I charge you, O ye daughters of Jerusalem ...
that ye stir not up, nor awake my love,
till he please (*'ad she-yehpats*). 2:7

When we let ourselves be thus suffused by the 'sweet fragrance of love's spiced wine' (to paraphrase the *Song of Songs*), we may become truly bewildered: can we recognize in these ancient verses the voice of our tradition? Do not these powerful sensuous verses talk in a language and imagery that had been frowned upon by the Sages, the venerable offspring of the Biblical lover and beloved? And since no one can deny that these verses have been canonised by our Sages of old as part of our sacred Scripture, albeit – it must be said – not without controversy,[2] how are we to reconcile the open eroticism contained in them with the seemingly low-key piety and the modest inconspicuousness prescribed upon sexual or erotic utterances, let alone behaviour, by our religious mentors? Are we not taught to revere the Holy Scriptures and to approach them with a pious purity of heart and mind that excludes sexual profanities?[3] How are we to understand – granted the religious canonicity given it – the direct, instinctual, earthly utterances exchanged between the lovers of the *Song of Songs*? The male and female lovers, who are constantly in search of one another; who only rarely meet one another, but when they do, there are no apologies about the triumph and joy with which they consummate their love-desire:

> By night on my bed I sought him whom my soul loveth
> I sought him, but found him not ... 3:1

or this:

> Open to me, my sister, my love, my dove, my undefiled,
> for my head is filled with dew ...
> I have put off my coat, how shall I put it on?
> I have washed my feet – how shall I defile them?
> My beloved put in his hand by the hole of the door *('al kappot ha-man'ul)*
> And my bowels were moved for him.
> I rose up to open to my beloved ...
> But my beloved had withdrawn and was gone ... 5:2–6

The purpose of this paper is to point out that notwithstanding the pious, lofty and allegorical interpretations which have piled up around this ancient text, one can detect behind them an attitude which has clearly endorsed the vibrant and fiery quality of the *Song of Songs*; more specifically, to point out that Eros has become identified, especially in mystical circles, with the motive, the dynamic and the goal of the so-called spiritual, or mystical, quest.

2. See, Mishnah Yadayyim 3:5 (tr. Danby, Oxford 1933, pp. 781–2); cf Abot de rabbi Nathan 1:4 (tr. J. Gldin, Yale University Press, 1983, p.5)
3. On the possibility that the rabbis prohibited youths from reading the *Song of Songs* see G. Scholem, 'The Age of the *Shiur Komah* Speculation and a Passage in Origen' in *Jewish Gnosticism, Merkabah Mysticism and Talmudic Tradition*, New York 1965; cf. also D. Halperin, *The Faces of the Chariot*, Tübingen, 1988, pp. 31ff.

This discussion will focus mainly on Jewish material which bears upon these points. Yet let us remember that although Christianity and Islam may have developed their own sets of images, symbols and vocabulary to describe the yearning of the soul for the Divine Beloved, at heart, the erotic fire which has motivated or symbolized the mystical quest has not only been alive in all three religious traditions, but has also been one of the most apparent passages for cross-fertilization between them throughout the centuries.

We are told in many pieces of Midrash (exegesis, homiletic exegesis) which have been compiled around the *Song of Solomon*, that he indeed wrote it through the inspiration of the Divine Spirit (*be-ruah ha-qodesh*), which revealed to him the true nature of the love between God and the Congregation of Israel, a love-affair so intimate, tender and passionate that it could not be conveyed in any other way:

> Had Solomon composed [the Song of Songs] out of his own mind, it would have been incumbent on you to incline your ear and listen to them; all the more then since he composed them in the holy spirit. (*Song of Songs Rabba*, tr. M. Simon, Soncino edition 1939, I,1,8, p.9)

An ancient tradition, linked with R. Akiba and his school, sees in the *Song of Songs* the most sacred Scriptural testament of this love affair:

> ... the whole world only existed ... for the day on which the Song of Songs was given to it; why so? because all writings are holy, and the Song of Songs is the holy of holies ... of all the wisdom of Solomon the 'fine flour' is only the Song of Songs of Israel. The Song of Songs – as if to say: the *best* of songs, the *most* of songs, the *finest* of songs (ibid., p. 18)[4]

Some sages went even further and maintained that this was no earthly poem at all, and that it was written by no earthly king, but by the Heavenly King Himself: *Shlomo = she-hashalom shelo*, 'He whose name is Shalom'. These verses were taken then to be God's own words spoken 'directly' to the Congregation of Israel, as well as the response of the Congregation of Israel addressed directly to God:

> In all other [biblical] songs either God praises Israel or they praise Him ... Here, however, they praise Him and He praises them: 'Behold, thou art beautiful, my beloved' (1:16), and they praise Him: 'Behold thou art beautiful, my beloved, verily pleasant (1:17) (ibid., p. 19)

The sages also say that this intimate dialogue of love-play took place at the most sacred, most numinous experience in the life of the Jewish people, namely, during the awesome events of the Exodus from Egypt. R. 'Akiba who, as we shall see, is one of the main exponents of the mystical interpretation of the *Song of Songs*, went so far as to say, that had the Torah not been given to Israel at all, the *Song of Songs*

---

4. See also *Mishnah, Yadayyim*, 3:5

would have fulfilled its function and holiness.[5] Without bearing this in mind, it may be difficult for us today to take seriously such interpretations of the first verse of this poem as, for example, the following, ascribed to one of the early Tannaites (first – second century C.E.):

> 'Let Him kiss me from the kisses of His mouth' : If you absorb yourself in the words of the Torah so that your lips are well armed *(menushshakot)*[6] with them, in the end all will kiss thee on the mouth. (ibid., p. 28)

Similarly, we read in the Midrash:

> 'Behold, thou art beautiful, my beloved': you are beautiful in precepts, you are beautiful in deeds of kindness ... in positive precepts ... in negative precepts ... in religious duties of the house ... and of the field ... etc ... (ibid., p. 175),

and one can cite many more similar passages.

In the early historical contacts between Judaism and Christianity, and especially in the context of the earliest theological polemics between the two religions, the transcendental, allegorical interpretation of the *Song of Songs* played a very important role. This exegetical tradition was endorsed by Origen, one of the early Church Fathers, who lived in Cesarea at the end of the third century C.E, and from him it passed on to many of the Christian Church Fathers.[7] At that point in time Cesarea occupied one of the Palestinian Rabbinic centres. Origen, a highly influential Christian teacher and writer, compiled both a commentary and a collection of homilies on the *Song of Songs*.[8] He settled in Palestine about a century after the Bar-Kokhba revolt. The grim aftermath of this revolt – known also as the Second Revolt – and the devastation which befell the Palestinian Jewish communities in its wake, heralded a cataclysmic transformation in the religious arena of the world of Late Antiquity. One of its immediate and long lasting results was the consolidation of one particular theme in Christian theology: the belief that these events were a sign of God's retribution. God had forever removed His love from the physical, sinful Israel and had bestowed it on the 'new', Spiritual Israel, namely the Christian Church.[9] This theological principle, which conceives of the Christian Church as the 'true', spiritual Israel, who has come to replace the rejected physical Israel, is closely linked with the development of the allegorical interpretation of the *Song of Songs*.

---

5. See Schechter, ed., *Aggadat Shir ha-Shirim*, p.5; see also E.E. Urbach, *The Sages, Their Concepts and Beliefs*, Jerusalem, 1969, p. 131 (in Hebrew).
6. There is an implicit pun here between the Hebrew root *n-sh-k* in the sense of 'kiss' and the same root in the sense of 'arms', 'weapon'.
7. See N.R.M. DeLange, *Origen and the Jews: Studies in Jewish-Christian Relations in Third Century Palestine*, Cambridge, 1976.
8. See Origen, *The Song of Songs: Commenatry and Homilies*, tr. R.P. Lawson, London 1957
9. See e.g., M. Simon, *Verus Israel*, (tr. H. McKeating), Oxford 1986, esp. pp. 65ff.

Origen maintained close links with some of the Tannaites of his time and place. These embodied the second generation of disciples of the great second-century rabbis: R. Akiba, R. Ishmael and other eminent sages who, according to the Rabbinic tradition, had been ruthlessly executed by the Romans. From these third-century sages Origen learned methods of scriptural commentary, namely, Midrash. In his writings he sometimes quotes explicitly from Tannaitic traditions. It is now well known that with Origen the allegorical interpretation of the *Song of Songs* was introduced into Christian circles.[10] As in the Rabbinic tradition, the poetic expressions of the *Song of Songs* had been stripped of their earthly sensuality, and were given a 'clean', allegorical and transcendental meaning. But in Origen's teaching this interpretation acquired a new, polemical message: it was the Church, not Judaism, which had now become the legitimate heir of the Congregation of Israel in the holy matrimonial love affair between God, or Christ, and Christianity. Origen interprets the opening verse of the *Song of Songs* in the following way:

> 'Let him kiss me from the kisses of his mouth': It is the Church who speaks here as a collective person. She says: I am tired of the gifts I have been given as dowry for my wedding, since, when I was getting prepared for my wedding with the King's son, his holy messengers brought me the Torah for my wedding gift ... now I pray and beseech Thee, my father my bridegroom, that you should stop talking to me via your servants, the angels and the prophets, and that you should come yourself and 'kiss me from the kisses of your mouth' ... The kisses are Christ's kisses which are given to the Church ...[11]

This material is cited not only because of its scholarly interest, but because it is highly probable that it provides us with a clue to the intriguing metamorphosis of the *Song of Songs* from an enchanting, sensual love poem exchanged between two earthly lovers, into a sublime poem about a transcendental, sacred Matrimony. It may provide us with an insight into the deep collective depression in the life of the Jewish nation during the first centuries of the common era. Depression not only in political, social or economic terms, but in acute psychological terms: a collective psychological trauma in the face of the *loss of a national sense of historic continuity* vis-à-vis the growing confrontational strength of Christianity. This process must have brought about a complete change in the mental and spiritual profile

10. See e.g, A. Louth, 'Eros and Mysticism: Early Christian Interpretation of the Song of Songs' in J. Ryce-Menuhin ed., *Jung and the Monotheisms: Judaism Christianity and Islam*, London 1994, pp. 241–254.

11. On the origins and implications of the *Song of Songs* interpretation in Christian circles see E.E. Urbach, 'Rabbinic Exegesis and Origenes' Commentaries on the Song of Songs and Jewish-Christian Polemics' in *Tarbiz* XXX, 1960–1, pp. 148–170 (in Hebrew); the above citation is quoted from this paper, p. 153.

of Judaism. It is at this very moment in the life of the Jewish nation, that spiritual and theological traditions, which had surely existed long before, acquired the stamp of Rabbinic authority and canonicity and were accepted as normative. Somewhere in the crystallization and the consolidation of the comforting allegorical tradition concerning the *Song of Songs* one can find the footprints of the deep and prolonged collective grief.

This, however, is only one aspect of the issue. The 'sublimation' of the *Song of Songs* and the symbolic interpretation of its eroticism were undoubtedly fed by yet another source: the concrete and mystical aspiration of the soul to unite with its highest 'image', the Heavenly Beloved. In the Jewish tradition this mystical aspiration is linked once more with the name of R. 'Akiba. This is not the place to go into a detailed elaboration of the place R. 'Akiba occupies in so many facets of the Tannaitic tradition, halakhic, exegetical and mystical. Suffice it to reiterate, that it was R. 'Akiba who had placed the *Song of Songs* above all other biblical scriptures, and on a par with, if not above, the Torah itself. It was R. 'Akiba who, in his devotional fervour, decreed that 'he who trills his voice and makes melodies of the *Song of Songs* in taverns and public places may not inherit the World-to-Come' (*Tosefta, Sanhedrin* 12).[12] It is R. 'Akiba about whom it was related, that in the mystical ascension of his soul to the upper realms, he was brought 'into the King's chambers'.

There are many traditions concerning the mystical experiences of R. 'Akiba. He is one of the two main protagonists of early Jewish mysticism, which is also known as the Hekhalot mysticism (i.e., the ascent into the Divine Palaces).[13] The best known tradition of the Hekhalot literature, over the interpretation of which much ink has been spilled, is probably the one about 'the four who entered Pardes'. According to this tradition, which has been recorded in many Rabbinic sources including the Babylonian Talmud, R. 'Akiba was the only Tanna whose soul completed successfully its mystical ascension: 'He ascended in peace and descended in peace'.[14] All of the other three rabbis who had attempted the mystical ascent perished in one way or another. The reason for their failure seems to be that they were not spiritually ripe for the highly ecstatic and highly bewildering experiences which were showered upon them. In the rabbinic tradition biblical verses are quoted to typify each of the four rabbis. The verse

12. See, e.g., Shechter (ed.), *Aggadat Shir ha-Shirirm*, p.5.
13. On the Merkabah and Hekhalot literature see the encyclopaedic study by D. Halperin, *The Faces of the Chariot.*
14. The most exhaustive study of this tradition so far has been Y. Liebes, *The Sin of Elisha.* (in Hebrew), Jerusalem, 1990; see also G.G. Scholem, 'The Four who entered Paradise and Paul's ascension to Heaven' in *Jewish Gnosticism*, pp.14–19; cf. D. Halperin, *The Faces of the Chariot*, pp. 31ff et passim.

which has been chosen to typify R. 'Akiba is, naturally, from the *Song of Songs*: 'Draw me, we will run after thee, the King hath brought me into His chambers' (1:4). The suggestive expression 'The King's Chambers' has indeed acquired a deeply numinous significance in the Jewish mystical tradition throughout its different phases.

However, R. 'Akiba – and this has always moved me – also comes across in the Talmudic tradition as a human lover. His love for his wife Rachel and her love for him has become proverbial. He was a poor shepherd in the service of Rachel's father, one of the rich men of Jerusalem before the destruction of the Second Temple. She fell in love with him and betrothed herself to him against the will of her father. She was then banned from her father's home and possessions. They were poor and had nowhere to live. Winter came and they found shelter in a barn, and every morning – so the Talmud tells us – 'Akiba used to pluck out straw from her hair'. Eventually Rachel urged her illiterate husband to go and study Torah. He was forty when he first learnt how to read and write. He vowed to Rachel that when he became learned and wealthy he would buy her 'a golden Jerusalem' – a piece of jewellery in the shape of Jerusalem. For years she waited for him in poverty, but eventually he came back with thousands of disciples. Then he kept his promise, and the 'Jerusalem of Gold' with which she adorned herself, probably with great pride, caused the wife of Rabban Gamliel, the Patriarch, great distress and envy. How did Gamliel defend himself? He said to his wife: 'Would you have done for me what she had done for him, that she sold her long hair so that he could study?' This, in any case, is what the Talmud tells us, in its typical down-to-earth manner. (P.T., *Shabbat*, 6:1).[15]

R. 'Akiba's agonizing and brutal death at the hands of the Romans is also presented as an act of love. This was, for him, the highest experience of divine love. He died, according to the Talmudic tradition, while experiencing the full depth and virtuality of the biblical commandment: 'Love the Lord your God with all your heart, and all your soul, and all your might' (Deut. 6:4–5) [ B.T. *Berakhot*, 61b].

In his *Major Trends in Jewish Mysticism* Gershom Scholem quotes from the writing of a twelfth-century Jewish mystic from Ashkenaz (Germany), R. Eleazer of Worms, a passage on divine love :

> The soul is full of love of God and bound with ropes of love, in joy and lightness of heart. He is not like one who serves his master unwillingly, but even when one tries to hinder him, the love of service burns in his heart, and he is glad to fulfill the will of God ... For when the soul thinks deeply about the fear of God, then the flame of heartfelt love bursts in it and the exultation of innermost joy fills the heart ... And the lover thinks not of his advantage in the world, he does not care about the pleasures of

15. See also B.T. *Kethuboth* 62b; B.T. *Nedarim*, 50a.

his wife or of his sons and daughters, but all this is as nothing to him, everything except that he may do the will of God ... and all the contemplation of his thoughts burns in the fire of love for Him. ( p.95)

Scholem goes on to explain that 'the relation of the mystic to God is described in terms of erotic passion ... The earthly love, which [the mystic] describes in considerable detail ... [becomes] a complete allegory of the heavenly passion ...' Quoting the Ba'al Shem Tov, Scholem goes on to say '... if the force of sensual love is so great, how great must be the passion with which man loves God'. (ibid., p. 96)

It is clear enough that in these quotations we see yet another approach to the love of God, different from the lofty, allegorical interpretation of the Tannaitic sources or the Christian tradition. Although both may be polar aspects of the same essential attitude, a fundamental difference can be discerned. In the allegorical exegesis a somewhat mental method of 'equation' is employed: the earthly king *equals* the Heavenly King; the earthly Jerusalem *equals* the Heavenly Jerusalem ... In the later mystical tradition, however, the allegory becomes *a reality on another level*: the very same passion, which in our human experience we identify as 'erotic', is transferred, in the rapture and intoxication of a mystical experience, onto God. Whether we can identify with this kind of mystical passion or not, we are bound to accept that this is indeed an experience which has its place in human phenomenology. The evidence of so many mystical traditions makes it a universal phenomenon. Although such an experience can never be prescribed or taught, it has been documented in abundance, and can therefore be validated as an authentic experience of individuals whose *spirituality* has been kindled by the erotic fire.

'The yearning of the soul to the Divine Beloved' and, by the same token, 'the yearning of the Divine for the soul of His human lover' allude to the inner drama which takes place between two separate entities, reaching out for one another. They reach out because their completion cannot be brought about unless they unite. The intensity of this drama and the urgency and overwhelming nature of the 'reaching out' is at most periods of our life dimmed out, we are not fully aware of it. But there are times when we are bound to confront our fundamental existential incompleteness, our fundamental, 'primordial', state of separation. All mystical systems, and for that matter all art forms, all creative expressions, start from this point of departure. From its very inception, our inner life has been stamped with an agonizing stamp of 'longing' for completion, longing for a fulfilling union with the beloved 'other'. For most of us this 'longing' reveals itself in situations which are not necessarily mystical. But in times of great lucidity, or, conversely, in times of great distress, we may become aware that the experience of our incompleteness, coupled with a longing for fulfillment, lie, like an existential programming, at the very roots of our human experience. It seems to me, and this impression is backed up by the evidence of so many mystical representations, that somewhere in our depths we carry a reflection, or an image, of completeness, together with a vague memory of a state in which we were utterly fulfilled.

It is possible that in pure psychoanalytic terms this 'longing' may be interpreted as a yearning to return to the womb; or as an incestuous yearning to unite with the father or the mother, according to our gender. This is most probably true. However, it is also possible that the 'yearning to return to the womb', or the incestuous longing and desire, may be understood as an internal, psychological *metaphor* for a 'primordial' state of union with the beloved. In other words – based on the evidence of mystical testimonies as well as of depth analysis – it is quite possible to turn the psychoanalytic interpretation of the erotic drive on its head. That is, rather than interpret all erotic experiences as a metaphor, projection, transference, or sublimation, of an incestuous desire, the 'erotic', in whichever way it becomes activated, may be seen as a metaphor, or even as an 'acting out', or enactment of the mystical yearning for a primordial state of union. Logically and phenomenologically this is as valid as the more popular understanding of modern depth psychology: neither can be conclusively demonstrated as absolutely true, and both are deeply inter-related. This 'reaching out' which lies at the root of our *instinctive* erotic experiences, and of which the *Song of Songs* gives such a poignant, heartfelt expression, also lies at the very roots of our *spiritual* quest. And this is the reason why the spiritual quest has never been solely about moral conduct or theological principles or even practical precepts; but also, and perhaps primarily, about a *concrete* experience of the erotic yearning of the soul.

# THE LUST FOR ASCETICISM IN THE HASIDIC MOVEMENT*

*David Biale*

Research into the history of asceticism has already proved, one can say, that there are as many types of asceticism as there are ascetics.[1] The significance that the various ascetics attribute to their customs is not static but changes according to the traditions that mould the religious mentality of each specific ascetic movement. From a very general point of view, each ascetic approach tries to train the body – this is the original meaning of the word 'Askesis' in its ancient context – in order to prepare it for a higher spiritual goal than this world. Although many forms of asceticism are supposedly based on aversion to the body in particular and the material world in general, the attempt to be independent of the body very often involves intensive occupation with the different functions of the body itself. It might even be possible to go as far as to say that asceticism is an inverted worshipping of the body.

Sexual asceticism presents a complex of specific problems in the general study of asceticism. Contrary to sleeping, eating and drinking, which also play an important part in various ascetic doctrines, one can totally abstain from sexual activities without endangering one's life. It is possible that this is the reason why sexual asceticism, more than any other ascetic doctrine, advocating the total abstinence from any possible sexual activities, involves imaginary temptations.

* This article is a translation from Hebrew which is, in turn, a considerably revised version of a chapter of David Biale's *Eros and the Jews*, (Basic Books 1992)

1. See Vincent L. Wimbush ed., *Ascetic Behaviour in Greco-Roman Antiquity: A Source Book*, Minneapolis, 1990, pp. 1–14. For a more detailed study see Susan Harvey, *Asceticism and Society in Crisis*, Berkeley, 1990.

That is why many ascetic traditions emphasise control over erotic thoughts as much as control over the body itself. Furthermore, some traditions, like the Hindu tradition, try to achieve control over sexuality by exercising sexual activities without deriving any pleasure or reaching orgasm.

Asceticism in the Jewish tradition is still awaiting a complete and exhaustive study. The accepted view is that the Rabbinic tradition since the Talmud sees the body in a positive light, particularly when contrasted with the Christian view of that time. It is true that abstinence as an ideal, as it appears in the Christian Canon, is almost completely missing in Rabbinic Judaism, because of the commandment to 'be fruitful and multiply' *(p'ru u'rvu)*, and the obligation to satisfy the woman's sexual needs *(ona)*. But as Steven Fraade showed there are echoes of asceticism in Rabbinic texts,[2] although less extreme than in the literature of the Sects and the Hellenistic Judaism of the same time. This also applies to the various streams in Jewish Philosophy and the Ethical Literature of the Middle Ages. Obvious ascetic expressions can be found in all the above.[3]

The Jewish mystical tradition *(Kabbalah)* presents a particular problem.[4] On the one hand, following the philosophy and also the vestiges of Gnosticism, the Kabbalists perceived the material world as the source and the location of evil. On the other hand they claimed that there is a theurgic relationship between the physical actions of the body and the spiritual body of the Godhead. This intricate and ambivalent standpont is particularly prominent in the attitude of the *Kabbalah* to sexuality, our topic. The devotees of Kabbala gave a spiritual explanation to the sexual act as paralleling the relations of the Sefirot and as having a direct influence on them. They assumed that the relationship between man and woman is a microcosm of the relationship between the Sefirot. They created a space for the use of sexually explicit language in their theology. However, particularly because of the heavy charge that sexuality carried within the *Kabbalah*, each and every sexual transgression, albeit in the mind alone, had far more threatening consequences than within the *Halakhic* tradition.

2. Steven Fraade 'Ascetical Aspects of Ancient Judaism' in Arthur Green, ed., *Jewish Spirituality*, New York, 1986, vol.1.
3. See my book *Eros and the Jews: from Biblical Israel to Contemporary America*, New York, 1992, chaps. 4 & 5, and Georges Vajda, 'Continence, Mariage et vie mystique: selon la doctrine du Judaism' in *Mystique et Continence: Travaux scientifiques du VIIIe Congres International d'Avon*, Paris, 1951.
4. See Moshe Idel, 'Sexual Metaphors and Praxis in the Kabbalah', in David Kramer ed., *The Jewish Family Myth and Metaphor*, New York, 1989.

## Hasidic Asceticism

This tension found one of its most extreme expressions in the Hasidic Movement of the eighteenth century. [5] Indeed, this statement might seem surprising, as it is well known that the Hasidic movement started as a moderate reaction to the radical asceticism of the wandering moralistic preachers in Poland during the first half of the eighteenth century. On the basis of a particular stream in the earlier *Kabbalah* the Baal Shem Tov and his followers developed the dialectic terminology of 'worship through corporeality' *(avodah begashmiyut)* and 'uplifting of sparks' *(haalaat nitzotzot)* as substitutes for the absolute rejection of the materialistic world in other circles. One obvious example of this positive approach appears in the following paragraph by Benjamin of Zalozce:

> When the body derives great pleasure from the fleeting and impermanent corporeal things, how can it not do its work for the Eternally Blessed Lord in happiness and pleasure and consequently by experiencing corporeal pleasures he would realize how to worship the Blessed Lord with spiritual pleasure. [6]

However, this doctrine acquired an increasingly ascetic interpretation, particularly with Dov Baer, the Great Maggid of Mezhirech, and with his students. [7] This approach was not accepted by all the different Courts of the first generations of Hasidim. However, the Maggid's ascetic doctrine had a great influence on the minds of the early Hasidim, as it filtered through the large numbers of his disciples who themselves set up Courts. In their hands the doctrine of 'self-abrogation' *(bittul hayesh)* could have led to the negation of the material world, or, in more dialectic expressions, like those of Shneur Zalman of Lyady or Jacob Isaac the Seer of Lublin, it could acquire a two-fold meaning that could both validate and negate this world at one and the same time. [8]

This ascetic tendency is particularly prominent in anything related to sexuality. According to the Maggid; 'during intercourse a man should be a non-being *(ayin)*', [9] i.e. one should shake oneself free from the corporeality of the body and cleave to the divine *ayin*. What emerges from this standpoint is the need for sexual practice without physical enjoyment. This need appears explicitly in the commentary

5. Some of the material presented here is published in greater detail in *Eros and the Jews*, chap. 6.
6. *Ahavat Dodim*, Lemberg, no date p.35 a-b. (Hebrew).
7. See Rivkah Shatz, *Hasidism as Mysticism*, Tel Aviv, 1962.
8. On total '*bittul hayesh*', see Gershom Scholem, 'M. Buber's interpretation of Hasidut' *Dvarim bego*, Tel Aviv, 1985, pp.361–382. For a more dialectic expression of the concept see Rachel Elior, *Torat Achdut Hahaphakhim*, Jerusalem, 1993.
9. *Zava'at Ha-Ribash*, par.101.

of Elimelech of Lizhensk (the Maggid's most important pupil) on the verse in Genesis 'And Adam knew Eve his wife; and she conceived, and bore Cain ...' (Genesis 4:1). The word 'knew' seemed strange to him. If the Biblical verse wanted simply to express intercourse, it would have used that specific verb. On the other hand the word 'knowledge' symbolises a negative action. The correct way in sexual intercourse is to think exclusively about the Higher Worlds and not to 'know' that one was with one's wife. Since Adam knew that he was with his wife, that is to say that he felt her physically, the issue of that intercourse was Cain, who is called in the Zohar '*keina demesavuta*', the nest of uncleanness, (*Zohar* III 60a). Adam's sin was not sexuality itself but the desire and physical enjoyment that was aroused in him while having intercourse.

The catastrophic projection of this 'knowledge' causes a destruction in the upper worlds. The only way to correct this destruction was by the correct ascetic behaviour of the Righteous (*Zaddikim*) i.e. the leaders of the Hasidic movement.

Menahem Mendel of Kotzk, who was possibly the most ascetic of the first generations of Hasidim, supported this approach. He understood the biblical prohibition of adultery as extending to the legal wife.[10] Although he does not make this explicit in the text under discussion, from many other texts one can conclude that he had in mind only such relationships with the legal wife when a man experienced desire or physical pleasure.[11] As we will see below, such desire is a betrayal or an act of adultery against the *Shekhinah* (the indwelling presence of God).

A similar standpoint was adopted by Zvi Elimelech of Dinow who grappled with the famous question as to why our Sages did not institute a blessing over intercourse, given that one should say a blessing over anything that brings pleasure. He concludes that the Sages did not institute such a blessing deliberately since 'according to the Torah it is better not to enjoy'. More precisely one should distinguish between the commandments of *pru u'rvu* and the inferior physical enjoyment which accompanies the fulfilment of the commandment. The absence of this blessing is to prevent the erroneous impression that it is permitted to experience pleasure, an error that he still found with 'the majority of the masses that still retain desire'. However, since it is difficult not to experience pleasure, a man must recite the blessing in a foreign language and furthermore the exact wording should not be written down but conveyed by word of mouth.[12] These

10. Menachem Mendel of Kotzk, *Emet Ve'emunah*, Jerusalem, 1970, par.635.
11. On abstinence in Mendel, see A.B. Heschel, *Kotzk*, Tel Aviv, 1973, vol.1, pp. 243–247.
12. Zvi Elimelech of Dinov, *Agra dePirka*, Lemberg, 1870, par.197.

manoeuvres are designed to indicate that sexual enjoyment actually belongs to the outside world, to the unholy world of foreign languages. Apparently, the assumption is that one can train the body to diminish the pleasure derived from the act by changing and altering the usual version of the blessing. In other words, the senses are susceptible to linguistic influences as well as to physical chastisements. Nahman of Bratslav's standpoint with regard to the *Zaddik*'s sexuality is even more extreme. He held the opinion that one should train oneself not only to have intercourse without pleasure, but to suffer actual pain:

> He also stated that copulation is difficult for a true *Zaddik*. Not only does he have no desire for it at all, but experiences real suffering in the act, suffering which is like that which the infant undergoes when it is circumcised. The very same suffering, to an even greater degree, is felt by the *Zaddik* during intercourse. The baby has no knowledge, therefore his pain is not so great, but the sufferings of the *Zaddik* who has knowledge are greater than those of the baby.[13]

The sexual act becomes holy only when it is accompanied by the pain of the covenant and never through physical enjoyment. In his *Guide to the Perplexed* Maimonides suggests that the pain inflicted on a baby during circumcision is essential in order to curtail his sexual desire as he grows older.[14] Nahman takes this approach further; the *Zaddik*'s sexuality is the sexuality of circumcision, i.e. sexuality that is experienced as a physical pain.

It is of course possible to explain Nahman's comparison between circumcision and sexual intercourse in Freudian terms as castration anxiety. Indeed, it would appear that the paragraph cited above was written shortly after Nahman's marriage at the age of thirteen, the accepted age for marriage amongst the Jewish élite in Eastern Europe.[15] It is possible that Nahman's argument presents a deliberate repression of his sexual desires, as he himself states, or it may be that he transposed his sexual fears into an all inclusive pedagogical doctrine.

In any case, the texts we have read suggest an unprecedented attempt in Jewish thought to create sexual activity without physical enjoyment. However, one can find expressions, both in philosophy and early *Kabbalah*, of condemnation of those who favoured physical enjoyment while advocating concentration of thought on God. And yet it seems to me that in none of these texts was any thought given to the idea of intercourse without physical feelings or through suffering and pain. These teachings are not limited to the élite. Theoretically, at

13. *Shivchei Ha-Ran*, par. 17.
14. *Guide to the Perplexed*, III ch. 49.
15. On Nachman's youth see Abraham Green, *Ba'al Haysurin*, Tel Aviv, 1981. On the marriageable age in Eastern Europe and its effect, see n. 22 below.

least, this is guidance exported to the masses. Even Nahman who proclaims the asceticism of the true *Zaddik*, concludes his words thus 'and it is said that every man can be worthy of achieving this level ...'

## Abstinence Within Marriage

It was possibly easier to preach such behaviour than to actually carry it out. The tension embedded in this teaching was possibly instrumental in advocating another solution similar to the one found in early Christianity, i.e. total abstinence within marriage, once the commandment of procreation had been fulfilled. One can find precedents of separations in earlier periods. The Babylonian Rabbis for example, would stay away from their homes for longer periods of time than appeared to have been permitted according to the *Mishnah*. However, these incidents point more to rivalry between the study of the Torah and family life rather than to aversion to a sexual life. In Hasidism, stories of the abstinence of the *Zaddikim* are emphasized to an unprecedented extent as symbols of holy asceticism.

Many of these stories appear in Hasidic hagiograhical literature and should not be given historical credence. Nevertheless, as stories of the deeds of the *Zaddikim* they helped mould ideals for society, even if not a single such incident actually occurred. In the 'Praises of the Besht' *(Shivchei HaBesht)*, for example, the Besht is related to have stayed away from his wife during the last fourteen years of their marriage. After her death his Hasidim tried to convince him to marry again. His reply was: 'A wife I need? I stayed away from my marital bed for fourteen years and Hershele my son was born by the Word'.[16] This story is omitted from later revisions of the book possibly because of its Christian resonances.

A more detailed story which appears in different versions is told about the angel Abraham, the son of the Maggid of Meseritz. Apparently, the designation 'Angel' originated from his abstinence from sex. According to one version he got married at the age of thirteen, but after the wedding:

> He raised his voice in a great cry that it was difficult for him to humiliate himself with an act of physical intercourse, and from this crying, his bride fainted and was ill for a long time. ... And after a while when he was about to have intercourse again he was crying at that time too ... and he begat two sons ... and the Angel did not know his wife again and he abstained for the rest of his life.[17]

16. *Shivchei HaBesh't*, Nusach Kapust, 36:B.
17. *Seder hadorot hechadash*, Lemberg, no date, p.19b–20a. Also see Horodetsky, *Hachasidut vehachasidim*, Tel Aviv, Vol.2, p.53.

Similar stories appear about Mendel of Kotzk and Israel of Ruzhin.[18] One of the stories about the latter is that he got married at the age of thirteen but refused to approach his wife, claiming that he wanted to be like Ben Azai, i.e. married to the Torah. His mother went to Abraham Joshua Heschel and pleaded with him to exert some influence over her son. Heschel promised that her son would have sons. However later on he reflected thus: 'Who knows if I will not be punished for having brought down a holy soul like this one into the realm of this World'.[19]

Prior to Hasidism, such extreme expressions, an opposition to the *mitzvah* to 'be fruitful and multiply', must be sought in the literature of the sects of the Second Temple period. For Rabbinic Judaism, that proclaimed the commandment of procreation as the first commandment, such an approach would appear to come close to heresy and constitute a real innovation.

## The Mitnaggedim

The Hasidim were not the only ones during that period who were called upon to practice sexual asceticism. It is instructive to note that sometimes the *Mitnaggedim* imitated their opponents (the Hasidim). The Gaon of Vilna, whose position amongst the *Mitnaggedim* was similar to that of the *Zaddik* amongst the Hasidim, served as a model for negating the mundane matters of this world. According to his son's testimony he was amongst those 'who left the ways of this world and its concerns behind in order to labour in the *Torah* and commandments'.[20] He purposely neglected his family and did not show any interest in them. Although we do not have any direct testimony about his sexual life, it has been said about him that he fought a difficult war against his body and against the machinations of his impulse. One may assume that just as he limited his sleeping hours to not more that half an hour at a time, so he also restricted his sexual activities to the absolute minimum.

The descriptions of the Lithuanian *Yeshivot* point to the fact that the ideal of sexual abstinence played an important part in the social-religious atmosphere that they created.[21] This tendency was derived from the term *bittul Torah* ( failure to study the Torah) that elevated the study

18. A.B. Heschel, *Kotzk*, Tel Aviv, 1983, vol.1, pp.246–247.
19. See Horodetsky, *Hachasidut vehachasidim*, Tel Aviv, vol.3, p.102, for further bibliography.
20. The introduction to the Gaon's commentary on *Shulchan Arukh*.
21. A description of the *Yeshivot* is found in Ephraim Daynard, *Memories of my People*, St Louis, 1920. On the family life of Lithuanian *Mitnaggedim* see Emmanuel Etkes, 'Marriage and Study among the Lithuanian Lomdim in the Nineteenth Century' in Kraemer, ed. *The Jewish family*, pp.78–153.

of the Torah onto a paramount position. It set aside any other occupation and necessitated the limitation to the bare minimum of any other occupation that was not necessary for the study of the Torah, including other positive commandments. Obviously the physical pleasures of the body were at the top of the list of possible diversions from the study of the Torah. This term functioned in a similar manner to the term *Dveikut Be-Elohim* (Cleaving to God) in the Hasidic Movement, and the similarity between the two strengthens the impression that a similar dynamic operated within the two opposing movements.

## Adolescent Problems as an Incentive for Asceticism

The question arises why so many movements in Eastern Europe were attracted to extreme sexual asceticism in the latter part of the eighteenth century? I would like to suggest two possible answers to the question although there might be more. One explanation is social-psychological and the second is religious-theological. I would like to argue that one of the reasons for the creation of new religious movements came about because of the disillusion with the system of early marriages that had been typical among *Ashkenazi* Jews since the Middle Ages.[22] It is obvious that this was not the first time that opposition to this custom had been voiced. Nor should one conclude that all those who were part of the Hasidic movement, the Lithuanian *Yeshivot* or the Enlightenment movement, acted in this way because of marital problems. However, it is clear that at the end of the eighteenth century, when the leadership of the traditional congregations in Poland crumbled and various other religious movements sprang up, many people were battling with such problems and this wrestling found an ideological expression.

Movements such as the Hasidic movement not only provided a legitimate escape for the youth who experienced their marriages as problematic from a young age, but also gave an ideological framework that justified such an escape. In a few cases, as we have already seen, we have evidence of the connection between ascetic expressions and early marriages, as in the cases of Abraham the Angel and Nahman of Bratslav. However, ordinary Hasidim were also drawn to the *Zaddik*'s Court for the same reason. Eliezer Zweifel, whose approach to the Hasidic movement was more positive then other *Maskilim* pointed out that many of those who joined the Courts were young boys who had recently been married.[23] Because they were

---

22. On age for marriage in Eastern Europe and for development of my argument here, see my book *Eros and the Jews*, pp.127–130, including the bibliography in the notes.
23. Eliezer Zweifel, *Shalom al Israel*, (Zitomir, 1870) vol.2, Part III, pp.30–31.

disturbed by youthful sins, i.e. masturbation and wet dreams, they were drawn to the *Zaddik* as the model of ascetic sexuality.

Hasidic sources corroborate the connection between the ascetic ideology and the mass of adolescent Hasidim. Menahem Nachum of Chernobyl based his life on the Talmudic tradition according to which the Sages of Babylon would go to the *Beit Midrash* (academy) for a lengthy period directly after their marriage. He thus explains the custom:

> ... this was in order to break down desire by means of circumcising the heart, setting their moral lives aright and especially uplifting any fallen love through the study of the Torah ... After these qualities were in their proper place, they returned home to produce offspring, fulfilling this commandment of their creator just like any other, filled with love of God and with nothing extraneous.[24]

Whatever was right for our Sages (of blessed memory) was obviously suitable for the young boys who were drawn to the *Zaddik*'s court. According to this approach, marriage is essential to fulfil the commandment of procreation but it is also dangerous, for without the right training a husband might distort his values because of his desire for his wife. The study of the Torah, or dedication to the *Zaddik* circumcises the heart, an explanation reminiscent of the connection made by Nahman of Bratslav between circumcision and the pain endured by the *Zaddik* when he had intercourse with his wife. 'The circumcision of the heart' means lessening the sexual desire to such an extent that intercourse would not awaken more physical reaction than any other commandment connected with the body like *tzitzit* or *tephilin*.[25]

Similar expressions are found in Israel of Koznitz[26] and Mendel of Kotzk.[27] Mendel demanded that his Hasidim enter his Court immediately after their wedding, at the time when the sexual desire is at its highest, for then he would be able to break it once and for all. Such phrases serve as clear evidence of a very powerful ideology which was moulded as a response to the problems of adolescent Jewish males in Eastern Europe.

## The Erotic Theology of the Hasidic Movement

The development of erotic asceticism within the Hasidic movement was rooted not only in sociological, but also theological problems. Obviously these two components – the spiritual and the sociological – were not separated from each other, and it is difficult, if not impos-

24. *Meor Einaim*, Lech-Lecha p.24.
25. Ibid., see also *Zava'at Ha-Ribash* par.101 (a discourse attributed to the Maggid).
26. See *Mishmeret Itamar* 1:1.
27. Heschel, *Kotzk*, Tel Aviv, 1983, vol.1, pp.246–247.

sible, to determine which was the chicken and which the egg. What is important is that suppressing physical sexual enjoyment was not the suppression of Eros. On the contrary, in the Hasidic Movement, similar to mystical movements in other traditions, erotic energies found their place on the divine level. The impulse to sexual asceticism within the marriage was a direct result of mystic theology that emphasised more strongly the erotic coupling between the Hasid and God. Based on the earlier *Kabbalah*, the Hasidic literature described the *Devekut* (cleaving) with God in erotic language, which starkly contrasted the revulsion of many Hasidic philosophical leaders towards sexuality on a human level. However, as we will see below, in contrast with the *Kabbalah* of the *Zohar*, in which human beings are the theurgic aid for the Hieros Gamos, in the Hasidic texts there is a clear sense of the opposition between the sexual demands of God and those of the human female. It seems to me that the novelty here is the almost exclusive emphasis on the union between the Hasid and God for the sake of diminishing the copulation of man and woman. Marital relationships are possibly the starting-point of the process towards union with God, but only with the stipulation that at the end the Hasid will succeed in depleting them of anything relating to this world.

The motif of the sexual union of the Hasid with God is repeated in all the genres of Hasidic literature. This may be illustrated, for example by Yaakov Yitzhak, the Seer of Lublin, who took a particularly extreme ascetic-erotic position:

> We have explained the verse 'and in sin my mother conceived (*yehemateni*) me' (Psalms 51,7) that repentance is called a command, for since man was made as if a new creature that has just been born and it is known that one needs great desire for the worship of God, and desire comes from the evil inclination, that is the meaning of 'and in sin (in heat) my mother conceived me' it gives me 'heat' for the Lord, Blessed be He, to worship Him with enthusiasm. And this is the meaning of 'Command Aaron and his sons etc.' this is a terminology of exhortation, for the desire that comes from the evil inclination is called *tzav* 'command'.[28]

It is an interesting fact that the sexual 'heat' or excitation mentioned in the Biblical verse takes on a clear theological explanation here: the evil inclination transposed into erotic 'heat' for God.[29]

28. Yaakov Ytzchak of Lublin *Divrei Emet*, p.81. Also see Rachel Elior, *From Lublin to Izbezia: Between awe and love and depth and variation – Changes in the religious thought of the Hasidism in Poland* (this text is not yet published). The Seer was much less ascetic than other Hasidic leaders and also preached against too much sexual asceticism. On this see *Zot Zikaron* p.126. On the Seer's Hasidism which was positive about the material world see Rachel Elior, 'The Doctrine of the Zaddik the Seer of Lublin' in Ada Rappaport-Albert and Steven Zipperstein eds. *Jewish History Essays in Honour of Chimen Abramsky*, London, 1988, pp.393–455.

29. Harnessing the evil inclination to God's worship is an important motif in early Hasidism that was adapted from ethical-kabbalistic literature. See for example *Shnei Luchot Ha-brit* p.49a-b and p.110a.

The most surprising text that talks about the communion between God and the Hasid in erotic terms is attributed to the Besht himself, although this attribution is somewhat problematic:

> Prayer is a form of intercourse with the *Shekhinah* (God), and just as at the beginning of intercourse one moves one's body, so it is necessary to move one's body at first in prayer, but afterward one can stand still, without any movement when there is a great union with the *Shekhinah*. The power of his movement causes a great arousal, for it causes him to think: ' why am I moving myself?' [And he answers himself:] 'Because perhaps the *Shekhinah* is actually standing in front of me.' And from this great power, he comes to a great passion.[30]

The Mitnaggedim appear to have known this text from the *Zava'at Ha-Ribash* and distorted it by claiming that the Besht instructed his Hasidim to imagine that a woman was standing in front of them during prayer, and the *Devekut* described here actually led to ejaculation.[31]

Indeed, even in that Hasidic text, *Zava'at Ha-Ribash*, the union with God is described as a metaphorical orgasm, that takes one close to death: 'And it is only out of grace from God blessed be He, that a man remains alive after prayer, since from a physical point of view, he should die, for he loses all his life force in prayer ...' (*Zava'at Ha-Ribash*, para 38). The loss of the life force during intercourse is a well-known theme in ancient medicine which left its mark on the beliefs and opinions of the Middle Ages. Within the Hasidic context, this opinion is given an extra dimension: if direct human sexuality is so threatening how much more threatening would be union with the *Shekhinah*. If so, what a great achievement it would be for the young virile Hasid to unite with the *Shekhinah* and survive. Furthermore one might go so far as to suggest that this is a spiritualized version of a typical male fantasy dealing with the conquering of the unattainable erotic woman – i.e., the *Shekhinah*.

Therefore, it is not surprising that such dedication to the *Shekhinah* to the point of death could remove any interest in sexuality of this world, as is testified in one of the sayings of Aaron Halevi, a Hasid who was an opponent of Chabad Hasidism: 'The real end of the individual soul that hands itself over, willingly and in its entirety, with all the strength of its ten faculties; should uproot its own life in order to be absorbed in the body of the king (God). That soul should detest its life, even the essential part of life that is crucial for the study of the Torah and worship and for the continuation of the species, and it has no wish for any life except that which is necessary to adhere to the source.' (*Avodat Halevi*, 17, 1-2).

The connection between asceticism in this world and the erotic desire to be united with God appears in many places in Hasidic lit-

30. *Zava'at ha-Ribash*, par.68.
31. See Mordechai Wilensky, *Chasidim vemitnaggedim*, Jerusalem, 1970, vol.2 p.108.

erature. I will cite two examples with the same subject. Jacob Joseph
of Polonnye belonged to a less ascetic stream of early Hasidism, but
his explanations on Mishna *Kiddushin* 'a woman can be acquired in
three ways: by money, or by document or by intercourse' (*Kiddushin*
1:1), attributes a higher value to the union with the *Shekhinah* than to
human union.[32] The beginning of man's life has to be material and
is symbolised by money. Specifically, the material value here is the
desire for women. From sexual desire one has to rise up to the next
stage, the document, i.e. the study of the Torah. But the final and
highest stage is *biah* intercourse which signifies here the exact opposite of a carnal act of intercourse, i.e. spiritual intercourse with God.
Therefore the main aim is to transform the desire for physical union
to a desire for spiritual union and to turn the subject from women to
God. In this way sexual asceticism facilitates spiritual union.

Another example is the commentary of the Maggid of Mezeritz
on the Talmudic saying: 'I have studied the Torah with my ten fin-
gers and I did not enjoy it, not even with one finger' (*Ketubot* 104a).
He concludes that the 'little finger' is the male sexual organ. In order
to explain the text he cites another well-known saying: 'There is a
small organ in man, when you starve it, it is satisfied, when you satisfy it, it is hungry' (*Sukka* 52,b). He maintains that only by 'starving
the organ' at the time of intercourse can one satisfy the desire for
God. The requirement to desire God is accompanied by the requirement for sexual asceticism.[33]

As is implied in the above cited passage from *Avodat Halevi*, rejection and abhorrence of this world can lead into transgression of the
*mitzvot* themselves. Indeed, although the majority of the Hasidic
leaders were careful not to advocate an antinomian doctrine, there
were certainly such echoes among some of them. Mordechai Yosef of
Izbezia claimed that there is no absolute truth, but different, even
contradictory truths.[34] There is even one truth that exists beyond the
*Halakha*. On this level which he calls '*or barur*', clear light, the prohibitions on forbidden marriages become permissible: 'because in the
Clear Light, there are no prohibitions nor restrictions'.[35] Therefore
he justifies the case of Judah's relations with his daughter-in-law
Tamar (Genesis 38) as incest which serves a holy purpose. The terminology of forbidden marriages (*Arayot*) is connected in his view to
'doubts' that have a positive and essential place in his theology.[36]

---

32. *Toldot Yaakov Yosef* (Jerusalem 1965) vol.2 p.559.
33. *Maggid Devarav leYaakov* par.55, pp.76–77.
34. See R. Elior, *From Lublin to Izbezia*.
35. *Mei HaShiloach* Part I *shemini*, 34a.
36. I am grateful to Rachel Elior who drew my attention to these texts and showed me
    her manuscript mentioned above.

However, his antinomian doctrine needs to be qualified. In spite of the supposed similarity to Shabbatean or Frankist doctrines, there is no Messianic impulse in Mordechai Yosef. His standpoint is a direct result, albeit an extreme one, of the earlier doctrines of *devekut* such as those of the Seer of Lublin and Mendel of Kotzk as has been demonstrated by Rachel Elior. It is possible that this is an indirect influence of the Shabbatean movement, since many traditional terms underwent change because of its influence. However, Izbezia's radicalism is embedded in the ontological and epistemological state of this world and is not of the 'Messianic Era'.

A second qualification, and a more important one for our subject, is the relationship between theory and action according to Mordechai Yosef. If indeed he allows antinomian actions in the relationship between men and women – and it is difficult to claim this conclusively – he repeats and emphasises the importance of asceticism in such activities: 'in any case where a man needs clarification, the advice given him is first to remove all contact which gives him pleasure because God, blessed be He, will be able to clarify that even what was done against the law, was also good, because "It is time to act for the Lord, they have breached your Law"' i.e. in a place where a man goes against the Law because it is time to act for the Lord he is not allowed to derive pleasure.[37] Such a dialectical antinomian approach is found in his explanation of the incident concerning Zimri. Zimri was killed by Pinhas because of the sin of Ben Pe'or (Numbers 25) 'and one should not think, God forbid, that Zimri was an adulterer, God forbid, because God, blessed be He, will not call a *parasha* in the Torah after an adulterer'. Although according to the Bible Zimri fornicated with the daughter of a Midianite, Mordechai Yosef turns this Biblical story on its head. Zimri, and not Pinchas is the real hero of the story. The esoteric interpretation that exonerates Zimri is that 'Zimri guarded himself from all evil desires'.[38] Therefore, only the person who knows how to afflict himself and remove from himself all physical pleasures is allowed to surrender to the evil inclination, subtly operated by God Himself, in order to achieve His will.

Mordechai Yosef of Izbezia was undoubtedly unusual in his opinions, but even this conspicuous antinomian is careful to maintain the distinction between physical pleasures and sexual behaviour. The erotic tension that Hasidism created between the Hasid and his God was possibly too threatening on a practical level and therefore demanded an extreme asceticism in order to limit it to the spiritual world.

---

37. *Mei HaShiloach, lech,* 7b.
38. Ibid., Part I, Pinchas, 54a.

Hasidism did not develop this radical seed, and over the years shook itself free from the sectarian stance that characterised it at the beginning. But the tension between the desire for God and sexual pleasures in this world continued even to this century, as is testified by Samuel Bornstein in his book *Shem Shmuel*: 'The two desires, i.e. the desire for God, blessed be He, and the desire for external lust, cannot coexist in one heart'.[39] Therefore the strong craving for union with the Shekhinah that took hold of the masses of people that swarmed into the courts of the *Zaddikim* was inextricably linked with an equally strong desire for abstinence and asceticism on a human level. Thus it is that the seemingly paradoxical phrase 'the lust for asceticism' is of cardinal significance for understanding the Theology of Hasidism.

39. Shem Shmuel, *Shabbat Teshuvah*, 1913, p.77.

# HOMOSEXUALITY AND LESBIANISM

# JUDAISM AND HOMOSEXUALITY
## Some Orthodox Perspectives*

*Alan Unterman*

Jewish homosexuals and heterosexual traditionalists often seem to find 'dialogue' about sexual mores very difficult, because it has to take place across the gap between two completely different emotional and cultural spaces. In this, it is not so very different from most gay/straight confrontations, but the Jewish dimension obviously has its own dynamic. The specifics of that dynamic are what make traditionalist Jewish space seem so claustrophobic for homosexuals, and gay space seem so agoraphobic for Jewish traditionalists.

## Reproductive Sex

The pressure on young, and even not so young, Jews to marry is no mere social convention but has its roots deep in the Jewish religion. For traditional Judaism, sex is pleasurable but it is also a celebration of God's world, the bringing together of two people to become 'one flesh' in companionship, the uniting of two families via the marriage bond of their children; and sex is above all reproductive. Among Ashkenazim, parents are thought to derive *nachas* ('joy', 'content-ment' or 'vicarious glory') from the achievements of their children, but also directly from the mere existence of their grandchildren.

In Jewish consciousness, procreation is regarded as fulfilment of God's blessing to Adam, 'Be fruitful and multiply' (Genesis 1:28). It is also the foremost weapon of Jewish demography and one of the

* This chapter was previously published in *The Jewish Quarterly*, Autumn 1993.

most efficient survival techniques for any minority. Procreation needs to be supported by the marriage of all members of the ethnic group. Failure to marry and to reproduce is thus not merely the avoidance of a positive commandment, it is akin to communal treason.

The value placed on marriage and reproduction finds a common expression in the pinch on the cheek, the knowing smile and the 'Please God by you' uttered at family celebrations. It is ironic that *simcha* is a Yiddish and Hebrew cognate for 'gay'. If anything, the confrontation with well-meaning family members at a *simcha* is likely to disturb the equanimity of gays, and of closet homosexuals, even more than it disturbs unmarried heterosexuals. (Of course it is *meant* to disturb the latter and spur them into action.) Those estranged gay men and women who return to the traditionalist space to attend the engagement, wedding or circumcision of a relative may find their own space seriously violated by these pinches.

As Jewish gays grow older, the pinch on the cheek becomes weaker but heterosexual Jewish space hardly becomes safer. Rarely is there a point when someone who is not married is simply accepted as someone who does not wish to marry. For traditional Judaism, all unmarried members of the community are *nebich*, not yet married. All childless couples are *nebich*, not yet parents. All parents are, 'Please God by you', grandfathers and grandmothers in the making.

## Dialogue Across the Gay *Mechitzah*

Contemporary Judaism, even contemporary Orthodoxy, has no central authority and no single voice. The various gay groups too, have many spokesmen and spokeswomen but no single voice. Almost by definition, the closet homosexual is not represented by the 'gay and proud of it' homosexual. Nor the reverse. It is thus unclear whether traditional Judaism can satisfy the demands which gays make on their religion, even minimally, or whether traditional-minded gays can respond to any of the demands which even a liberal Orthodoxy makes of its sons and daughters.

It is possible that it is still too early for gay people, emerging from straight family backgrounds, to define for themselves exactly what they want of Judaism, and particularly of traditional Judaism. Judaism is certainly still trying to find its own response to the various sexual revolutions in western society and particularly to the phenomenon of gay subcultures on the periphery of Klal Yisrael.

Some kind of mutual listening is necessary even if merely to clarify the antagonisms. Otherwise there will be a withdrawal of gays from active participation in institutions of traditional life and the backtracking of Orthodoxy into homophobic slogans. Accusations and counter-accusations, anger and disgust, simply reinforce mutual suspicions.

From an Orthodox perspective, it is quite clear that ways must be found to enable people to come nearer to God and to his Torah. This should be done without compromising religious values or the dignity of those struggling to find a path to God. Such an attempt to maintain contact between people on the sexual periphery of Judaism and the traditional centre was attempted in the mid-eighteenth century by R. Jacob Emden. He wrote a responsum advocating the reintroduction of a form of concubine marriage (*'She'elat Yavetz'* II no. 15). This would involve a couple agreeing to live together as sexual partners without any religious ceremony of *ketubbah.* The relationship could be dissolved without the need of a *get*, and thus there would be problems of children born out of adulterous relationships (*mamzerim*).

Emden supported his position by arguing that it was a *mitzvah* to publicise his ruling in order to save Jews who had been influenced by a promiscuous Gentile environment, or by anti-nomian and orgiastic Shabbatean sects. If easier forms of permitted sexual relationship could be found, Emden argued, then people would prefer not to break the prohibitions of the Torah. Later authorities, it must be added, did not support Emden's position by allowing such concubine partnerships.

## Can Someone Be a Jewish Gay?

The answer to the question, 'Can someone still be Jewish and gay?', is a simple 'Yes'. Whatever the attitude of traditional Judaism to the sexual activities of gay people, and however much some Jews may disapprove of Jewish gays, this does not affect their status as Jews, albeit as Jewish sinners.

It has never been an issue for Judaism whether gays can *daven* in straight *shuls.* They can. Or whether they can participate in home-based family rituals. They can. Should they *daven* regularly? They should. Must they keep *kashrut*? They must. Does God forgive gays for their sins when they repent, as He forgives straights for their sins when they repent? He does.

All this does not get us very far but it does help to deal with the vast burden of guilt felt by some Jewish gays about their lifestyle. To be engaged in a form of sexual activity which is outlawed by one's religion obviously sets up tensions, and guilt feelings are inevitable. There is a form of guilt which helps a person turn to God in contrition, but gay guilt often casts up a barrier between man and God that makes any traditional Jewish life seem impossible for those on the wrong side of the barrier. As far as the *Halakhah* is concerned, the situation of gays is, in most respects, not fundamentally different from that of straight Jews who sin.

One of the most obvious non-*halakhic* differences between straights and gays, however, is that some gays define themselves as a group of sinners. Not in the positive way that the liturgy recommends, by which man stands before God and declares, 'Help me Lord, for I have sinned, have mercy on me, O Merciful One, for I am a transgressor'. Gay self-definition may not involve penitence for homosexual behaviour itself. It is more like: 'Help me, O Lord, for I am gay *and* I am a sinner.'

Certainly Orthodox straight people sin, they commit adultery, they eat non-kosher food on *Yom Kippur*, they cheat the Inland Revenue, they steal the life savings from little old pensioners, they break the speed limit, they fail to wear *tefillin*, they do not go to the *mikveh* before having sexual relations, and they also indulge in homosexual acts. All these are sins incidental to their identity, however, whereas gays define themselves specifically by their sins.

Some gays who engage in homosexual activity see their love for members of the same sex, and its consummation, as constitutive of their very identity. It is this which brings them sharply up against the prohibitions found in the Bible and in the writings of the rabbis. It is rather as if groups were formed within the Orthodox community which defined themselves as 'The Union of Jewish Adulterers', 'Jewish Lovers of Pork' or '*Pesach* Bread-eaters'.

## How Does the *Halakhah* View Homosexuality?

Traditional Judaism does not recognize homosexuals because it does not recognize heterosexuals. The different sexual categories it recognizes have to do with the physical make-up of people rather than their sexual preferences. The two main categories consist of males (defined as those who have a penis and testicles) and females (those who have a vagina and lack a penis and testicles). The two sub-categories consist of androgynes (those who have both a penis and a vagina) and *tumtums* (those who have no clearly defined penis or vagina).

Males and females are forbidden to have same-sex relations, so permitted sexual relations are exogamous between them. Sexual intercourse between males is regarded as an abomination and prohibited in the biblical verses, 'You shall not have sex with a male after the manner of sex with a woman' (Lev. 18:22) and 'A man who has sex with a male, after the manner of sex with a woman, they have both committed an abomination, they shall surely be killed' (Lev. 20:13). Maimonides formulates the law against male homosexual behaviour as follows:

> [A man] who has sexual intercourse with a male, or who brings a male on him for sexual intercourse, once penetration has been effected (if both the men involved are adults) then they are both punished by death through stoning.
>
> This is true whether he has sexual intercourse with a male or with an androgyne, if it was anal intercourse with the latter, but he is free from the death penalty for vaginal intercourse with an androgyne. The *tumtum* is a doubtful case and so for sexual intercourse with a *tumtum*, or for vaginal intercourse with an androgyne, one would be punished by a rabbinical beating. An androgyne is allowed to marry a woman (*Hilkhot Issurei Bi'ah* 1:14–15).

Lesbian sexual relations are not directly prohibited by the Torah but are thought by the rabbis to come under the category of 'deeds of the Land of Egypt' (Lev. 18:3) which Jews should not imitate. As Maimonides expresses it:

> It is forbidden for women to mutually masturbate [lit. 'rub each other'], and this is a deed of the land of Egypt that we were warned against. ... Our sages explain that what they used to do [in Egypt] was that men used to marry men and women used to marry women ... Although this deed [i.e. lesbian masturbation] is forbidden no lashes are prescribed for it, for there is no specific negative commandment about it and no sexual intercourse is involved. Women who engage in lesbian practices are not forbidden to marry priests because of harlotry, nor are wives forbidden to their husbands because of this, since there is no harlotry here. It is fitting to punish them by a rabbinical beating as they have performed a forbidden act. A man should be strict with his wife about this matter and should prevent women who are known for such lesbianism from coming in to her and prevent her from going out to visit them (*Hilkhot Issurei Bi'ah* 21:8).

The above passage seems to rule out any place for homosexuality within Orthodox religious space, even if we recognise that punishments for sins are not meted out any more. In the face of such a condemnation, it is not surprising that many homosexual men and women feel unable to associate in any way with a traditional community which rejects them so radically. In so far as people regard themselves as having a distinct identity, as gay Jews, part of that identity will have to remain in abeyance within a traditional environment or conflict with traditional norms will inevitable ensue.

The situation does not appear so stark, however, if we consider the harsh things said in *halakhic* codes about people who break Shabbat publicly, or who eat non-kosher food, or who shave with

an open razor, or who engage in pre-marital sex, or who eat leav-
ened products on *Pesach*, or who have sexual relations with Gentiles,
or who doubt the Mosaic authorship of the Pentateuch, or who
watch immodest shows in the theatre, cinema and on television, or
who work on the second day of *Yom Tov*, or who drink non-kosher
wine, etc. This does not prevent people who do some, or all, of
these things from attending synagogue, engaging in Jewish religious
life, and even occupying positions of leadership in the Jewish community in Britain.

It is just as unlikely that the *Halakhah* will ever approve of the host
of besetting sins of Anglo-Jewry as it will approve of non-heterosexual
sex. Sinners may complain that they do not really see what is so wrong
with wearing *shaatnez* today, with boiling meat and milk together, or
with driving a car on Shabbat. Similarly, homosexuals may complain
that they simply cannot see what is so wrong with gay sex.

There will always be parts of the totality of the commandments
which seem incomprehensible to a particular generation, or to a particular sub-group. The commitment of the Orthodox community to
Torah is not a consciously selective one, but relates to a whole tradition, parts of which may seem obvious and relevant and parts obtuse
and irrelevant. What happens in practice, in the modern Orthodox
community at least, is that individuals, families and sometimes whole
congregations focus their religious energies only on those areas they
can make sense of, downgrading or ignoring the rest.

It should be possible, in theory, for those gays who desire as full
a Jewish life as possible to emphasise those parts of the tradition
which help them to develop spiritually, and to carry over their arguments about their sexual lifestyle into their private prayers. It does
not seem, however, that there is a greater demand among gays for
some, at least tacit, approval for their lifestyle from the *Halakhah*
than among other dissatisfied sinners.

As long as gays are simply regarded as males and females, homosexual acts are prohibited to them. In order for the practice of homosexuality to be approved by the *Halakhah*, homosexuals would have to
be recognised as a separate, endogamous, sexual category, or as two
separate categories for males and females. This would contradict so
many *halakhic* assumptions that it simply does not seem on the cards.

The sexual sub-categories of androgyne and *tumtum* were not
assigned separate status although views are found in talmudic literature that each should be considered a third sex and *sui generis*. Even
people who have undergone transsexual surgery are not recognised
by the *Halakhah* unambiguously in their new sexual identity (see J.
Bleich, 'Transsexual Surgery and Ambiguous Genitalia', in his *Judaism
and Healing*, 1981). Had *halakhists* been willing to accept the existence

of a third sex, however understood, this might have created a precedent for a completely new way for the *Halakhah* to look at gays.

## How Orthodox Jews View Gays

Failing any *halakhic* breakthrough, the attitudes of Orthodox Jews to gays will fall within a range which varies from 'sympathetic' to 'extremely hostile'. The response that recognises gay people as most equal to straight traditionalists is also the one least sympathetic to homosexuality. It maintains that though there are people with different sexual appetites and preferences, the Torah prescribes how we are permitted to express these preferences. It is not forbidden to be sexually attracted to members of one's own sex, but it is forbidden to act on such preferences. Similarly, it is not demanded that one should be sexually attracted to members of the opposite sex, but it is demanded that, attracted or not, one should still get married and have children.

There are a number of Orthodox people, whom the gay community would class as gay because of their sexual preferences, who yet live in heterosexual relationships within the traditional Jewish community, and have families. Whether they are as happy and sexually fulfilled as they would be were they part of the gay community is not at issue. Sexual expression within Judaism is only one of many aspects of life and what is more central is the attempt to live a life guided by God's teachings.

The most sympathetic Orthodox response to homosexuality is also the one least acceptable to large sections of the gay community. It recognizes that Jewish gay people are substantially different from straight people, and should not be blamed for their sexual behaviour. Homosexual preference and practice are to be viewed as symptoms of a sickness, whether psychological or physical in nature. Gays, although they should not have same-sex relations, may not be entirely responsible for their actions because they are subject to a form of compulsion. Thus their activity cannot be condemned, abhorrent though it is to Orthodoxy, but neither can it be condoned and homosexual marriages in an Orthodox synagogue would always be anathema. Gay Jews, according to this approach, should be encouraged to seek treatment for their condition and ultimately return to the fold as heterosexuals (see Norman Lamm, 'Judaism and the Modern Attitude to Homosexuality', in *The Encyclopaedia Judaica Yearbook*, 1974, pp. 194–205).

Some traditional homosexuals themselves may well subscribe to the 'homosexuality is a sickness' approach, and it may help assuage guilt. Most gays would resent the patronising implications of being regarded as ill. Sickness, after all, is at least in part a convention and therefore, from a gay point of view, heterosexuals may be the sick ones. The idea that forbidden sexual activity could be motivated by 'a spirit of foolishness' is cited approvingly by the Talmud (*TB Sotah* 3a). Nevertheless even such a partial acknowledgement of sin as sickness threatens to undermine the central Jewish teaching that a person is always responsible for his actions.

I have no doubt that God loves gays as He loves straight people. I would like to believe that Orthodox Jews, for all their hang-ups, can practise *imitatio dei* and make traditional Jewish space less claustrophobic for gays. They can do this by holding out a hand to all those who wish to come in under the shadow of the *Shekhina* and mourn their absence in the words of King David's pained eulogy for his friend:

> I am sorely distressed for you, my brother Jonathan.
> Your company was so very pleasant to me.
> Your love for me was a wonderful thing,
> Surpassing the love of women (2 Samuel 1:26).

This is often quoted by gays as testifying to biblical homosexual love but is understood by classical commentators as a reference to the love which transcends all physical expressions of Eros.

# A STRANGE CONJUNCTION*

*Mark Solomon*

Time and again in the history of Europe, Jews have had to justify their very existence. Unlike English-being, French-being or German-being, Jewish-being demanded explanation, both to ourselves and, if we were to survive, to the world outside. For Jewish existence, and Jewish persistence, were patently a mystery, glorious if one were a Jew and infuriating if one were an anti-semite.

Homosexuals, too, have been seen as an anomaly demanding explanation and justification. Long before the term 'homosexual' was coined in the nineteenth century, gay men and lesbians, by whatever name they were known, had to defend their right to exist in the midst of the heterosexual majority. Frequently, the same periods and places which saw persecution of the Jews also witnessed attempts to extirpate homosexuality, culminating in Hitler's massive programme of racial and sexual purification.

Yet, despite the common fate that has attended both Jewish and gay existence, homosexuality has always been for Jews the non-Jewish vice *par excellence*. The chapter in the Torah which includes the prohibition (as the rabbis understand it) of anal intercourse between men is prefaced by the verse: 'After the doings of the land of Egypt, wherein ye dwelt, shall ye not do; and after the doings of the land of Canaan, whither I bring you, shall ye not do; neither shall ye walk in their statutes' (Lev. 18:3). The rabbis saw in this verse a prohibition of lesbianism, which is nowhere mentioned explicitly in the Torah, but which evidently struck them as an Egyptian and Canaan-itish sort of behaviour.[1] When Rabbi Judah, in the second century CE,

* This chapter was originally published in *The Jewish Quarterly*, Autumn 1993.
1. Sifra to Leviticus 9:8.

pronounced that two bachelors should not sleep under the same blanket, the rest of the sages demurred, asserting that Jews are not suspected of homosexual activity.[2] Although the *Shulchan Arukh*, written in sixteenth-century Palestine, qualified this with the warning that 'in these generations, when licentious men are numerous, one should be careful not to be secluded with a male',[3] the Jewish perception remained that homosexuality is quintessentially non-Jewish. Jews just don't do such things. Jewish lesbians and gay men are thus doubly an anomaly, outcast among the outcast.

And yet, we exist. I am writing this article not as a disinterested academic, but in the full reality of my being as a Jew and a homosexual – or, as I prefer to say, eschewing the stigmatizing medical jargon of the last century in favour of the more positive, if somewhat laughable, terminology of liberation; a gay man.

Many Jewish lesbians and gay men sacrifice one aspect of their being to the perceived demands of the other. Some deny their homosexuality as incompatible with a Jewish life, or find a tortured sexual outlet in surreptitious, fleeting encounters. Others jettison Judaism, seeing it as inimical to a satisfying and mature emotional life, and finding in the community only rejection and ignorance. For me, as for many who have accepted, or are trying to accept, their dual religious and sexual identity, there is a drive, an imperative almost, to seek for the meaning in this strange conjunction of peculiarities, and discover its potential.

After more than a century of scientific study, the aetiology of homosexuality is still moot, with psychoanalytic, genetic and hormonal theories, among others, contending to explain the diversity in human sexual responses. Serious Jewish consideration of homosexuality is much more recent, and was only triggered by the gay liberation movement of the late 1960s and 1970s; when, that is, it was patently no longer possible to maintain that 'Jews are not suspected of homosexuality'. Nevertheless, here too there is a similar variety of explanations for the Torah's prohibition of homosexuality and the application of that prohibition today. I shall try to present here the more notable of these approaches and to engage with them from my vantage-point as a gay rabbi.

Leviticus 18:22 states: 'Thou shalt not lie with mankind, as with womankind; it is abomination.' *Halakhically* speaking, this verse refers exclusively to anal intercourse, whether active or passive; other homosexual acts resulting in the emission of semen would be forbidden by the law against masturbation. Many treatments of the

2. Babylonian Talmud (henceforth B.T.), *Kiddushin* 82a.
3. Even ha-Ezer 24.

subject concentrate on the word 'abomination' ('*to'evah*' in Hebrew), which seems to function in the verse as an explanation. The talmudic comment on this interprets '*to'evah*', by the rabbinic technique known as *notarikon*, as a conflation of the words '*to'eh atah bah*', 'you err by it'.[4] This explanation itself obviously demands explanation, and three are commonly cited.

The most recent, that of R. Barukh Halevi Epstein, understands it to indicate the anatomical unnaturalness of homosexual intercourse – or, as it has been called, the argument from plumbing.[5] Our genitalia, runs the argument, were clearly meant for heterosexual intercourse, and don't function well any other way. The satisfactory experience of countless people, straight as well as gay, with non-vaginal intercourse would seem to be adequate refutation of this argument, unless it is taken in a prescriptive rather than a descriptive sense. This is ruled out, however, by the fact that the Talmud permits – though not without qualms – anal intercourse between husband and wife.[6] In a related argument, the word 'cleave' in the verse, 'Therefore shall a man leave his father and his mother, and shall cleave unto his wife, and they shall be one flesh' (Genesis 2:24), is interpreted 'cleave – but not to a man'.[7] Rashi, followed by Epstein, explains that since the passive partner in anal intercourse derives no enjoyment, he cannot be said to 'cleave'.[8] Again, many could testify that this explanation rests on a false premise. As an irreverent quip puts it, if God had meant us to have anal intercourse, he would have given us anuses.

Another, more weighty interpretation of 'you err by it', given by *Tosafot* and R. Asher b. Yechiel, is that '[men] leave their wives and go after homosexual intercourse'.[9] That homosexuality can have a disruptive effect on marriages is shown by the many couples, still today, who separate or divorce, often with great trauma, because one partner is gay. It could be said, however, that the fault lies not with the gay partner, but with the social and religious forces that compel homosexual people into marriages to which they are not sexually suited, and which are therefore doomed to failure. If the distress caused by broken or unfulfilling marriages is the rationale behind the Torah's prohibition of homosexuality, then it is the prohibition itself that is the abomination, not homosexuality.

The third and most important explanation of 'you err by it' is that found in the *Pesikta Zutrata*: 'you err by it – for from it you can

4. B.T. *Nedarim* 51a.
5. Torah Temimah on Lev. 18:22.
6. B.T. *Nedarim* 20b.
7. B.T. *Sanhedrin* 58a.
8. Rashi, ibid.
9. Tosafot and Peirush ha-Rosh, ibid.

have no offspring'.[10] This charge is echoed in later *halakhic* works,[11] and has become, in the thinking of the present Chief Rabbi, Jonathan Sacks, the principal Jewish objection to homosexuality. In his powerful vision of Judaism, the family occupies the central position. 'Be fruitful and multiply' is not only the first command in the Torah; it is the fundamental imperative of Jewish existence. In choosing to have children, to take responsibility for their welfare and education, and to work for a world fit for them to live in, we find the root and fount of our entire ethical enterprise. In the light of this, 'the ideals of heterosexuality ... are written into the entire fabric of the biblical vision,' and hence 'traditional sexual ethics become ... the only persuasive way of life for those who want to engage in the ethical undertaking'.[12]

This grand, sweeping vision, which disqualifies *all* people who, for whatever reason, choose not to have children from being counted as truly ethical human beings, nevertheless begs great questions with regard to homosexuals.

Sacks' position implies, first, that marriage and procreation are physical and emotional possibilities for all gay men and lesbians, an assertion that is questionable and *prima facie* improbable. Those who are incapable of having children, whether through infertility or other disability, must, even for Sacks, be exempt from this obligation. Would he insist that those for whom marriage is physically possible but emotionally damaging must nevertheless venture upon it in order to 'engage in the ethical undertaking', regardless of the cost to themselves and their families? An underlying assumption seems to be that not only homosexual acts, but homosexual orientation itself, is freely chosen, and that a different choice would make marriage feasible for all lesbians and gay men. I believe it is intellectually and ethically valid to maintain, on the basis of my own experience and scientific evidence, that this is simply not the case. Many of us, men and women alike, yearn for the joy and responsibility of parenthood, and if we felt that marriage was a viable and responsible option, no hedonistic consideration would deter us from taking on that blessed and awesome task. Many of us consider, and some pursue, other ways of becoming parents, such as adoption, fostering or artificial insemination, sometimes by arrangement between a lesbian and a gay man who wish to have a child together. Such avenues, however, are fraught with enormous legal and practical difficulties that place parenthood beyond the reach of most of us. Of course, many gay men, and especially lesbians, *are* parents, and continue, even when

10. Cited in Torah Temimah on Lev. 18:22.
11. See, e.g., Sefer ha-Chinukh, 209–10.
12. Jonathan Sacks, *Tradition in an Untraditional Age*, London, 1990, pp.169–70.

their marriages have ended, to care for their children, educate them and work for a better world for them to live in.

A more important general point, however, is that all of us, whether or not we have children, are members of families: those in which we grew up, and those which we form ourselves through our partnerships and friendships. It is through receiving care that we learn to give it; in being educated that we learn to teach; and by living in the world that we gain the will to preserve and improve it. Homosexuals are no less capable than others of ethical endeavour, and tend, if anything, to have a disproportionately large presence in caring professions such as nursing, teaching and social work. Above all, it is through our sexuality, our capacity for love and intimacy with those of our own sex, that we discover, as others do in marriage, the fullness of the covenantal relationship which embodies the deepest mystery of human and Jewish existence.

Sacks' vision of marriage and the nuclear family as the *sine qua non* of ethically responsible Jewish life would create a fundamentalist Procrustean bed for a community, many of whose members not only want, but *need,* quite a different form of sleeping accommodation.

Since the various explanations of '*to'eh atah bah*', 'you err by it', have failed to yield a morally compelling argument, what of the word '*to'evah*', 'abomination', itself? Here, too, I shall consider three approaches.

The first approach is that of Norman Lamm, the leader of American modern Orthodoxy, in his seminal and highly influential 1974 article 'Judaism and the Modern Attitude to Homosexuality'. After presenting the interpretations we have previously noted, he writes:

> It may be, however, that the very variety of interpretations of *to'evah* points to a far more fundamental meaning, namely, that an act characterized as an 'abomination' is *prima facie* disgusting and cannot be further defined or explained ... It is, as it were, a visceral reaction, an intuitive disqualification of the act ...[13]

The question this begs is, of course, whose intuition, and whose viscera. The thought of gay sex may have an upsetting effect on Lamm's digestive tract, but can he so blithely attribute to the divine Author a judgment so aesthetically subjective, and proceed to make it the basis of a law with the potential to blight the lives of countless individuals? Needless to say, the intuition and innards of gay men and lesbians experience no disgust whatever at the contemplation of sexual acts which to them are both natural and highly pleasurable.

Lamm goes on to argue for an understanding attitude towards gay people based on a view of homosexuality as sickness, which dimin-

---

13. *Encyclopaedia Judaica Yearbook,* 1974 (quoted here from *Contemporary Jewish Ethics,* ed. M.M. Kellner [New York, 1978], p.383).

ishes slightly the culpability of the practitioner. He recommends that
laws against 'sodomy' be kept on the statute books (in the United
States), but rest unenforced, signalling society's abhorrence of the sin
but compassion towards the sinner. This has remained the mainstream Jewish approach to homosexuality to the present day.

The subjectivity of Lamm's approach to '*to'evah*', and the deficien-
cies of some of the other views mentioned above, have led to an
interesting new approach by Joel Roth, a leading American Conservative rabbi and scholar. His magisterial responsum on homosexuality played a key part in the recent decision of the Conservative
movement in America not to allow the ordination of gay and lesbian
rabbis.[14] Roth acknowledges that homosexuality cannot be considered *inherently* abominable, but asserts that the Torah simply *attributes*
the quality of abominableness to homosexuality, placing the prohibition beyond the reach of any extra-legal considerations that would
favour its abandonment. Like other rabbinic authorities who admit
that homosexuality is not really a 'curable' condition, Roth's last word
to the gay person is that 'Jewish law would have you be celibate'.

It is truly an extraordinary spectacle to see a leading Conservative
rabbi retreat, on this issue, to a position of extreme and formalistic
fundamentalism, and maintain that the words of the Torah must be
upheld, in the face of manifest suffering and injustice, although they
are, as best we can ascertain, meaningless labels. Rabbi Eliott Dorff,
in a dissenting responsum, finds the results of Roth's reasoning
'unbelievably cruel'.

The third such approach I shall mention is that of R. Moshe Feinstein, the most widely revered and accepted *halakhic* authority of the
post-war Jewish world. In a responsum dated 1976, addressed to a
young man who had asked for help in dealing with his homosexual
impulses, Feinstein offers three reflections which will help him resist
his 'evil inclination'. The first is to reflect on the seriousness of the
sin, indicated by the statutory penalty of stoning which it entails. It
is, moreover, one of the most disgusting of sins, from which even
non-Jews are bidden to abstain. The second is that it is inconceivable
for one to have any natural desire whatsoever for homosexual liaison, which is utterly contrary to the way in which human beings
were created. This is why it is called an abomination, unlike the
other forbidden relationships in the Torah, which at least arise from
the natural heterosexual impulse. Even ordinary sinners do not
indulge in homosexual practices, which have no root in the human
sex drive, but are performed simply *because* they are forbidden, in

14. *Papers on Issues Regarding Homosexuality*, Committee on Jewish Law and Standards
of the Rabbinical Assembly (U.S. Conservative), 1992.

wanton rebellion against God. The third salutary reflection is that all, even the wicked, despise homosexuals; indeed, even homosexual partners find each other despicable.[15]

One can only hope that R. Moshe's correspondent found comfort and strength in these thoughts.

The issue of the unnaturalness of homosexual acts, raised by Feinstein, Lamm and others, is one of the oldest and most common charges levelled against gay people. There is no space here to discuss the concept of nature, or Nature, with reference to sexuality. Suffice it to say that, if nature is understood in an empirical sense, descriptive of what is, rather than an ideal sense, prescribing what should be, then any view of it must take account of the existence, in all periods and places, of a substantial minority of people primarily attracted to members of their own sex. To such people, it is heterosexual activity that is unnatural, whereas homosexual acts feel, and are, perfectly natural and spontaneous.

It is my deeply-held belief, shared by many lesbians and gay men, that this homosexual nature was implanted in me by my Creator. The purpose and precise means of this are open to endless speculation but the fundamental conviction remains that God created me, and wills me to be, gay. What, then, of the divine will as expressed in Lev. 18:22? A variety of responses is possible.

Some, reluctant to abandon their belief in the Torah's divine immutability, but unable to deny themselves all sexual outlet, resign themselves to living with a bad conscience, much like the many United Synagogue members who guiltily drive to the synagogue every Shabbat (an offence likewise incurring the biblical death penalty). Yet other gay men adhere to the letter of rabbinic exegesis and avoid anal intercourse while permitting themselves the very many other possible acts of homosexual intimacy.

In contrast with these dubious strategies, sustained reflection on my situation led me, for the sake of religious and sexual survival with integrity, to reject the commandment altogether. Such a prohibition, resulting in centuries of needless deaths and ruined lives, is utterly incompatible with the nature of the God whom I love and worship. Creation is the overflowing of divine love and goodness, and the divine image in which we are created impels us to love others created in the same image. This love reaches its highest intensity and meaning in a partnership involving sexual intimacy – a partnership which gay men and lesbians can enjoy only or primarily with a person of the same sex. It would be contrary to the very nature of God and the rationale of creation to suppose that God makes women and

15. Iggerot Moshe, *Orach Chayyim* vol. 4, no. 115.

men only to frustrate the realisation of their human potential by a cruel and pointless command. This prohibition, then, is not divine, but all too erringly human.

The logic of this position led me to revise my whole conception of the Torah, which I have come to regard not as the unmediated revelation of God's immutable will, but as an earthly record of the sustained encounter of our people with God, at times expressing the highest wisdom, beauty and goodness of which inspired humanity is capable, at others reflecting the prejudices and fallacies of a primitive and patriarchal society. The present instance is clearly of the latter type. Whether the prohibition of homosexual intercourse is motivated by a loathing of pagan cultic practices, disapprobation of the rape of defeated enemy warriors, or simply revulsion at the idea of man being 'womanised' in a society where women were regarded as necessarily passive and submissive, it certainly has no claim whatever on the conscience of any gay person today.

This realisation did not, of course, come to me all at once. The years of isolation, crushing guilt, self-hatred and self-pity – when every social relation was poisoned by the thought, 'but if they knew …', and every prayer became an ordeal of spiritual self-flagellation – did not fall away in an instant. 'Coming out' was a long and tortuous process of learning and maturing. But I am fortunate in being able to identify one moment of breakthrough.

Alone one Friday night, I had made *kiddush* and was sitting for a while in thought before continuing the Shabbat meal. Of a sudden, strangely moved, I spoke aloud quite without premeditation, and said: 'Thank you, God, for making me gay.' I was shocked and confused by what I had said, not having realised that I had even accepted the fact that I was gay, let alone come to feel *grateful* for it. In that moment of illumination, however, I became conscious that my whole being – my capacity for love, understanding, creativity and spirituality – was bound up with my sexuality; that, were I not gay, I would not be *me*, and that I was glad and grateful to be me.

Pride in being gay makes as little sense, and as much, as pride in being Jewish. I chose neither and can take credit for neither. But I *am* proud of the achievement of Jewish people and gay people alike in surviving – with courage, humour and creativity – the forces of bigotry that would have wiped all of us out. And I am proud, in laying claim to my identity as a gay Jew, to commit myself to the quest for wholeness, and to join the struggle for freedom and equality for all people.

# THE JEWISH HOMOSEXUAL AND THE HALAKHIC TRADITION
## A Suitable Case for Treatment*

*Rodney Mariner*

Ask 'What is the Jewish attitude to homosexuality?' and you are more than likely to be referred to two verses in the Book of Leviticus; others may prefer to waft some of the fire and brimstone of Sodom and Gomorrah in your direction and consider the question even more emphatically answered (ignoring the fact that for Jews across the centuries, the sin of Sodom was not sexual but criminal inhospitality, rendering the very word 'sodomy' a misnomer). Those who would count themselves among the more *halakhically* informed, may direct you to the Talmud, *Kiddushin* 82a, which states that 'Israelites are not suspected of either sodomy or bestiality', which effectively means that a Jew engaged in an act of sodomy, is either not a Jew or (despite appearances) engaged in some other activity. In any event, it will quickly become apparent that for those who would seek to enlighten you, not only is sodomy to be equated with homosexuality but to speak about a Jewish homosexual is to be involved, quite literally, in a contradiction of terms, to speak as it were of 'the Jew who never was'.

If, on the other hand, you were to check the sources for *mishkav zakhur* (sodomy) and its variants in a male/male context, such as *ba al* (he mounted), not only will you find that in *halakhic* terms the 'Jew who never was' certainly 'was' but the very vehemence his presence engenders in a legal system more often marked by mercy than strict

* This text is based on a lecture delivered at the Leo Baeck College, November 3 1993

justice, suggests that there is no room in society for the sodomist who
is, as it were 'the Jew who must not be allowed to be'.

It should be noted that in our time, when political correctness
demands that where possible 'gender-inclusive' language should be
used, a discussion of homosexuality is a singular exception that
'proves the rule'. *Halakhah*, in common with most legal systems, dis-
plays a considerable imbalance in its attitude to, and consequent
treatment of, male homosexuals and female homosexuals. D. J.
West, in his study *Homosexuality* (pp. 14–15), notes: 'Lesbians owe
their immunity from arrest and imprisonment to the masculine pride
of legislative authorities who tend to resist the public admission that
many women prefer to bestow their sexual favours elsewhere'.
There is no evidence to suggest that rabbinic legislators were not
similarly considerate of the male ego, both their own and the ego of
those for whom they legislated.

Consequently, while sodomy in both Torah and Talmud carried
the death penalty for the active and the passive partner, lesbianism
was a very different matter. There is no direct reference to female
homosexual practice in the Torah; rabbinic Judaism derived its prohibition against such activities from its interpretation of Leviticus
18:3: 'After the doings of the land of Egypt wherein you dwelt, you
shall not do and after the doings of the land of Canaan, whither I
bring you, you shall not do'. *Sifra* 9:8 describes these 'doings' as
including lesbianism. In comparison with the severity with which
male homosexuality is viewed, the female equivalent is regarded as
a 'mere obscenity' ( *Yebamot* 76a and *Shabbat* 65a and b) which, it was
suggested, might serve as a disqualification for marriage with a
priest, yet even this possible disqualification was overruled.

To return then to the 'Jew who never was or never should be', as
the Jewish homosexual might be characterised on the basis of his
treatment in *Halakhah*. Part of the problem lies in an *Halakhic* mis-
categorisation or, more precisely, an attempt by moderns to find
*Halakhic* sanction for the prohibition and condemnation of Jewish
homosexuality. The error arises from the misconception that
*Halakhah* actually has an answer for every question, so that it may be
treated as if it were a universal problem-solver, a giant punch-card
computer that only requires a question to be fed in at one end for an
answer to appear at the other. The trouble is that too frequently this
*Halakhic* computer appears to be perfectly capable of fulfilling the
task of an 'Enquire within'. By way of an example, if one were to ask
'Is an oral contraceptive permitted by Jewish law?', it is just a matter
of putting the question and in no time at all the reply comes back
'Yes!' Similarly, 'Is driving permissible on the Sabbath' would produce a resounding 'No!' while 'Does Judaism condone homosexual-

ity?' would evoke a 'Definitely not!' How simple it all is. However, if we examine the terms of the question and the terms of the response in each case, we may well find that something 'similar' is not necessarily the same thing. Thus, the permission to use an oral contraceptive may be found to rest on the *Halakhic* computer drawing an analogy between an oral contraceptive and a sterility potion (*Yebamot* 65b) or Sabbath travel requiring that a car be equated with a donkey which, *Mishnah* concludes, may not be ridden on the Sabbath lest one is tempted to cut a switch from a tree to urge it on (*Betzah* 36b). Finally, and of direct relevance to our discussion, homosexuality would need to be equated with sodomy.

To some, the distinction between oral contraceptive and sterility potion, car and donkey, will be more obvious than that which lies between homosexuality and sodomy. That this is so is reason enough to warrant a fuller examination of both the terms of the 'homosexual question' and the terms of the 'homosexual answer'.

To begin to answer our original question, we need first to examine not what the Torah says on the subject or even the Talmud, but what is meant by the word 'homosexual' itself. Only then does an examination of the sources become relevant; only when we know what it is that we are looking for, will we know whether we have found it. The results of such a study force an examination of the principle of sexuality itself and no doubt will be challenging to some.

Homosexuality is a sexual orientation, while sodomy is a sexual practice that may be engaged in by both homosexuals and heterosexuals (though it is in fact illegal in Britain for heterosexuals to do so). Even in using such terms as 'homosexual' and 'heterosexual' we have, as it were, already moved from the world of the Torah about as far as a car is from a donkey or from the world of the Talmud, the distance between an oral contraceptive and a sterility potion. According to Alfred Kinsey, the word 'homosexual' and, as a consequence, the concept it defines, is relatively young – only about one-hundred years old in fact – and in usage it 'has been applied to sexual relations, either overt or psychic, between individuals of the same sex'. Thus, 'homosexual' is a term for same-sex orientation and is not itself a description of sexual practices. Indeed, it is possible for an individual to be a lifelong homosexual without ever giving physical expression to their homosexuality as too, of course, may a heterosexual. As we have come to learn that sexuality is more about images in an individual's head and feelings in their heart than modes of sexual satisfaction, to define sexuality by the means chosen to express it is a nonsense.

The difficulties of definition become even more apparent in any attempt to distinguish between 'homosexual' and 'heterosexual' as terms used to describe a relationship between two people. A homosexual relationship can no more be defined by what the individuals do to give sexual expression to that relationship, than a heterosexual relationship could be given adequate definition by such a single criterion. Excluding the possibility of procreation (which is by no means a given in all heterosexual relationships), both heterosexual and homosexual relationships share many potentials, such as permanence and impermanence; loyalty and promiscuity; loving concern and indifference. While Judaism is predicated on a heterosexual family unit, to those who can set their prejudices to one side it is clear that a homosexual relationship has the same capacity for stability, growth and the affirmation of God and God's creation as a heterosexual relationship would have for the two individuals who comprise it.

It should be stated categorically that while those who formed the great chain of tradition that transformed the Torah into the minutiae of law would not have understood the distinction between homosexual and heterosexual, it is more than likely that they were themselves more inclined towards the latter than the former, if we are to judge by the legislation that has come down to us. How then, in the light of a contemporary definition of homosexuality, are we to understand the Levitical statements upon which it is claimed that Judaism's anti-homosexual stance and, as a consequence, that of Christianity rests?

The statements appear to be quite explicit and consistent in their wording. The first occurs in a list of forbidden sexual unions in *Sidra Acharei Mot* and states: 'You shall not lie with a man after the manner of a woman, it is an abomination' (Leviticus 18:22) and the second, which is found in *Sidra Kedoshim* in a similar context, includes the penalty for such a union when it states 'If a man also lie with a man as one lies with a woman, both of them have committed an abomination; they shall surely be put to death, their blood shall be upon them.' (Leviticus 20:13)

It could be argued that the apparent clarity of these statements is like that of many Torah translations, illusory; that the expression *mishk'vey ishah*, literally 'lyings of a woman', only occurs in these two almost identical contexts. Thus, without a wider range of contexts, it remains a matter of conjecture as to its precise meaning (at least one Talmudic discussion applies it to the two modes of intercourse of an hermaphrodite!) The precise disapprobative weight of *to'evah* is also questionable, ranging from an expression of disgust indicating an instinctive visceral reaction, to a condemnation of an action which represents betrayal or disloyalty to the group. Setting those issues aside, even granting that these texts are clear and unambiguous, is this a description of homosexuality or of sodomy?

Certainly, the *Acharei Mot* text, even without the 'linguistic gymnastics' of exegesis, can carry the meaning of non-consensual sodomy, that is 'sodomite rape' of the order used by victorious armies both ancient and modern to degrade and emasculate the enemy by 'womanising them'. Surely, this is far from representing a loving and nurturing homosexual relationship, just as similar behaviour by a heterosexual would be remote from representing not even the ideal but the normal heterosexual relationship.

The *Kedoshim* text, which is found in a passage that includes seven forbidden categories of sexual union, states that the punishment for both the active and the passive partner is death. The implication here is that the forbidden mode of intercourse has involved the consent of both parties. However, this could hardly be true of the last two unions (man/animal and woman/animal) where 'consent' on the part of the animal is at best dubious, while the first four unions involve the violation of legal relationships (man with neighbour's wife/father's wife/daughter-in-law/a woman together with her mother). Male/male unions here and, as we shall see, elsewhere in Jewish Law, represent a 'very special case'.

Again, in the light of the *Kedoshim* statement, it should be emphasised that the Torah makes no explicit attempt to speak of the nature of the relationship between the parties involved in a sexual union. Despite media stereotypes, an abhorrence of promiscuity is not confined to heterosexuals and even the disapprobation implicit in this legislation (though not its Draconian penalty) would find support among homosexuals in some circumstances.

Before examining the 'special treatment' accorded this 'special case' by the Talmud, it is useful to note the comment of the great nineteenth-century exegete Meir Malbim (d. 1879), even though the '*illui* from Volynia' would have felt distinctly uncomfortable being quoted in this context. Malbim, in a restatement of a debate between Akiba and Samuel as to whether the Levitical expression *mishk'vey ishah* (lyings of a woman) describes both partners in an act of sodomy or only the active partner, suddenly applies, despite the anachronism of the suggestion, a Buberian I-Thou, I-It dichotomy to the language of the *Acharei Mot* statement. In essence Malbim says that there is a difference between the expression *shakav im* and *shakav et* and that the usage in the statement *v'ish asher yishkav et zakhar* (a man who lies with a male) is that which would seem to indicate a natural manner of lying.

Malbim elaborates this conclusion by saying that while one would have thought that *im* (with) would have been more appropriate than *et* (an indicator of the object of the verb), it is not the case, for the text uses it to say something about the active partner, namely that the mode of intercourse (mechanically speaking) is not unnatural for the active partner and that he may derive pleasure from this mode of intercourse. Malbim writes:

It might appear that *v'im zakhar lo tishkav* is more apt but the difference of this expression is self-evident, the word *et* instructs us about the active partner and it teaches that in normal intercourse his female partner is gratified and derives enjoyment from it. When the intercourse is unnatural it would not be correct speech to say *she-shkav ottah* (literally 'he laid her', denoting mutual enjoyment) rather, *she-shakav immah* (literally 'he lay with her', denoting the enjoyment of only the active partner) for the one lain with is not gratified. Therefore, that which is written here is *et zakhar*, for in this case the passive partner does not enjoy this mode of intercourse. *Ha Torah V'Hamitzvot* 109

To some Malbim's argument may seem contrived, but in terms of our question its contribution is crucial as it looks beyond the sexual act and defines natural in terms of mutual gratification, the pleasure afforded both parties by a loving act. While as a heterosexual it may have been beyond him to conceive of both parties deriving mutual gratification through an act of sodomy, Malbim's analysis of the *Acharei Mot* passage lends support to the view that it proscribes the use by one man of another, as an object for sexual gratification through sexual abuse.

While there are many incidental references to the Levitical sodomy passages in the Talmud, adduced as proof for teachings as remote from each other as a belief that homosexual cult prostitutes existed in the days of the First Temple, to legislation related to a woman's capacity for two modes of intercourse – *ckdarkah* (natural) and *lo ckdarkah* (unnatural) – the whole issue is largely avoided, as has already been mentioned, by the 'Jew-who-never-was' passage of *Kiddushin* 82a. It is important to quote this text as it has been used to 'short-circuit' debate on homosexual practice up to and including our present time.

> *Mishnah:* An unmarried man must not be an elementary school teacher nor may a woman be an elementary school teacher. Rabbi Judah said: An unmarried man must not tend cattle nor may two unmarried men sleep together under the same cover but the sages permit it.
>
> *Gemara:* What is the reason? Shall we say on account of the children [i.e. fear of pederasty]? Surely it was taught, said they to Rabbi Judah, Israel is not to be suspected [*necheshdu*] of either *mishkav zakhur* [sodomy] or bestiality. An unmarried man [is forbidden] on account of the children's mothers [who bring them to school] and a woman on account of their fathers.

Thus when it comes to 'special cases' Israel itself is a 'special case' like no other on earth. Not only does it not indulge in *mishkav zakhur* (male 'lying') – note, *Gemara* only uses the expression *mishk'vay ishah* when quoting *Kedoshim* and *Acharei Mot* – it may not even be suspected of doing so. In itself this is even more special as this concept in other legislative contexts (such as *Bava Metzia* 71a and *Avodah Zarah* 22b which caution the widow against keeping a pet dog or taking in a male student as a boarder) is usually taken to mean that one should not behave in a manner that might cause even the suspicion of indulging in a proscribed activity and thereby provoke malicious gossip. Secondly, ignoring the contextual link with bestiality, the discussion does not actually refer to sodomy as such but sodomy with children. This distinction is not a matter of special pleading or even pedantry, but it is important to note (as translations frequently do not) that there are considerable differences between sodomy and pederasty. Most notably, a sodomiser can be either an active partner or a passive partner, while a pederast is almost invariably an adult male who takes the active role with a pre- or post-pubescent child. In other words, this classic source of 'proscription by denial' against homosexual conduct among Jews turns out to be a proscription against the sexual abuse of a child by an adult in *loco parentis*, a proscription that would be endorsed by most homosexuals who are no more pederasts than they are transvestites or child-murderers or defilers of Communion wafers!

The Talmud itself goes on to ignore its own disclaimer by making direct reference to the practice of sodomy, but when it does so it reveals the almost unique loathing with which it was viewed. *Yebamot* 25a reveals the uncharacteristic severity with which the sodomist was viewed: '[If a man stated], "so-and-so committed sodomy against my will", he and any other witness may be combined to procure [the sodomist's] execution'. In all but a few cases Jewish law requires the testimony of two witnesses to secure a conviction. This appears to be the only instance in the Talmud involving capital punishment whereby the victim of an offence can be a witness with another and obtain a conviction. Perhaps the best example of the way in which the Talmud legislates to ensure that the 'Jew who never was shall never be' is to be found in a passage from *Sanhedrin* 73:

> *Mishnah:* The following must be saved [from sinning] even at the cost of their lives: he who pursues his neighbour to slay him [or] another male [for sodomy] [or] a betrothed maiden [to dishonour her]. He who would pursue an animal [to sexually abuse it] or who would desecrate the Sabbath [which carries the same death penalty in *Torah* as sodomy], or commits idolatry must not be saved at the cost of his own life.

The *Mishnah* and the *Gemara* both emphasise that the maiden must be betrothed. If she were not, and below the age of twelve years and one day, she would not be classified as a 'maiden'. If she were between twelve years and one day and twelve years and six months, her ravisher would pay a fine and be compelled (if her father agreed) to marry her. If she were above twelve years and six months, he would only be required to pay her compensation for 'pain, suffering, shame and blemish' (*Ketubot* 39a). The degree of latitude enjoyed by the ravisher in this context surely reflects a masculine heterosexual bias that would be offensive to any contemporary, civilized person.

The *Gemara* also excludes the High Priest in hot pursuit of a widow and an ordinary priest in pursuit of a divorcee from those who may be slain to protect themselves. Rabbi Papa asks Abaye 'Does not a High Priest dishonour a widow?' He is answered 'The Divine Law sought to protect her from great dishonour but not from a little dishonour.' (*Sanhedrin* 73b)

The *Gemara* makes no concessions to the sodomitic rapist. The law stands uncompromisingly adamant, no hedging, no mitigation; either the intended victim or a third party may kill if they believe there is a danger of sodomy being committed, a suspicion of non-consensual sodomy constitutes grounds for justifiable homicide. For a society that claimed to contain no sodomists, this legislation surely reveals a considerable fear of them.

That same fear is reflected in a late Response from Chayyim Pallaggi (1788–1869, Smyrna) which in a way brings this discussion full circle as it returns us to the very circumstances that produced the *Kiddushin* disclaimer. Pallaggi writes:

> It most certainly seems to me that where we found that a certain person had succumbed to the temptation of sodomy, and if he were a teacher or one of the rest of the professions, then under no circumstances would one allow him a further opportunity to be alone with a male ... Is it not fitting that one who has succumbed to temptation in his professional life should not be allowed to return to his former post ... It seems that anyone who errs in such a situation, even though he made complete repentance, is nevertheless under a ban against seclusion with a male. He would need to take a solemn and binding oath that he will never allow himself to be alone with a male by day and even more by night. Only then will his repentance be recognised. *Ruach Chayyim*

Maimonides' paradigm of perfect repentance is that of a man who has committed a sexual sin who, as a result of his repentance, is able to be with the same woman, in the same circumstances and, as a result of his repentance, is able to resist temptation. It would seem that while it might be possible to give the benefit of the doubt if a woman was the sex object, fear of ravishment by even a penitent sodomite was too much for a heterosexual male to be expected to risk.

To return to our original question 'What is the Jewish attitude to homosexuality?' On the basis of this brief excursion it could be argued that while Judaism had a horror of sodomy, and in particular non-consensual sodomy, it never addressed the issue of homosexuality until recent times; when it did so in literalist circles, it viewed the issue through the prism of previous sodomy legislation. Outside of the non-fundamentalists, there has been little understanding that ancient Jewish legislation operated from an incomplete understanding of the nature of human sexuality. They, and many of their spiritual heirs, knew of only one sexual orientation, which we would call heterosexual, and anything that deviated from that was by definition deviant and unnatural. Thus in our own time, those seeking to give legitimate expression to innate heterosexual homophobia, rather than address and confront the limitations of their own sexuality and their consequent bias, believe they have found in Jewish law an emphatic 'No!' to the question of the legitimacy of Jewish homosexuality even though actual sexual orientation, in contra-distinction to sexual practice, is beyond choice. At best non-Orthodox *halakhists* have been prepared to move from seeing the homosexual as a sinner, a criminal, a willful offender, to being the victim of a tragic illness. As long, however, as homosexuality is not seen as a different sexual orientation, it will continue to be seen, at best, as immature heterosexuality or, at worst, as willfully aberrant deviation in need of treatment.

Can homosexuals be 'cured' of their homosexuality? To ask the question is almost to be beyond the reach of the answer. There is no shortage of those who claim to have a cure, but their clients often turn out to be transitional homosexuals; adolescents experimenting with their sexuality or situational homosexuals, men who are in totally male environments who achieve sexual gratification through same-sex activities. Some years ago aversion therapy based on a Skinnerian model was used as a 'cure'; while it produced a short-term aversion to homosexual images, it was unable to create a concomitant desire for heterosexual images. More recent genetic research has supposedly isolated the so-called homosexual gene; this would suggest that such a gene would create a predisposition to homosexuality which, while it might be strengthened or weakened by nurture or environment, will continue to exist independently. Sadly, instead of this discovery leading to a revision of ill-founded attitudes to homosexuality as a perverse deviance, there has already been a call for more research into genetic engineering to enable the eradication of this significant gene. Homosexuality, it seems, maintains its special status even on the genetic level. There have been no similar calls from these new advocates of genetic engineering for the eradication of illnesses that are both real and tragic, such as hemophilia, spina-bifida or cystic fibrosis.

Finally, has *Halakhah* ever changed its mind about anything? The answer to that is a resounding 'Yes!' and the range of such items of legislature so changed is truly vast. For our purposes one in particular represents a suitable model for revising a *halakhic* response to the issue of Jewish homosexuality, namely the *Cheresh* (deaf mute). While it is unfortunate to have to refer to a pathological example, the comparison holds on more significant levels. In the Talmud the *Cheresh* is always classed with the minor and the imbecile as having no testamental capacity and as a consequence unable to engage in such activities as marriage, making contracts, buying property or many of the rituals of Jewish life, as they lacked the capacity to communicate or be communicated with. These laws did not anticipate the advent of electronic hearing aids or the advancements in the education of deaf children that are commonplace today. In the nineteenth century some *halakhic* authorities had already said that if the *Cheresh* can communicate, then h/she is not mute and therefore not subject to all the limitations of the *Cheresh.* In the last decade there has been a call to abolish the category altogether and allow the deaf unrestricted access to Jewish life. Rabbi Shlomo Goren has opened the way for change in declaring 'Now that this (communication) has been developed through reading, writing and sign language, I am convinced from a *halakhic* point of view we can give the deaf equal status to the hearing and speaking'.

Moses Isserles, the great Ashkenazi commentator to the *Shulchan Aruch* wrote:

> If anything arises that the former teachers knew not or were not called on to decide, then surely a change is necessary as any alteration mentioned in the Talmud, for the reason that the former authorities had not the present condition in mind when they introduced the custom. (*Teshuvot Rema,* Chap.12)

The history of homosexual legislation in Judaism is as confused as it is benighted. The continued discrimination and bigotry it engenders is as damaging to the heterosexual community as it is to homosexuals. Many Jewish homosexuals have now found their 'voice' and science has now confirmed what the ancients could never have known, namely that the homosexual is neither 'the Jew who never was or the Jew who never must be' but the Jew who can take his place in society and, if treated equitably, labour as well as the next man or woman for the coming of the Messiah.

The issue of the Jewish homosexual is indeed a suitable case for treatment; it is not, however, the homosexuals who need the treatment but those heterosexuals who are still unable to confront the primitive nature of their own homophobic prejudices and thereby begin to overcome them.

# Bibliography

Johnson A., *Sexual Attitudes and Lifestyles*, Blackwell Scientific Publications, Oxford,1993

Kinsey A. G., Pomeroy W. B. and Martin C. E., *Sexual Behaviour in the Human Male*, Philadelphia, 1948

Wellings K., *Sexual Behaviour in Britain*, Penguin, London, 1994

West D. J., *Homosexuality*, 2nd edition, Harmondsworth, London, 1968

# JUDAISM AND LESBIANISM
## A Tale of Life on the Margins of the Text*

*Elizabeth Sarah*

What has Judaism got to say about lesbianism? Few people asked that question thirty years ago. Today, after a quarter of a century of feminism, and lesbian and gay liberation, Jewish lesbians are coming out as Jews and interrogating their inheritance. This is one reason why it is necessary to insert the conjunction 'and' and explore the relationship between the body of received tradition called 'Judaism' and lesbianism. The other reason emerges from the relationship between Jewish teaching on lesbianism and Jewish teaching on women. On the one hand, Jewish law views lesbianism as a sub-category of homosexuality; on the other hand, the treatment of lesbianism within Jewish law is an extension of the treatment of women. And so a general study of homosexuality and Judaism is not sufficient: it is essential to consider what Jewish teaching has to say *specifically* about lesbianism.

Interestingly, sexual intimacy between women was not mentioned at all in Jewish texts until 1,500 years ago. When we turn to the first source of Jewish teaching, the Torah, the Five Books of Moses, redacted either as early as the tenth century or as late as the fifth century BCE, we find that the sections which outline prohibited sexual unions (Leviticus 18 and 20) do not include a single word about lesbianism. Leviticus 18:22, addressing the individual male, states clearly: 'You shall not lie with a male as with a woman. It is an abhorrence' (*'to'evah'*). And Leviticus 20:13 adds: 'And a man who lies with a male as with a woman, both of them have committed an

---

* This chapter was originally published in *The Jewish Quarterly*, Autumn, 1993.

abhorrence: they shall surely be put to death; their blood shall be upon them.' The context of each verse is a lengthy statement detailing prohibited sexual unions; the operating rationale is the separation of Israel from the peoples around them, and their consecration to God. And it is here, right at the beginning of the story of homosexuality and Judaism, that we find a clue to the assumptions underlying Jewish teaching on lesbianism which emerged centuries later: women are included in the texts of Leviticus 18 and 20, of course, but with the exception of the case of bestiality (Lev. 18:23), women are the *objects*, not the *subjects*, of the different types of sexual union, and there is no mention at all of women *in relation to one another*.

The first fleeting allusion to sexual contact between women is made by the rabbinic sages in *Sifra* (*Acharei Mot* 9:8), a work of *halakhic Midrash* (that is, rabbinic exegesis of legal biblical material) which comments on the Book of Leviticus and was edited no earlier than the end of the fourth century CE (when the Jerusalem Talmud was completed). Here, referring to the 'laws' of Egypt and Canaan which the Israelites are prohibited from following (Lev. 18:3), the text cites as an example that 'a man would marry *(nosei)* a man, and a woman a woman' – a clear reference not only to same-sex intimate *acts*, but also to on-going *relationships* between same-sex partners.

The next brief comments are found in the Babylonian Talmud – edited about one hundred years later in two different tractates: *Shabbat* and *Yevamot*. *Shabbat* 65a/b refers to the father of Samuel (Samuel being the pre-eminent authority among Babylonian Jewry in the middle of the third century) not permitting his daughters 'to sleep together'. The text offers two explanations for his position: one view links it to a teaching of Rav Huna (a disciple of Samuel's principal colleague, and sparring partner Rav): 'For R. Huna said: "Women that play around *(hamesolelot)*[1] with one another are unfit *(pesulot)* for the priesthood [i.e. to marry a High Priest]."' The majority of the sages, however, reached a different conclusion: 'No: it was in order that they should not become accustomed to an alien body *(gufa nuchra'ah)*.'

*Yevamot* 76a makes it clear *why* the law does not follow Rav Huna. After quoting his teaching the text adds:

> And even according to Rav Eleazar, who stated that an unmarried man who cohabited with an unmarried women with no matrimonial intention renders her therefore a prostitute *(zona)*, this disqualification ensues only in the case of a man, but when [the case] is that of a woman [playing around with another woman] the action is regarded as mere obscenity.

---

1. I have chosen a common English euphemism for sex, 'play around', to translate the rabbinic euphemism *hamesolelot*.

Rav Huna's teaching is rejected because, unlike heterosexual co-habitation, sexual intimacy between women does not render the individual women concerned 'unfit'; it is *peritzuta*, 'obscenity', not *zenut*, 'unchastity' or 'harlotry'. And if the women's behaviour does not render them 'unfit', they are not thereby debarred from marrying a High Priest (who must only marry a virgin – that is, a woman who is 'fit').

Interestingly, the expression 'play(ing) around', *hamesolelot*, is a rabbinic euphemism for sexual behaviour (sometimes translated as 'making sport' or 'committing lewdness') and is only used of women who engage in intimate acts with each other or with their 'little sons'.[2] While the term is very dismissive (in its simple form, the root, *Samech Lamed Lamed*, means to 'swing', to 'be light'), it is not at all ambiguous.

After the completion of the Babylonian Talmud at the beginning of the sixth century, there were no further textual references to lesbian behaviour until Moses ben Maimon (1135–1204) (known as Maimonides or Rambam) clarified the *halakhic* position in his code, the *Mishneh Torah* (*Hilkhot Issurei Bi'ah* 21:8). He wrote:

> For women to play around with one another is forbidden and belongs to 'the practices of the Egyptians' concerning which we have been warned, 'You shall not copy the practices of the land of Egypt' ... But though such conduct is forbidden, it is not punishable by lashing since there is no specific prohibition against it and in any case no sexual intercourse takes place at all. Consequently, such women are not forbidden to the priesthood on account of unchastity, nor is a woman prohibited to her husband because of it, since this does not constitute unchastity. But it is appropriate to flog such women since they have done a forbidden thing. A man should be particularly strict with his wife in this matter, and should prevent women known to indulge in such practices from visiting her, and her from going to visit them.

Maimonides's formulation of the *Halakhah* was upheld by Jacob ben Asher (1270?–1340) in his *Arba'ah Turim* a century later (*Even ha-Ezer* 24), and by Joseph Caro (1488–1575), whose *Shulchan Arukh* (*Even ha-Ezer* 24), published in 1563, became the authoritative guide to *Halakhah* throughout the Jewish world – a status it still occupies within Orthodox Jewry today. The *Shulchan Arukh* was the 'final word' on the subject for four hundred years.

Torah is silent on the subject of lesbian behaviour; subsequent Jewish teaching has had very little to say. But it is clear: sexual acts

2. The expression *hamesolelot* is used in the *Tosefta* (collection of Tannaitic teachings parallel to the *Mishnah*) and in both the Jerusalem and the Babylonian Talmuds as a euphemism for women who engage in proscribed sexual acts – the examples being 'a woman that plays around with her son' (*Tosefta Sota* 5:7; *Sanhedrin* 69b; *Yerushalmi Gittin* VIII, 49c) and 'women who play around with one another' (Shabbat 65a; *Yevamot* 76a). Note that Maimonides uses the same expression: '*Nashim hamesolelot zo bezo asur*' – 'For women to play around with one another is forbidden' (*Hilkhot Issurei Bi'ah* 21:8).

between women came to be regarded as 'forbidden' (*asur*). And the reasons for the prohibition are quite apparent in the different key texts.

First, the *source* of the prohibition is drawn from the Torah: while the Torah omits any explicit reference to female sexual unions, the 'practices' and the 'laws' of Egypt and Canaan – which are not detailed in Torah – may be understood to include sexual relations between women (*Sifra: Acharei Mot* 9:8, *Mishneh Torah: Hilchot Issurei Bi'ah* 21:8) even if women who 'played around with one another' were guilty of 'obscenity' only and not of 'unchastity' (*Yevamot* 76a).

Second, the *purpose* of the prohibition seems to be to ensure that 'they should not become accustomed to an alien body' *(gufa nuchra'ah)* (Shabbat 65b). In my view, the argument here makes most sense if put in the context of the line of reasoning articulated throughout the Book of Leviticus (see especially, 18:3–5, 24–30, 20:22–26): just as the people of Israel must separate themselves from the *alien* nations surrounding them (their *neighbours* with whom they might otherwise *identify*) in order to be 'holy' to God, so individual females must separate themselves from *alien* bodies – other *females* with whom they might otherwise identify – in order to become attached to individual males.

While the prohibition on lesbianism articulated in *Sifra*, the Talmud and the later codes is primarily justified in terms of the same rationale used in Leviticus for outlawing sex between men, it is clear that lesbian behaviour is not regarded in the same way as male homosexual behaviour. A crucial reason for the difference stems from the rabbinic interpretation of the first commandment of the Torah: 'Be fruitful and multiply and fill the earth' (Genesis 1:28). On the face of it, this command is given equally, to 'male' and 'female' alike (1:27). But after the eating of the fruit of the forbidden tree, the Torah does not continue in this even-handed manner. With the exception of Lot's daughters,[3] and Judah's daughter-in-law, Tamar[4] – none of whom may be regarded as 'daughters of Israel' – sexual ini-

3. Genesis 19:30–38 relates how Lot and his two daughters dwelt in a cave after the destruction of Sodom and Gomorrah. Because they believed their father to be the last man left on earth, the daughters got him drunk and had sex with him, in order to ensure the birth of heirs. The firstborn bore a son and called him Moab – the father of the Moabites – the younger daughter bore a son and called him Ben-ammi – the father of the Ammonites.

4. Genesis 38:12–30 relates how Tamar, the widow of Judah's first-born, Er, pretended to be a prostitute in order to get her father-in-law, Judah, to sleep with her when he failed to marry her to his third son, Shelah, as he promised. The second son, Onan, having been killed by God for spilling his seed, Judah represented Tamar's only hope for a child. If one goes beyond the Torah to the text of the Bible as a whole, one finds other examples of women taking a sexual initiative – e.g. Ruth, the Moabite, a descendant of Lot's eldest daughter, when she 'uncovers' Boaz's feet at the threshing floor during the night (Ruth 3:6–15).

tiative is a male preserve in the Torah. And so 'fruitfulness' became the responsibility of men too. Indeed, Genesis 28:1–10 relates God's lethal punishment of Onan, Judah's second son, for 'spilling' his seed on the ground rather than impregnating Tamar, his dead brother Er's childless wife.

In the main, the narrative of the Torah makes it clear that men are the central actors in every sphere of life – sexual, social, economic, political.[5] And this picture is reinforced by the law – first set out in the Torah and later developed through the *Mishnah*, the Talmud and the medieval codes. With the exception of widows and divorcees (with a *past* attachment to a man), single women and married women do not have an independent existence, but are rather defined in relation to their fathers and husbands, respectively, who have authority over them.[6]

Herein lies the reason why sexual intimacy between men is explicitly mentioned in the Torah – and condemned – while no reference is made to sexual intimacy between women: women are not seen to *lie together* because, unlike men, they do not officially *relate together* in any other area of life.

And yet, as the text from *Sifra* indicates, by the end of the fourth century, the rabbis were aware that among the nations of Egypt and Canaan, at least, 'A man would marry a man, and a woman a woman' (*Acharei Mot* 9:8). And the references in the *Gemara*, the commentary on the *Mishnah* (*Shabbat* 65a/b and *Yevamot* 76a), suggest that the sages of Babylon were wary of young girls 'sleeping together' and knew of Jewish women who 'played around with one another'. It seems that while in theory women were completely subject to the authority of men, in practice women may have had a little more freedom of action.

But even though legal texts from *Sifra* onwards acknowledge both the *possibility* and the *reality* of sexual intimacy between women, the tone of the pronouncements is very different from the savage rejection of sexual acts between men first articulated in Leviticus. The

5. Of course, there are strong women in the Torah, in particular, Sarah, Rebecca and Miriam. But of these three, Miriam alone is named '*nevi'ah*' ('prophetess'), remains unmarried and acts in relation to the community of women (see especially, Exodus 15:20–21). And yet, compared to the lengthy treatment accorded her younger brothers, Aaron and Moses, Torah says very little about her. There are only four short narrative texts: Exodus 2:1–10, concerning the saving of the baby Moses; Exodus 15:20–21, describing Miriam leading the women in a song and dance with timbrels after the crossing of the Sea of Reeds; Numbers 12:1–16, focusing on Miriam's (and Aaron's) challenge to Moses's leadership; and one verse at the beginning of Numbers 20 – after a lacuna in the text of thirty-eight years – relating Miriam's death at Kadesh in the wilderness of Zin.
6. See Exodus 21, Numbers 5 and 6, and Deuteronomy 21:10ff. for the key legal sources in Torah outlining the dependent position of women.

clue to this difference in tone may be found in what Maimonides had
to say: 'But though such conduct is forbidden, it is not punishable by
lashing since there is no specific prohibition against it and *in any case
no sexual intercourse as such takes place at all*. When a man 'lies with a
male *as with a woman*' (Lev. 18:22), sexual intercourse takes place
and *both* men may be deemed to have 'spilled' their seed. As we read
in Leviticus, sexual acts should only take place between a man and
a woman who is not 'near-kin' (Lev. 18:6). In this way the procreative purpose may be ensured. Not only are women free of the
responsibility of ensuring procreation, but two women cannot lie
together as a man does with a woman: sexual intercourse in the
sense of penile penetration and ejaculation of semen does not take
place; and so sexual intimacy between women is 'obscenity', *peritzuta*, and not 'unchastity', *zenut.*

However, as we have already seen, although intimate contact
between women is not sexual intercourse, it is 'obscenity', it is 'forbidden' *(asur),* and it must be prevented: *Shabbat* 65a reveals that
Samuel's father 'did not permit his daughters ... to sleep together';
Maimonides urges husbands to keep their wives away from women
known to engage in lesbian behaviour. Indeed, Maimonides, in particular, seems to suggest that not only was 'obscenity' between
women a recognized phenomenon, but women who customarily
engaged in intimate relations with other women were also known in
the community. What is more, while Jewish teaching on same-sex
intimacy focuses on individual acts, not on relationships – Torah
does not consider for one moment that men who lie with one
another might be engaged in a long-term liaison – two rabbinic comments hint at other possibilities: as we have seen, *Sifra* (*Acharei Mot*
9:8) speaks of the 'laws' of Egypt and Canaan whereby 'A man
would *marry* a man, and a woman, a woman'; *Shabbat* 65b suggests
that young women might sleep together on a regular basis and so
become 'accustomed to an alien body'.

While Jewish teaching on male homosexuality and lesbianism has
not changed in the last four hundred years since codification of the
laws was officially completed, the twentieth century, and in particular the past thirty years, have seen a massive transformation both in
the roles of women and men, and in personal lifestyles and domestic arrangements. In this climate, lesbians, in common with women
in general, have been claiming the right to define their own lives; in
these circumstances, lesbians, like their gay brothers, have been
'coming out' and asserting their desire not only to engage in same-
sex intimate acts, but to live as lesbians and establish lesbian relationships. Some of these lesbians are Jews, not only by birth, but by
choice and conviction (whether 'cultural' or 'religious', or both).

Indeed, like other Jewish women, lesbians today are taking an increasingly active part in Jewish communal life – including becoming rabbis and cantors. So far, 'Judaism' has had very little to say which is new in response to this new phenomenon. The time has come for new Jewish teaching which recognises the aspirations, the integrity and the Jewish commitment of Jewish lesbians and gay men. The time has come for new Jewish teaching which acknowledges the limitations of legal enactments framed in different times and according to imperatives – such as the need to forge a separate identity in an 'alien' environment – which are no longer relevant or appropriate in the 1990s.

Fortunately, there is evidence of new approaches – but only on the part of those who do not feel bound by the *Halakhah* as set out in the sources. The progressive movements in both Britain and United States have begun to tackle the legal prohibition against same-sex intimacy.[7] Individual scholars are attempting to create a new Jewish sex ethic, both by *reinterpreting* Torah – for example, the meaning of '*to'evah*', usually translated as 'abomination', or the prescriptions against 'uncovering nakedness' (Lev. 18) – and by drawing on *other* Torah teachings, such as humanity made 'in the image of God' and 'love your neighbour as yourself'.[8] It is a beginning.

7. See Dr Wendy Greengross, *Jewish and Homosexual*, London, Reform Synagogues of Great Britain, 1979 (currently being updated); *Where We Stand on Homosexuality*, London, Union of Liberal and Progressive Synagogues, 1990; *Report of the Ad Hoc Committee on Homosexuality and the Rabbinate* adopted by the Central Conference of American Rabbis, 25 June 1990; *Homosexuality and Judaism: The Reconstructionist Position; The Report of the Reconstructionist Commission on Homosexuality*, Federation of Reconstructionist Congregations and *Chavurot*, Reconstructionist Rabbinical Association, 1992; *Homosexuality and Judaism: A Reconstructionist Workshop Series*, ed. Rabbi Robert Gluck, Reconstructionist Press, 1992.
8. See, for example, Sharon Cohen, 'Homosexuality and a Jewish Sex Ethics' and David A. Teutsch, 'Rethinking Jewish Sexual Ethics' (both articles are published in *Reconstructionist*, July-August 1989); Rebecca T. Alpert, 'In God's Image: Coming to Terms with Leviticus', in *Twice Blessed. On Being Lesbian, Gay and Jewish*, ed. Christie Balka and Andy Rose (Boston, 1989); Robert Kirschner, '*Halakhah* and Homosexuality', *Judaism*, Autumn 1988. My sermon on the double Torah portion '*Acharei Mot-Kedoshim*' at the *Erev Shabbat* service of the Thirteenth International Conference of Gay and Lesbian Jews, 30 April-3 May 1993, explored the implications of interpreting the Torah's preoccupation with 'uncovering nakedness' (*Acharei Mot*, Lev. 18) in the context of the command 'You shall love your neighbour as yourself' (*Kedoshim*, Lev. 19:18).

# WHAT IS OUR LOVE?*

*Sheila Shulman*

How else should I begin but with a story?

> Rabbi Bunam said to his disciples: 'Everyone must have two pockets so that he can reach into one or the other according to his needs. In his right pocket are to be the words: "For my sake was the world created," and in his left pocket, "I am dust and ashes."'

I have been complaining all my life that women's clothes are not made with enough pockets. I complained for practical reasons; long after I had found this story I still did not realize the full dimensions of the problem. It is no wonder there are strictures in our tradition against women wearing men's clothing. God forbid we should ever say 'For my sake was the world created.' It would probably start a revolution. And it has, it has.

That remarkable sentence, 'For my sake was the world created,' comes from the *Mishnah* (*Sanhedrin* 4:5). The legal context is the urgency of admonishing and warning witnesses in capital cases to give truthful evidence. The anonymous rabbis of this *Mishnah* support their case for this urgency with a *midrashic* discussion about why at first only one human being was created. The burden of the discussion is the preciousness of each unique human life both for its own sake (to save or destroy a single soul is to save or destroy a whole world), and as that unique life manifests the greatness of God.

> ... for man stamps many coins with one die and they are all alike one with the other, but the King of the king of kings, the Holy One, blessed be He, has stamped all mankind with the die of the first man and yet not one of them is like another. Therefore every one is in duty bound to say, 'For my sake was the world created.'

* This chapter is based on a lecture given at the Leo Baeck College, 14 February 1990.

How should we understand this text? There are a number of possibilities; the *Mishnah* is lucid but not necessarily explicit. The first
thing to do is sort out the gender problems in the grammar. Hebrew
is a highly gendered language, and the rabbis were not slow to exploit
that unfortunate but accidental phenomenon. We cannot permit that
exploitation to continue, either for our own sake, or for the sake of
our tradition, which demands justice. The central image hinges on the
phrase *adam ha-rishon*, usually translated 'the first man' and refers
back, of course, to the creation story in Genesis. In what is by now a
definitive article, the feminist theologian Phyllis Trible has used structural analysis to clarify, once and for all, that in Genesis 1:27, usually
translated 'So God created man in His own image, in the image of
God created He him; male and female created He them', the phrase
'male and female' is structurally and semantically parallel to 'in the
image of God'. This parallelism links the two phrases so that they necessarily resonate with each other. Therefore 'man,' *et-ha-adam*, in the
first part of the verse, has to be translated 'humankind,' or something
like that, and that *ha-adam*, the *adam-ha-rishon* of our *Mishnah* passage,
is not 'one single creature who is both male and female, but rather
two creatures, one male and one female.' Trible reinforces this reading of the text by pointing to the plural form in the previous verse:
'Let us make humankind (*adam*) in our image ... and let *them* have
dominion.' (Trible, 75ff) On one level this is old hat. On another, if
we look at it together with our *Mishnah* text, that is, if we connect the
idea that each woman of us is made in the image of God, with the
idea that each woman of us is as unique and beloved as the first
human being, then something else emerges – an imperative to love
ourselves, to consider ourselves precious and unique, an imperative
that runs flatly counter to the dominant male strain in our tradition,
an imperative which is usually the last thing to occur to any of us
because we have been so remorselessly taught otherwise.

If each of us is duty bound to say, 'for my sake the world was created,' what does it mean? Let us try it this way. We are, it seems to
me, duty bound to take on a number of understandings, and live
accordingly. First, each of us is a unique being, the centre of a world,
the elements of which it is our God-given task to name, to look after,
to learn from, to be sustained by. Second, each of us is in a central,
primary, and unmediated relation to the awesome and loving energy
of creation. Third, each of us flames with that divine energy, unique
and undiffused, as if we were at the beginning of creation. I am of
course speaking extravagantly, though not altogether. I know we are
all tired, and cluttered up by the details of our lives, and remote from
any such perception. Still, to talk about love is to talk about the centre of our own being, which in each of us could do with a bit of

warming by unaccustomed truths. Such truths often must be stated violently in order to be heard at all.

If, as women, we are going to talk about love, for me there is only one place to start, with ourselves, with our own experience, with the necessity to make ourselves central in our own lives. We have to start with loving ourselves, by which I do not mean an extra allowance of bath oil, though that is all very well, or some therapeutic platitude about mothering ourselves, although that cannot hurt. What I mean is somehow getting to know and understand, and to live in the understanding, that each of us is made in the image of God. It makes little difference whether we understand that in a formally 'religious' sense or not. All human language for the divine is metaphorical. But what does make a difference is what we take that notion to mean. One of the conventional understandings of 'being in the image of God' goes something like 'As God is merciful and compassionate, so you shall be merciful and compassionate.' That is, we are meant to imitate, in our human way, God's attributes of concern – for others. Well and good; there are all sorts of things men have still to learn. But as women we have been told and taught, and it has been enforced upon us for millennia, that it is the very point and essence of our being to be for others. 'Being for others', which in the case of women has excluded any sense of being for ourselves, has resulted in myriads of wasted and destroyed women's lives.

No. As women we have to look for some other understanding of what it means to be 'made in the image of God'. However we think about God, one image inherent in our understanding is that of intentional creative energy and power. That is where we should look, and where we have been prevented from looking, for an understanding of how we as women are made in the image of God. We too are creators, and not merely by virtue of our reproductive systems. We too share in the energy and power of the original creation. We too are meant to name, to build, to make, to work, to order the creation, to stand at its centre. We have been kept away from that primary power for so long that to most of us it feels deeply illegitimate to claim it. But until we can claim it for ourselves, love will be a largely meaningless, if not destructive, word, because it will contain neither power nor responsibility. That is what I mean by loving ourselves, and loving ourselves has to be the starting point for any discussion of love, particularly if that discussion is meant to take place in the context of Jewish tradition. As Jewish women, we cannot be in a passive relation to that tradition. Rather, our relation to it must of necessity be transformative if we are to live in it at all.

Because we have been invisible as persons, when we have not been maligned or destroyed as persons, our relation to Jewish tradition – which at least has the virtue of never having been monolithic or static – must be transformative if we are on the one hand to recover ourselves, and on the other hand not only continue to live within that tradition but participate fully in its development. In the simplest and most direct sense of the word, our task is creative, and therefore contingent upon an understanding of ourselves as central to the tradition in the way I have described. Our work, as far as I can see it, is not to get ourselves an equal slice of the pie; it is to rethink and reimagine ourselves and the world in the context of Jewish tradition, except insofar as that tradition violates us or our understanding of justice, at which point we have to step outside, say no, find buried sources, new understandings, do something so that we can continue to be Jews.

The most intractable element in our tradition is obviously *Halakhah*, the body of rabbinic law that in theory should govern every aspect of our lives. Halakhically, if we understand *Halakhah* in its strict legal sense, the problem about women is enormous. The best description of the difficulty I have seen comes not from a Jewish source at all, but from a brilliant book by the American feminist lawyer Catherine MacKinnon. The book is called *Feminism Unmodified*, and it is a collection of essays about the legal and meta-legal issues surrounding the controversy over anti-pornography legislation in America. The following passage is about the relation of women to the American legal system, but when I read it, it leapt off the page at me because of its obvious applicability to the relation of women and *Halakhah*. In her preceding paragraph, she has convincingly explained why, as if we did not already know, 'substantively considered, the situation of women is *not really like anything else*.' And then she continues:

> Doing something legal about a situation that is not really like anything else is hard enough in a legal system that prides itself methodologically on reasoning by analogy. Add to this the specific exclusion or absence of women and women's concerns from the definition and design of this legal system since its founding, combined with its determined adherence to precedent, and you have a problem of systemic dimension. (MacKinnon, 167)

Since there is a whole tractate of the Talmud called *Nashim*, women, this would appear not to be the case in *Halakhah*. But that is an illusion. Women had no part in the discussions and decisions that make up either the tractate itself or the subsequent commentaries and responsa. We do not exist as persons within that body of text. We exist as objects, possibly as animals or demons, which will not do. So as far as I can see the problems inherent in the relation of women to American civil law and to *Halakhah* are precisely analogous, and we too are faced with a problem of systemic dimension.

There are two possible responses to such a situation, both open to us, both potentially transformative. One is to work as MacKinnon does, passionately determined to change not only the law, but its exclusive dependence upon analogy and precedent. In order to do so, we have to be convinced that the law is not immutable. We also have to feel that we are or should be bound by that law. In civil society, we have little choice. We know that civil law is to say the least man-made, that it is very much an on-going process and that we have no option but to be bound by it. As Jewish women our situation is different. We understand *Halakhah* along a pluralistic spectrum; at one end are women who understand it as divinely ordained down to its last jot and tittle, and feel utterly, irretrievably bound by it; at the other end women who regard it as irrelevant and ignore it as an anachronism, a sterile relic.

I do not suppose any of us is in either of those extreme positions. Communities without law, implicit or explicit, do not exist. I have known self-identified Jewish atheist socialists to become quite passionate about some minute point of ritual, and then blush, as if at a fit of atavism. I am not poking fun; I think that response points to ambivalence, to ambiguity, and such a passion is real. I am also ambivalent, and full of questions. If I had that kind of head, which I do not, I would as a Rabbi try to take on that 'problem of systemic dimension' directly. As it is, the most I can do in that direction is recognise it, point it out loudly, clearly, in detail, at every possible opportunity, and nonetheless look for what I can love, respect, and even feel bound by in the *Halakhic* area of our tradition. There is, I find, more than I would have thought possible. For the rest, let me read you part of a moving statement by the heterosexual woman Rabbi of the Los Angeles gay congregation, the result of her five years' work with them. Here again, the analogy is obvious:

> ... I could find no published rabbinic statements declaring homosexuality an acceptable Jewish way of life. And so I had to decide: how much did it matter to me that the voice of my tradition, without exception, ran counter to the evidence of my experience and the deepest promptings of my conscience?
> For me the choice was clear. I could not be guided by laws that seem profoundly unjust and immoral ... I cannot accept that law as authoritative. It is part of my history, it belongs to me, but it has no binding claim on me ... This attempt to grapple with a law I find abhorrent in a tradition to which I am utterly committed has taught me a lesson: liberal Jews can rationalise or equivocate only so long. There comes a time when our deepest convictions demand that we break with *Halakhah* – and do so without apology, without attempts to unearth a minority legal opinion somewhere that supports our position. Reverence for tradition is no virtue when it promotes injustice and human suffering. (Balka and Rose, 215)

The point at which I as a woman break with *Halakhah* is wherever I am denied as a person, made in the image of God, for whose sake the world was created; wherever my experience and/or my being is defined for me; wherever my gender is used as a rationalisation for any kind of spiritual or political constriction, and whenever I am told how or whom I may love.

All of that happens with appalling frequency. So, for the remainder of this chapter I will be concerned not with *Halakhah* but with other sources in our traditions – Jewish and feminist – which will, I hope, allow us to think fruitfully and transformatively about love.

In the *Sifra*, a collection of *midrashim* on Leviticus, there is a discussion between Ben Azzai and Akiva about which is the most inclusive commandment. Ben Azzai says that the verse we have been looking at, 'In the image of God made He them' is more inclusive than 'Love your neighbour.' (*Sifra* 19:18) Certainly, as a woman, I share Ben Azzai's preference, for two reasons. The first is just an ironic thought I had about the relation of women to dicta like 'Love your neighbour.' How much time, energy, and love has each of us spent with women friends who were depressed, who were caught up in self-hatred, in complete failures of confidence, trying to tell them, to show them, with all our strength and faith, that they were loveable, viable people, whose life was precious, whose work was needed? I have seen those same women, full of self-loathing and terrified at the vacancy they perceived in their own lives, be courteous and gentle, attentive and caring, to friends, to children, to the most casual acquaintance, to anybody, yet remorseless with themselves. So I began to wonder after a while if it would not make more sense, for women, to hear that commandment the other way around – 'Love yourself as you love your neighbour' – be at least as decent to yourself as you are to anyone else. We have internalised so much of the misogyny that saturates the world that the last person we are usually decent to is ourself. Any of us could call up from our experience depth after depth of self-negation – I need not go into detail – except to say that none of it is spontaneous, it is taught, enforced, and damned hard to unlearn.

The second reason I prefer Ben Azzai's position has to do with the degree and extent to which the potentiality and actuality of our bonding with each other has been distorted and often destroyed by the woman-hatred, or at best the obliviousness to our existence as persons, that is embedded in our tradition. That woman-hatred, that obliviousness, has denied to each of us not only certain perceptions but the consequences of those perceptions. Just as we have been prevented from seeing ourselves as 'in the image of God,' just as I expect that for each of us there is a shock of non-recognition if we try

to say 'For my sake was the world created,' so we have been prevented from seeing each other in that light, as creative selves burning with holy energy at the centre of a world. We have been
prevented from seeing each other as potential sources of love and
enabling power. That is not entirely true, of course, but the very history and reality of female bonding has been obscured, buried, and
denied by those same forces, and it has required the immense labour
of a generation of feminist scholars to excavate the barest shards.

Our love for each other is the obvious corollary of our love for
ourselves. Just as we cannot really talk about love until, and unless
we talk about making ourselves central and primary in our own
lives, so we cannot really talk about love without talking about our
centrality and primacy to and for each other. Our love for each other
does not exist in the world of male discourse, through which the Jewish tradition has largely been articulated. In that sense the Jewish tradition is no different from any other patriarchal tradition, including
those of secular cultures, which are still saturated by the creation
myths that stand behind them, whether those origins are acknowledged or not. That whole ball-game is predicated on the myth of
androgyny, or complementarity, the substance of which is that
women must bond with men to:

> ... fulfil the supposed cosmic purpose of reunifying that which was myth-
> ically separated into male and female. Arguments supporting the pri-
> macy and prevalence of hetero-relations are in some way based on a
> cosmic male-female polarity in which the so-called lost halves seek to be
> rejoined ... All of life becomes a metaphor for marriage ... The two –
> female and male – must become one, whether in the bedroom or the
> board room. Hetero-relational complementarity becomes the 'stuff of the
> cosmos'. (Raymond, 12–13)

But the 'myth of androgyny', which spreads through our lives as
women like some kind of blight is, in the case of Jewish tradition,
contingent upon a reading of Genesis 1 which, as we have seen, is
neither structurally nor semantically accurate. It was neither an
androgyne nor a hermaphrodite that God created, but rather two
distinct and integral beings – and integral means that from which
nothing can be taken, whole, complete.

I said that our love for each other does not exist in the world of
male discourse, which is the only discourse we have ever been
exposed to, if and when we have been permitted, or taken, access to
any public discourse. That love does of course exist; it has a history
and a culture. But as Adrienne Rich says:

> Whatever is unnamed, undepicted in images, whatever is omitted from
> biography, censored in collections of letters, whatever is misnamed as
> something else, made difficult-to-come-by, whatever is buried in the mem-

ory by the collapse of meaning under an inadequate or lying language –
this will become, not merely unspoken, but *unspeakable.* (Rich, 199)

Well, for about twenty years now, this particular 'unspeakable' has
been being spoken, loud and clear. Across cultures, across classes,
across races, women are speaking of their bonds with each other,
and they are bringing back to life the histories of that bonding and
what it has accomplished out of their various individual and collective pasts. In a thoroughly inspiring book called *A Passion for Friends,*
Janice Raymond reminds us of our other tradition.

> The culture of female friendship is not an uninterrupted chronicle of
> wondrous happenings, nor is it a mournful tale of failure and disruption.
> It is an ongoing testament and testimony of women as acting subjects
> who, in relation to their vital Selves and each other, have created pas-
> sion, purpose, and politics. This tradition of female friendship and its
> ongoing life in the present needs to be thought about, lived, and cele-
> brated. (Raymond, 21)

Let me clarify what I mean by 'female bonding' or 'female friendship,' or, more simply, our love for each other. It may or may not be
sexual – that is another discussion – but it is neither romantic nor
sentimental. Romance inevitably involves a kind of sinking of the
self in the other that for us would mean a betrayal of the self we
struggle so hard to find, to make, to cherish. And it gets us nowhere.
As the American lesbian poet Judy Grahn said, '… romance, which
is so much easier, and so much less than any of us deserve.' Two
short poems of hers should put the whole issue into perspective.

> Love came along and saved me
> saved me          saved me
> However, my life remains the same as before.
> O What shall I do now that I have
>
> what I've always been looking for?
> I only have one reason for living
> and that's you
> And if I didn't have you as a
> reason for living
> I would think of something else. (Grahn, 140, 154)

These two poems tartly and effectively contradict a couple of mil-
lennia-old directives: a) the ancient and pernicious saw that our
(female) self is not integral and therefore requires completion, and b)
that love means a submerging of the self in the other. Or, as Andrea
Dworkin put it more pungently, 'Romantic fiction is about loving the
boot on your neck.' In 'romantic fiction' I also include the story of
Adam and Eve in Genesis 2. No, what I am talking about is love, a
capacity for friendship integrally related to our capacity to be a friend
to ourself, a lucid affection, full of thought and passion and worldli-

ness. If we understand thought as real conversation between 'myself and myself,' which is then materialised in the conversations and actions of friends talking and working together, and if we understand passion as a thoughtful intensity of delight in and commitment to the other as a result of which the integrity of each is not only maintained but furthered, we begin to see the outlines of our love for each other.

Worldliness, another necessary quality, needs a bit of defining. Obviously, it means being in or of the world, but how? Historically, traditionally, women have been confined to the private sphere, and kept out of the life of the community. In our own tradition, our grandmothers or great-grandmothers may well have supported the family, worked a market stall or even run a business, while their husbands studied. But we must not let our perception of this sustaining activity mask our understanding of their rigid exclusion from the public and active life of the community, political or religious. They were excluded from decision-making processes, from communal prayer, from negotiations with the powers that be. There was no way they could collectively influence events; they were neither visible nor effective. But it is more than a question of just claiming our right to be in the world as women together. As Janice Raymond has put it, our worldly integrity demands that we meet the world on its own turf, but not on its own terms. Describing women who are in some primary way committed to each other as 'inside outsiders', she goes on to say:

> The inside outsider lives in the world with worldly integrity ... paving the way for the entrance of women as women, that is, women on their own terms, into the world. As an inside outsider, a woman's work is characterised by the dual tension between her feminism and her worldliness. Her worldliness is dependent on her feminist vision, yet her feminist vision is actualised in her worldly location. (Raymond, 232)

Another crucial element of our worldliness is our solidarity with each other in need, not as victims, but as persons with a passion for justice. There is no other cry so harshly, so eloquently, so frequently articulated in our prophetic literature as the cry for justice, the demand that those in need do not suffer anymore. Therefore our love for each other is angry, and sees with precision how we are discarded, disregarded, in the world, sees how easily we are violated and murdered, sees how many of us die for want of that love that Judy Grahn calls 'our meat and potatoes'. Here is a section from a long poem of hers called 'A Woman is Talking to Death.' Part of the poem is put in the form of a 'Mock Interrogation', whether by death or by the police, it is not clear, and anyway they may be identical.

> You have kissed other women?

> Yes, many, some of the finest women I know, I have kissed. Women who were lonely, women I didn't know and didn't want to, but kissed, because

that was a way to say yes, yes we are still alive and loveable, though separate, women who recognised a loneliness in me, women who were hurt,
I confess to kissing the top of a fifty-five year old woman's head in the
snow in Boston, who was hurt more deeply than I have ever been hurt,
and I wanted her as a very few people have ever wanted me – I wanted
her and me to own and control and run the city we lived in, to staff the
hospital I knew would mistreat her, to drive the transportation system
that had betrayed her, to patrol the streets controlling the men who
would murder or disfigure or disrupt us, not accidentally with machines,
but on purpose, because we are not allowed out on the streets alone.

Have you ever committed any indecent acts with women?

Yes, many. I am guilty of allowing suicidal women to die before my eyes
or in my ears or under my hands because I thought I could do nothing
... I am guilty of not loving her who needed me; I regret all the women
I have not slept with or comforted, who pulled themselves away from me
for lack of something I had not the courage to fight for, for us, our life,
our planet, our city, our meat and potatoes, our love. These are the indecent acts, lacking courage, lacking a certain fire behind the eyes, which is
the symbol, the raised fist, the sharing of resources, the resistance that
tells death he will starve for lack of the fat of us, our extra. Yes, I have
committed acts of indecency with women and most of them have been
acts of omission. I regret them bitterly. (Grahn 124–5)

If our love for each other does not include that 'fire behind the
eyes' as part of our worldliness, it is worthless. 'In this poem, the
word "lover", purged of romantic-sentimental associations, becomes
a name for what human beings might mean to each other in a world
where each person held both power and responsibility.' (Rich, 251)

Finally, since we are talking about love, let us come home to our
bodies, and talk about eros, love in all its manifestations, the life-energy
in us of which sexuality, sexual behaviour, is only one expression.

The erotic [is] the life-force, the capacity for feeling, the capacity for joy
... a source of empowerment, a 'lens through which we evaluate all
aspects of our existence,' and so no longer 'settle for the convenient, the
shoddy, the conventionally expected, nor the merely safe.' (Balka and
Rose, 146)

The erotic is powerful, and dangerous. It makes connections, and
breaks boundaries. Erotic energy is a current that flows through all
activities that are important to us, in which we invest ourselves. 'True
intellectual exchange, common work, shared experience, are [all]
laced with erotic energy that animates and enlivens them. The bonds
of community are erotic bonds.' (Balka and Rose, 146) As Audre
Lorde says, erotic energy is a bridge across the false dichotomy
between the spiritual and the political. What we can most passionately feel, imagine, long for, demands embodiment in community.

The erotic energy of women has been stifled and constricted by
the hierarchical patriarchal systems we live in. We have been, and

are, subject to brutal controls and restraints, and our erotic energy has been, at best, relegated to the bedroom alone. It may be, says Judith Plaskow, 'that the ability of women to live within the patriarchal family and the larger patriarchal structures that govern Jewish life depends on our suppression of the erotic, on our numbing ourselves to the sources of vision and power that fuel meaningful resistance. Obviously, then, from a patriarchal perspective, erotic empowerment is dangerous.' But, she continues,

> From a feminist perspective ... the power and danger of the erotic are not reasons to fear and suppress it but to nurture it as a profound personal and communal resource in the struggle for change. When 'we begin to demand from ourselves and from our life-pursuits that they feel in accordance with that joy which we know ourselves to be capable of', we carry with us an inner knowledge of the kind of world we are seeking to create. If we repress this knowledge because it also makes us sexually alive, then we repress the clarity and creative energy that is the basis of our capacity to envision and work towards a more just social order. (Balka and Rose, 147)

Judaism and Jewish tradition present us with two possible models within which to consider our erotic lives, bearing in mind that the erotic suffuses all of our life, our work, our love. One model, I believe, leads to nothing but further suppression, falseness, and limitation; the other leads to potential transformation. The first possible model is the conventional talmudic/*halakhic* one, enshrined in Tractate *Nashim*, and subsequent derivative commentary, up to and including contemporary orthodox opinion. While early rabbinic thinking was no doubt advanced for its day, we have to ask advanced from what? Or to what? In any case, the whole lot is enough to make your blood run cold. It is entirely a model of male ownership and control of female (dangerous, unruly) sexuality, entirely a model for male acquisition and relinquishment of rights to that sexuality. It is a model of relationship between persons and objects, or persons and animals, or persons and slaves, or even persons and demons, but by no stretch of imagination is it a model of relationship between equally integral persons. I find it abhorrent, and wish I did not understand how some women can live by it.

The other possible model is the *Song of Songs*, which Rabbi Akiva called the holiest of all texts, saying 'the whole world is not worth the day on which the *Song of Songs* was given to Israel, for all the texts are holy, but the *Song of Songs* is the Holy of Holies.' (*Mishnah Yadaim* 3:5) The usual reason given for this apparently odd opinion is that the *Song of Songs* is an allegory of the intense and mutual love of God and Israel. That is, this utterly sensual poem, or sequence of poems, is not 'really' about human love at all, but rather coded language for another, different, spiritual love. Reading the *Song* as allegory is a gross oversimplification, a betrayal of its true force, centrality, and breathtaking beauty. The *Song* is indeed the Holy of Holies precisely because it is our tradition's central image of human wholeness, of the seamless inter-connectedness of the erotic and the spiritual. If in our human love of each other we truly honour the image of God in each other, the inviolable unique integrity of each other, the creative power in each other, and if that love is a source of joy and concern, then that love is also the love of God. And if, further, that unique love becomes a seal on our hearts of our commitment to others in community, then that love is also the love of the people for God, and a witness to God's loving presence within us. In this context, it is not a digression if I mention that Rabbi Sybil Sheridan has written a convincing paper strongly suggesting that the *Song of Songs* was written by a woman.

Our task, it seems to me, is to transform our tradition in the light of *this* model, and begin, if we have not done so already, the painstaking daily work of considering every aspect of our lives in that same light. One thing we must learn from the Rabbis of the Talmud; there is no detail, however minute, to which they did not pay attention. Our attempts to look at our lives, to decide what we want and need, to decide how we want to live and with whom, deserve exactly that kind of attention, so that we will be in no danger of ever settling for less than we deserve. At bottom, our love, for ourselves, for each other, and how that love is lived out – in thoughtful action, in passionate work alone and together – ought to be a source of something for which I have only heard a Russian word. In her memoirs, Nadezhda Mandelstam, a remarkable Jewish woman so painfully estranged from Jewish tradition that she had only Christian language to speak in, nevertheless spoke directly out of the heart of our tradition when she talked about being *zhizneradostny*, or 'life-glad,' to be glad in/about/with life. That 'life-gladness' is at the heart of our traditions's sanctification of every moment of our life, this life, our bodily life, here, now. Our way to participate in that 'life-gladness' is to find or make ways for us as women truly to live and love in the knowledge that on the one hand, we are made in the image of God, and on the other, that we can and should say, 'For my sake was the world created.'

# References

Balka, C. and Rose, A. eds, *Twice Blessed: On Being Lesbian, Gay, and Jewish.* Beacon Press, Boston, 1989.

Grahn, J., *The Work of a Common Woman.* Only Women Press, London, 1985.

MacKinnon, C., *Feminism Unmodified: Discourses on Life and Law.* Harvard University Press, Cambridge/London, 1987.

Plaskow, J., *Standing Again At Sinai: Judaism From A Feminist Perspective.* Harper and Row, San Francisco, 1990.

Raymond, J., *A Passion For Friends: Towards A Philosophy of Female Affection.* The Women's Press, London, 1986.

Rich, A., *On Lies, Secrets And Silence: Selected Prose 1966–1978.* Norton, New York, 1979.

Trible, P., *God And The Rhetoric of Sexuality.* Fortress Press, Philadelphia, 1978.

# GODLY AND GAY

*Rabbi Lionel Blue*

By helping people to be gay and Christian you are healing one of the many splits in present-day life. It is holy work, making people whole. By being gay and Christian, you may help others to be godly, gay and Jewish, and others yet, straight and gay, to marry religion to the reality of their lives. You may help many people to be religious and honest. Although these qualities should go together, in practice they are often split. In pursuing truth on the higher slopes of devotion, honesty on the lower slopes of fact is often overlooked or despised.

## The Split

The split between religion and life goes very deep now, and it falsifies even genuine piety. There is the split that Bonhoeffer pointed out between the ghetto and the boulevard, between where people are and where they are told they ought to be. There is a split between the advice in the public sermons of ministers, and the private advice they give in their rooms. There is a split between those who can give spirituality and those who need to receive, a crisis in its supply and demand. There is the fear which prevents gay Christians and Jews being open with their priests and rabbis and their fellow believers, and strains all relationships.

The examples are so many, that we take the split for granted and scarcely notice how harmful it is. We are used to commissions and committees who want to regulate gay life or judge it without con-

The Fourth Michael Harding Memorial Address, reprinted from a paper published by the Gay Christian Movement 1981.

sulting gays, or meeting them, or even knowing them. There are the ministers I know, who have to wear two hats – one when they are rabbis and one when they are counsellors, and are deeply troubled by it. There are the good and godly who condemn the gays they do not know, but regard those they do as different.

Gay people are only one example of this disjunction. Many now work out their salvation in relationships which have no benefit of clergy, for religion and reality have parted company and this affects homos and heteros alike. In my work I have to deal with people who seek to become Jewish. I ask them what happened to their former religion. Many do not know and look puzzled. They went to Sunday school, but in their early teens religion ceased to be relevant and the truth dwindled into a myth, and the myth into a nursery tale. Somewhere around the age of puberty, religion and reality parted company, and there was no one around to put them back together again, only to paper over the cracks. This split goes very deep. Few want to examine it. The silence around it is not the silence of contemplation but the silence of embarrassment.

## The Changes

A few years ago at an international Rabbinic meeting we were asked to lift the ban on Spinoza. Recently I was told that the Roman Catholic Church intended to rehabilitate Galileo. Now it is nice, though rare, when religious bodies have the guts to say 'Sorry, we were wrong!' As secular ideologies and political parties creak even more at the prospect, I do not underrate this late atonement. God always welcomes the repentant. But I doubt if these particular bells of heaven are going to go wild about it – the issues are too rusty. Spinoza and Galileo no longer need the Synagogue or Church, and whatever the forms of rehabilitation say, it is the religious establishments that need it, not their former victims. But I doubt if this will be openly stated – it needs inner security and courage to say one was wrong. Only now, as religion is coming to terms with the scientific revolution, do we see the tragedy and suffering caused by the divorce between the minds of people and their souls, and the cost of all that was not said, because at the time it was not opportune or safe, or would have caused a scandal; its only merit being, like the Kinsey Report, that it was true though inconvenient.

But the scientific revolution is being absorbed and the sexual revolution is on us; and it is now our task to join our bodies as well as our minds to our souls. Can we in our time do any better? The pace of change has quickened, and this revolution is certainly no easier to absorb. I have been a rabbi now for twenty years, and in that short space of time my earlier sermons have become redundant. The world they purported to describe owes more to *Little Women* or *Fiddler on the Roof* than it does to any Jewish suburban reality I know. With birth control and the conquest of V.D., sexuality and procreation have parted company, and sexuality has to be considered in its own right without its biological fig-leaf. They will never come together again in the old way. Women and men have escaped from their old tight roles. They have discovered each other in themselves, and are the richer for it. A man can do the washing-up, or see to the baby, and a woman does not have to look up at the ceiling. He can be tender, and she can be macho – they can now admit it, they are free. Last but not least, the sexual minorities have been able to come out of their darkness into the light of recognition and self-knowledge. Like the Hebrews, they have been redeemed from degradation, and from the blackmail and insults which had been forced upon them.

Our problem today is not the lack of truth, but its abundance and variety. It has flowed into us from mystics and Marxists, from rabbis and reformers, from laboratories and concentration camps and affluent societies. It is so various that our religions cannot contain it. It overflows our traditional compartments and categories.

There are many for whom religion means safety and not courage. Such people deplore this present freedom, and the liberation of women and gay people. They complain, they whine, they nag the Almighty, and their voice has a dying fall. There is always an attack on the open and permissive society, whose freedom they enjoy and under whose tolerance they live, and a bogus comparison with an age gone by, tarted up and cleaned up in their imagination.

Now problems exist for this society, but they are there to be solved, not to be deplored. In this organization [the Gay Christian Movement] you are trying to link the needs of your bodies and the needs of your souls. It is painstaking work, fitting two pieces of creation together. It requires devotion, patience and discipline, the faithfulness to the truth and precision that religion has to learn from science; but it is honest work, not rhetoric. It does not avoid or evade.

## A Caution

But this congratulation requires a caution which can be given and accepted because we try not to work for our own egos but for the truth. It is easy to score points off others; it is less easy but more important to make allowance for the motes in our own eyes. Because gay people have suffered, sarcasm for existing institutions comes easy.

It should be avoided. It leads nowhere. Many people have suffered injustice. It does not justify them in blowing up the world or even in blowing up society. Some of the injustice has to be absorbed – I can say this as a Jew – and with God's help it can be used.

We should not fall into the trap which has ensnared many followers of festivals of light. They forgot that both light and darkness dwelt within them. They spoke as if they were the light and the darkness was outside them, in others. Being right should not make us self-righteous, and may God keep us from that suspect emotion, righteous indignation.

We should remember that, though inspirational religion is revolutionary, institutional religion is slow, like all institutions, and cannot be otherwise. It is attached to what it feels is tried and tested. It is accustomed to preach the things that do not change, and preachers are not used to criticism. It therefore carries unwittingly attitudes of societies and systems whose creativity and vitality have ebbed away. It carries both the junk and the treasure of the past.

In any oppression the oppressed take on some of the characteristics of the oppressor. Because ecclesiastics have been glib about gays, gays should not be glib about complex issues to which many of them are linked not by personal experience but by political fashion. Male gays I know have taken fierce uncompromising stands about abortion. For many of them it is not directly relevant, and they have no special competence, possibly less.

## Scriptures

To guide us in this work of reconciliation the traditional scriptures in isolation are not sufficient, and indeed never have been. That is because they are external to us. Books stand still, experience does not. Every religion has required some device such as an oral law, an adaptive tradition, a legal fiction, a far-reaching commentary which goes behind the text, to fit the truths which come from both scripture and experience together, for they are one. All books can only speak of God's redemption to other people at other times. We have to supplement them with our own experience, which tells us how the same God redeemed us from our own Egypt in our own time.

While editing the Jewish Day of Atonement Service I came across these words:

> You open the book of memory, and it speaks for itself, for every man has signed it by his life.

It is these scriptures, signed by our lives, which are needed to connect the truth in the present to the truth in the past, the truth we have experienced to the truth of the community. The psalmist knew long ago that you met the same God in the Bible as you did in the late watches of the night. Saintliness can be found in a disco, and a blessing in a bar. This is no esoteric truth. We know it, straight and gay alike, from our own experience. We should not take fright at this abundance of grace, and lock God up in a historical cage, or reduce the cosmos to safe ecclesiastical proportions – parish size. The choice is always there, and always the same, between what is mean and what is generous, between what is expedient and what is true, and whether people can help each other or destroy each other. This is the plot. The Kleenex, the cosmetics, the furniture of piety, the dressing up, clerical or lay, only supply the incidental scenery to our own drama of salvation.

## A Mixed Blessing

With all this truth at hand we can begin to ponder certain questions, which are fresh but right, such as the religious vocation of gay people. Gays should waste less time in seeking the approval of religious institutions, and spend more in finding their special vocation in religion. When they have found their own vocation, they will get the recognition from others because they will have earned it. People do not experience their sexuality as an object of choice but as a given fact. For a gay it is part of the nature God gave him and must be used in His service. Like all things which come from Him, it should be a source of blessing. Now, counting our blessings is a luxury: using them is a duty. Use, not acceptance, is the aim.

For most gay people their sexuality is an unasked-for gift, and a mixed blessing. In all minorities there is an element of self-hatred, because being a little bit different, a little bit queer, is not easy in a frightened world. Jews, gays, and other minorities are always tempted to deny what they are and how God made them, in order to be accepted. Religious groups have been among the worst in penalizing the courageous truth and rewarding the opportune falsehood.

## Gay Vocation

If gay people examine their lives, they can thank God for many things which they can use for the growth of goodness within them, and for the well-being of others.

Through gay people God heals some of the divisions of the world. The difficulties and rejections which gays experience transcend the division of race, religion, colour and class, as any gay gathering can show. In this country, where class is so entrenched, this is truly a wonder. I have seen Arabs and Jews brought together, Germans and Poles, conservatives and communists. It was attraction, not ideology, which provided the occasion and brought some understanding and the seed of love. Authoritarians do not care for gays. They do not like their straying habits.

God can also use gays to heal some of the scars of a sexist society. It is natural to hate being persecuted, it is supernatural to hate being a persecutor even more. We should thank God, that though straights have burnt gays in the past, and still threaten stoning and occasionally practise it, gays have no desire to retaliate in kind. In my own experience, many hurt heteros turn to gays, for they bring no threat, only healing. So God's work is done through them. Gays can build a bridge of understanding and sympathy between the sexes if they are allowed to, and if they are willing to come out of their own ghetto.

Society has not given gays their self-respect. They have not inherited it or been presented with it. What they have, they have earned. It has come from the decency and trust that God creates in them with their consent. The sanction of their gay relationships was not provided by a law-court or a Prayer Book or a church blessing, but by such inner trust and faith a the parties could invoke. Such do-it-yourself religion cuts away the frills, and exposes the real price of sharing a home and a life. In a packaged society, such plain and simple truth is rare and valuable.

In gay people too, the value of friendship is restored. God may not bless them according to the formula of the traditional Jewish blessings like Ephraim and Manasseh, or like Sarah, Rebecca, Rachel and Leah, but as he blessed other same sex friendships and lives, whether the friendships had sexual expression or not; as he blessed Ruth and Naomi for example, or David and Jonathan, or Rabbi Jochanan and Resh Lakish, or Jesus and the beloved disciple. Particular friendships have to be rescued from suspicion and slander, and given more attention and understanding. In big towns and small families and bedsitters, friendship for heteros and homos alike is the way people give and receive, and redeem each other. It is not an official relationship, but it is of the same importance as marriage for the well-being of society. More and more in a modern town, a person's true family is her or his friends.

I hope that gays will also bring more honesty to religion. As I have said before, truth is partly catered for, honesty is not; and with honesty we could also do with some understanding. Nasty old men, cradle-snatching women and confused adolescents have been given a rough time in the past. Gays should never forget that they too were slaves in the land of Egypt, and should use this experience to help others who are still beyond the pale.

This is not an easy task, for while honesty, like the truth, makes you free, it does not make you cosy.

## Sex – Gay and Serious

I also hope that, just as boys will be boys, and girls will be girls, so gays will continue to be gay. Religion is a solemn affair, heavy with pretension, and lumpy with love. Listening to a religious debate on sex is like reading an academic thesis on jokes. It misses the point.

Now sex and sexuality need examination, but the text which needs most attention is the fabric of people's lives. If procreation is not present, which is the situation for most gays and many straights, what is left? A great deal more than a tumble in the hay! People sleep with each other and make love because they are lonely or tense; it is a way to make contact with another human being, to escape the confines of the ego, to give pleasure and receive it. It is a way to relax and get to sleep, and to listen to the body's needs. It is a way to give comfort and affection and warmth. It can be 'fun'.

Now fun is an unusual and difficult concept in religion. Like humour it is scarce. There isn't much in your scriptures or mine. God is angry or agonized. He is righteous or wrathful. He frowns, He judges and He favours. He rarely laughs and never winks – except perhaps at the end of the Book of Jonah. You have to go to the Talmud to find a real joke. Humour in religion is a welcome latecomer. Life is tough, especially if you are a member of a minority, and fun and humour, wherever you find them, can redeem you from all sorts of anger and grievances and grudges. A joke can cut you down to size as ruthlessly but less hurtfully than hours of kneework.

## Sex in Religion

Up to now approaches to sexuality have been heavy, and the language so clumsy with science or evasive with theology that the act itself is barely recognizable. Traditional religious systems have typed people by what is outward and physical, not by people's more subtle perception of themselves. Male and female have been defined by genitalia and procreation, not by feeling. In this, unrefined religion and hard porn have much in common. Neither does people justice. In a similar way the form of a relationship rather than its content or depth has been made the object of concentration. Some marriages are made in heaven and some are only made by money. Some deserve the name; with others it is only a name. Some are permanent in form but temporary in nature. Some are for convenience, without love. In some the bond is hostility, and the marriage is little more than a licence to destroy each other. The same phenomena apply to unmarried relationships too. The form tells you less and less as to which is which. Forms, of course, are easier to administer than content, so all institutions, whether religious or secular, concentrate on them.

Another problem is that the emphasis placed on sex in religion and in sexual propaganda *feels* wrong. It is either too light or too heavy, and does not accord with common sense. Sex is not a full-time activity, only a part-time one. The need for it is not constant in human life. It comes and it goes, and it is not the purpose for our life on earth. People can transfer energy from one activity to another in varying degrees. For myself, sex and food and prayer are outlets which can often interchange. Many times – not every time – I can choose. Sexual desire is immediate, and unless it is seen in a wider perspective it can lead to the numbers game, or manipulation, or the reduction of people to flesh, which does not do them justice. It is not a universal panacea.

On the other hand, the evasion of sex can cause even worse problems. When religion goes wrong, its real problems are power, ambition, sadism, masochism and violence, not sex. Its involvement with extreme nationalism, its unacknowledged taste for happenings, and its hankering after external authority more than after the truth, all seem to me evidence of a deep sexual insecurity and suppression. The fuss caused among a majority to accommodate the rights of a minority is so disproportionate, and the language and fervour so exaggerated, that I suspect the gay issue covers a secret sexual fear and distortion in the majority itself. The lack of faith shown by religion in its own institutions and its insecurity are frightening. Once again, it is right to unite your sexuality and your spirituality, and to bring the gay and Christian parts of yourself into dialogue. The price of castrating the body or the soul is too high. Fanatical religion and compulsive porn recommend this divorce. I have met people who have tried it but were wrecked. Even those who had a genuine vocation for celibacy could never speak the truth about their nature, in which their vocation had taken root.

I have spoken about sex and sexuality generally, because the gap between homosexual and heterosexual relationships is closing. There might be Berlin walls of theology which separate them: in practice the walls are more like those of Jericho. Experience can be translated from one expression to another with some adjustments. Most counsellors know this. Many religious spokesmen prefer not to.

There are many things gays and straights have to give each other. Gays are, in my experience, more straight and honest about their relationships. The straights carry more pretensions. On the other hand the reasonably monogamous marriage still takes the main strain of society, and gays should not knock it out of insecurity. Commitment, keeping faith, keeping your promises are not to be despised and should be honoured wherever they exist. More, not less, would be welcome in a gay bar.

## Judaism

But you have asked me here not for my own personal views, which are, I suppose, little different from your own, though expressed in an unfamiliar theological language. Increasingly we are posed the same questions, and give the same answers, despite our different traditions. You want to know if Judaism has any thing which can be relevant to you. We are serious people dealing with a serious issue, and I shall waste no time with ecumenical chit-chat or religious one-upmanship. The question is fair, because Jews were called to bring a blessing not just to themselves but to the world.

I cannot as easily give you a fair answer. There is no direct unanimous Jewish answer for gays. For traditionalists, homosexual behaviour is forbidden. The compassionate see it as an illness, and the rigorists as a sin. Neither permits it and the recommended therapy ranges from counselling to stoning. If the will were there, there could be a development in Jewish Law. Since interest is now allowed, and capital punishment abolished, polygamy forbidden, and slavery obsolete, then in theory a change in attitude could take place here too. But the will is not there. Like intermarriage and the food laws, and the sexual purity laws and the Sabbath observance laws, homosexuality is just another unresolved problem, set by an open and permissive society to a religious law which sought God's will in a closed and homogeneous one, drawn tight by external persecution and internal obedience. For the progressives and reformers in Judaism, there is a conflicting mixture of tradition, middle-class attitudes, fears for the family, fears for their own image, and a genuine sympathy with the minority and the underdog. They are struggling for an answer. They have not yet found one. Your experience could help us.

## Survival and Sex

I want to explain why this is so, why Jews as they weep over their six-million dead are scarcely conscious of the homosexuals in the camps who were tortured and killed beside them. Judaism is a small reli-

gion, one of the smallest in that exclusive club of the so-called
'Higher Religions', and for the last fifty years it has lurched from one
crisis to another. Its concern has not been sex but survival. In the
shadow of the camps, masturbation, birth control and homosexuality were not burning issues. Intermarriage worries Jewish leaders
more than premarital sex or homosexuality. The former threatens
the community, the latter issues involve only the parties concerned.

Seventy per cent of Jewry in Europe died in living memory, and
the survivors did not rush to consider homosexuality. Ghettos,
whether they are homosexual or Jewish, have their own order of pri-
orities. Seeing both is enlightening.

What does Judaism think of homosexuality? In Europe up to now
all one can say is that it doesn't, or not much. The teachers at my seminary told me it was a gentile weakness of which Jews were not suspect. In the same way, I suppose, for the English V.D. was a French
disease, and for the French a Neapolitan one, and it is presumably still
heading south on the old evasion route. Jews had enough problems
with the Inquisition and with Hitler, both of whom persecuted Jews
and homosexuals. Why compound homosexuality with Judaism and
get a double dose of punishment? Why get burnt twice?

So this evasion has survived despite some gay poems of great
medieval rabbis, the private lives of many public Jews, and the private
knowledge of many Jewish families, whose kindness usually overcomes
their astonishment for their gay sons, but not for their gay daughters.

There is not as much said in Jewish tradition as we might have
expected, though what is said is negative. In the Bible sodomy is
condemned as womanizing a man, and there are prohibitions about
clothes. There is little use in asking whether the prohibitions are
meant for homosexuals or for heterosexuals just being different, for
in the Bible there is no knowledge or discussion of homosexuality as
a person's orientation and personality. It legislated for a polygamous
society with concubines, where infant mortality was high and the
survival of the group precarious, where women were just ceasing to
be chattels who could be thrown out almost at will, and where adultery was seen as a kind of theft of another man's property. There is
no simple connection between the realities of that society and those
of our own. Scholarly argument about cult-prostitutes and the womanizing of defeated foes merely emphasizes the gap. The sin of
Sodom, incidentally, may not have been sodomy at all, but lack of
hospitality coupled with violence – which, you will agree, are not the
same thing at all.

Rabbinic law extends the biblical prohibition to lesbians, on a
somewhat shaky legal basis, and gets suspicious even of widows
keeping pet dogs. On the other hand it says that, as far as homosex-

uality in general is concerned, Jews do not do that sort of thing; which is certainly untrue now, and was probably inaccurate then. As in Christianity, a blight of scruples and suspicion settled over every-thing, including sex, though in Judaism it never went as far as in Christianity. The Inquisition and other persecutions helped to keep Judaism both straight and narrow.

If we approach all this deductively from the texts and impose them on people, it will not increase our understanding or their well-being. If we start from people's lives and possibilities and problems, and work our way back to the texts, then the result is more con-structive. In doing so, it is the scriptures themselves, with their call for honesty, justice and compassion, which make us go forward from the self-same scriptures. All honour to those Jewish reformers, whether they used traditional methods or not, who found ways to make the death penalty impossible, and slavery obsolete; who tried to give women equality, who ignored witch-hunting, and who made modern economic life possible. Their work too is Jewish tradition, and homosexuality should be added to the list. God worked through them. May we have the courage to let Him work through us. Our sci-entific and precise knowledge of human sexuality comes from mod-ern times, not from the scriptures, but is of no less religious value.

Yet, in an indirect way, Judaism can help gay people a great deal, if they examine it with discrimination, and they might also help Judaism in the process. Minorities need each other, and need to feel needed. Without each other's perspectives, life can easily be nar-rowed to a Jewish problem or a gay one.

## Jewish Society

Judaism has a certain domestic magic, made up of spirituality, cook-ing, gossip and kindness. This will not help gays with recognition, but it can help them to turn their house or flat into a home, and a gay gathering into a family, and a kitchen table into an altar. It can help gay people to build on their contact, to touch each other's lives and souls as well as each other's bodies.

You can learn from Jewish experience both positively and nega-tively some lessons and warnings about minority life. You need humour to cope with it. You have to know how to forgive the tres-passes of the majority against you, and how to accept some part of the role of the suffering servant with good grace, or you will be eaten away with bitterness or drowned in your own nostalgia. This is not so much piety as spiritual hygiene. When I go to church I have to lis-ten to the uncomplimentary remarks about Jews and Pharisees in the

Gospels. I don't protest about it, I take it. You will always have more problems than the majority. Be careful also of a tendency to retreat into a ghetto and lock yourselves in. In Judaism this produces intro- version, claustrophobia and prejudice. Think carefully about gay bars for men where women are not welcome, and houses for women where men are not allowed. The aim of gay liberation is to make people whole, not to increase their divisions and split the sexes apart. It is easy to escape from a ghetto imposed on you, and then to build one of your own because it seems safe and cosy.

One advantage of Judaism is that it has a long history, double that of Christianity. It is easier to see that institutions do not just drop from heaven. There is, of course, the spur of revelation and inspira- tion, but these require hard work, refinement, experience of life, and common sense, before they crystallize into social forms. Marriage, like the weekend, is taken for granted, but both had to be invented with trial-and-error and testing. The Five Books of Moses never refer to marriage explicitly – they talk of a man 'acquiring' a woman (the actual word, forbidden later by the Rabbis to be used, is 'buying' her). Before 'acquiring' was changed into 'hallowing', and marriage escaped from property law into status law, millennia had to pass, and prophets, scribes, writers, lawyers, reformers and Rabbis all had to make their contribution. Now gay relationships need the same real- ism and religion, to change a grab into a proposal, to find the forms which can satisfy and sanctify the partners by each other's promises, and to turn their house into a home, if they wish it.

Judaism is not a romantic religion. It is less concerned with peo- ple being in love than in 'the love' which, a text from the Jewish Reform Prayer Book says, 'you earn, as you earn your living, with the sweat of your brow.' This love is the end, not the beginning, of a relationship. It is the fruit of loyalty and of being able to appreciate the otherness of the other. It is an antidote to the kitsch and the infla- tion of love which occur in cheap religion, cheap romance, and cheap porn. In practice, sex does not always require love. It is nice, but arbitrary. Respect is more essential, and so is compassion, which is as necessary for sex as it is for prayer. Just because a marriage, for example, lacks love – for people fall out of love as they fall into it – it does not cease to exist.

Another aspect of Judaism is its communal character. Some Rab- bis and Christian ministers were discussing the subject of gay rela- tionships and their blessing. One of my colleagues pointed out that, if a blessing is required at the start of a gay relationship, religion is even more needed at its end. The community cannot only be involved when it suits people, and ignored when it doesn't. At first I found the idea odd – a sort of gay divorce – but on second thoughts there was more to be said for it. The break-up of a relationship affects and unsettles many people besides the parties concerned. It is not just their business. A blessing at the start of a relationship can be cosmetic or an exercise in public relations. To end a relationship decently, real religion is needed.

Another valuable aspect of Judaism is its discipline in working things out. A network of committees and fund-raising organizations supports homes for the elderly and welfare work, and cares for those who have fallen by the way (provided the way was straight and narrow). It is easy to scoff at the bazaars and the raffles, the fund-raising functions and the philanthropic tycoons: but they work. One glance through *Gay News* shows a similar network of concerned organizations. But they are starved of money and support. Gay people have not yet learned to give enough to their own.

Judaism also had a tradition of marrying religion to the realities of life, and of consummating the marriage in law. It undertook to find suitable partners for people, to provide for their dowries (especially if they were ugly) and to find them jobs. It had a language which could discuss sexual problems (of a heterosexual type) with precision and without embarrassment. This, present-day religion does not command. It is possible to discuss economics and sociology from the pulpit (in an imprecise way), but not four-letter words despite their respectable provenance in the *Oxford English Dictionary (Supplement)*. Religion is a middle-class affair today. Its good points are hard work and responsibility, and its bad points are hypocrisy, cowardice and evasion.

## A Gay Contribution

Now what can religion, including Judaism, gain from this encounter with gay people? – for all healthy encounters are two-way, benefitting both.

Religion in the West has had a bad record with minorities. Underlying modern political anti-semitism, there is a streak of a Christian anti-Judaism. It is only receding after the holocaust. In my own religion, both sides have used the power of the state against each other in religious disputes, and the pious are not averse to stone-throwing, fisticuffs and rugger tactics, nor are the enlightened immune from superiority and spite. Many religious groups want civil rights for themselves, not for others. I accept that much of their passion arises out of concern for the issues, but it is too partial to be helpful. With gays, religions have another chance to give a minority the understanding and sympathy that religions claim for themselves in a secular world: all religions have become minorities now.

Looking back over their achievements, gays have been a creative lot. Their contribution to religion has been significant, though unacknowledged; it could be even greater. Bursts of creativity often follow a liberation or a breakthrough. Such a liberation might also exorcise the unnecessary fear and insecurity which characterize the religious debate on sexuality.

Religion is at its best when it unites matter and spirit, the everyday things of life and the divine. This is the glory of Jewish law, and the freshness of the Parables. It is right to be concerned with the needs of the Third World, but not as an evasion of the problems on the doorstep. The former has the drawback that it is conveniently far away, the gay problem has the advantage that it is inconveniently near.

Involvement with the gay community would also bring an awareness that more truth has been revealed in our time than is officially allowed. The labels have been unfamiliar, but all truth is holy. In our time the redemptive and prophetic work of Judaism, for example, has taken place through such people as Freud, Wasserman, Emma Goldman and Magnus Hirschfeld. Although rarely mentioned among Jews, the last named, 'Tante Magnolia', is a shining example of courage and compassion, an outspoken doctor and reformer who redeemed people from their fears and anxieties, and who tried to make the crooked straight, even in Nazi times. We should be proud of such people, not hide them.

## Questions

Certain issues and studies are linked to the reconsideration of gays. They need a close attention to life as people actually live it, and precision. One such issue is the relation of sexual energy to religious energy – how far, for example, they are transferable. Another is to enquire what constitutes a marriage, whether one can define relationships by their content rather than by their form. Also linked to the problem is the separation of religion from the debris of past societies. If sexual abstinence is a help to spirituality, then why is it so and how? Can people keep faith in a marriage and not be 'faithful', or *vice versa*? These questions are not academic but practical ones for many. They require exact answers.

If religious people by a leap of feeling or imagination can look at their religion through gay eyes, they will see not only the caring side of their own religion but also its dark side. Most religions look at the relationships that they create and sanctify: they do not consider the relationships that they break or undermine. Gay relationships have achieved what stability they possess through inner religion, not through the external kind. It is the most valuable of insights for a community, as well as for an individual, to see the times when it is not as innocent as it thought – and that the oppressor is within.

The full potentiality of gay people for good has never been tapped. I believe the honest, caring, funny and humble aspects of gay life have much to give if they are allowed to find their place. There is also a caustic wit which is an antidote to humbug. It is possible that when religions have ceased to insult gays or to order them around, they might begin to enjoy them – they are great fun.

## Redeeming Each Other

People these days are looking around for gurus. They are imported from the East, and re-exported from the West. Everyone wants a bit of redemption to give meaning to her or his life and possessions. Many years ago I tried to track down the complete guru with great persistence, for I was a serious youngster. I followed up every clue I could find in the advertisements of the New Statesnan. The result was interesting but confusing. Gradually the truth dawned on me, that no one has the whole answer, but each of us has a bit of the answer; and, if we are allowed to, we redeem each other.

Have you watched an old person in a gay bar? Have you seen pride and power at work in religion? Both need the warmth and affection which they cannot generate in themselves. They need each other, and others yet.

When I was a child I used to say the traditional morning blessings. If you were a man you said: 'Blessed are You, Lord our God, King of the Universe, who has not made me a woman.' If you were a woman you said: 'Blessed are You, Lord our God, King of the Universe, who has made me according to your will.' If you knew you were gay, you had a long think, for you knew you were not wanted.

In a new revision of the liturgy, everyone now says: 'Blessed are You, Lord our God, King of the Universe, who has made me according to your will.' It is the only response which goes beyond the sociology of the past, and brings together women and men, straight and gay, into the fellowship of the divine.

# THERAPEUTIC VIEWS
# ON SEXUALITY

# FREUD, RACE AND GENDER

*Sander L. Gilman*

Freud's 'Jewish' identity has been long the topic for scholarly exegesis.[1] Recently Harold Bloom asked:

> What is most Jewish about Freud's work? I am not much impressed by the answers to this question that follow the pattern: from Oedipus to Moses, and thus centre themselves upon Freud's own Oedipal relation to his father Jakob. Such answers only tell me that Freud had a Jewish father, and doubtless books and essays yet will be written hypothesizing Freud's relation to his indubitably Jewish mother. Nor am I persuaded by any attempts to relate Freud to esoteric Jewish traditions. As a speculator, Freud may be said to have founded a kind of Gnosis, but there are no Gnostic elements in the Freudian dualism. Nor am I convinced by any of the attempts to connect Freud's Dream Book to supposed Talmudic antecedents. And yet the centre of Freud's work, his concept of repression as I've remarked, does seem to me profoundly Jewish, and in its patterns even normatively Jewish. Freudian memory and Freudian forgetting are a very Jewish memory and a very Jewish forgetting. It is their reliance upon a version of Jewish memory, a parody-version if you will, that makes Freud's writings profoundly and yet all too originally Jewish.[2]

My answer to Bloom's problem is only a very partial one. For Sigmund Freud, an acculturated Jewish medical scientist of late nineteenth-century Vienna, one of the definitions of the Jew which he would have internalized was a racial one and it is a definition which,

1. A more detailed discussion of these questions and the existing literature can be found in my, *The Case of Sigmund Freud, Medicine and Identity at the Fin de Siècle*, (Baltimore, The Johns Hopkins University Press, 1993); *Freud, Race and Gender*, (Princeton, Princeton University Press, 1993); and *Hysteria: A New History*, (Los Angeles, University of California Press, 1993) with Helen King, Roy Porter, George Rousseau and Elaine Showalter.
2. Harold Bloom, *The Strong Light of the Canonical: Kafka, Freud, and Scholem as Revisionists of Jewish Culture and Thought.* The City College Papers, no. 20. (New York: The City College, 1987), p. 43.

whether he consciously sought it or not, shaped the argument of psychoanalysis. Given Freud's own analysis of many of his dreams, the latent or manifest content of which reflect on the question of being Jewish in a violently anti-Semitic world, this question seems to have been first raised by Freud himself.[3] Thus we can respond to Peter Homans model of a response to an idea of "'Jewishness" after the fashion of a key to its wax impression or a statue to a plaster cast of the statue – psychoanalysis emerged as the negative image, so to speak, of its Jewish surroundings.'[4] Homan sees the de-idealisation of Jewish men to whom [Freud] had attached himself as the key to this movement; I see this de-idealisation, in part, as the result of Freud's struggle with the very definition of science which becomes central to his primary group orientation. The seeming fixation which Freud has on the biological explanation for psychological phenomena, a fixation which has greatly stirred the interest of historians over the past two decades, must be tied to his contemporary understanding of science as a domain in which debates about his own self are carried out.

For Freud in the 1870s the idea of race is a confining, limiting factor, as it implies a biological, immutable pattern of development. After the turn of the century, it comes to acquire a more positive valence as a sign of the special status of the Jewish way of seeing the world. It moves from a purely biological category to a purely psychological one. In 1886, about the time Freud was studying with Jean-Martin Charcot in Paris, Gustav Le Bon, the French anti-Semitic sociologist published his overt discussion of the inheritance of the psychological attributes of race, which he attributed as much to biology as to social environment.[5] Le Bon's views are central for Freud's later work on the psychology of mass movements which are his unstated analyses of anti-Semitism. Freud's experience in Paris was one which was as intensely anti-Semitic as his home in Vienna had been. Freud wants to reject Le Bon's biological view of race as 'the innumerable common characteristics handed down from generation to generation, which constitute the genius of a race.'[6] For Le

3. See, for example, Emmanuel Velikovsky, 'The Dreams Freud Dreamed', *Psychoanalytic Review* 30 (1941): 487–511 as well as the works by Masson and Loewenberg,
4. Peter Homans, *The Ability to Mourn: Disillusionment and the Social Origins of Psychoanalysis* (Chicago: The University of Chicago Press, 1989), p. 71.
5. Gustave Le Bon, 'Applications de la psychologie à classification des races', *Revue philosophique* 22 (1886): 593–619 as well as his *Role des Juifs dans La Civilisation* (Paris: Amis de Gustave Le Bon, 1985). See the discussion of Le Bon's attitudes toward the Jews in Robert Nye, *The Origins of Crowd Psychology: Gustave Le Bon and the Crisis of Mass Democracy in the Third Republic* (London/Beverly Hills, CA: Sage, 1975), p. 56 and Elisabeth Roudinesco, *La bataille de cent ans*, 2 vols. (Paris: Ramsay, 1982), especially her chapters 'L' inconscient à la française (de Gustave Le Bon à l'affaire Dreyfus)', 1: 181–221 and 'Judéité, israélisme, antisémitsme', 1: 395–411.
6. All of the quotations from Freud's works in this study, unless otherwise noted, are to

Bon, race stands in the first rank of those factors which help shape the underlying attitudes of the crowd. Racial character 'possesses, as the result of the laws of heredity, such power that its beliefs, institutions, and arts – in a word, all the elements of its civilization – are merely outward expressions of its genius.'[7] And yet for the older Freud it is within the psyche, not the body, that the difference between Jew and Aryan exists. And Freud does sense that there is a difference, unnameable perhaps, but a difference never the less. It is the unknowable essence of the Jew which anthropologists such as Richard Andree evoked. Unlike Andree, Freud provided this essence with a special, positive valence.

In 1926, Freud stated in an address to the B'nai B'rith on the occasion of being honoured on his seventieth birthday, that being Jewish is 'sharing many obscure emotional forces (*viele dunkle Gefühlsmächte*), which were the more powerful the less they could be expressed in words, as well as a clear consciousness of inner identity, the safe privacy of a common mental construction (*die Heimlichkeit der gleichen seelischen Identität*).'[8] His contemporaries, such as Theodor Reik (along with Freud and Eduard Hintschmann the only psychoanalysts to be members of the B'nai B'rith), were especially struck by these very words as the appropriate central definition of the Jew.'[9]

Freud's version of the ethnopsychology of the Jew twisted Le Bon's claims concerning the biology of race. It evokes the Lamarckianism of William James' view of the transmission of 'the same emotional propensities, the same habits, the same instincts, perpetuated without variation from one generation to another.'[10] It is the uncanny nature of the known, but repressed, aspects of the mental life of an individual – about which Freud wrote in his essay on the uncanny – which haunts Freud's image of the internal mental life which defines the Jew. As he writes to his Viennese Jewish 'alterego' Arthur Schnitzler: 'Judaism continues to mean much to me on an emotional level.'[11]

The debate about the meaning of what Phillip Rieff sees as the Victorian and Edwardian generalities about the 'persistent character of

---

Sigmund Freud, *Standard Edition of the Complete Psychological Works of Sigmund Freud*, ed. and trans., J. Strachey, A. Freud, A. Strachey, and A. Tyson. 24 vols. (London: Hogarth, 1955–74), here, 18: 74. (Referred to as SE). I have compared each quotation with the original as it appears in Sigmund Freud, *Gesammelte Werke: Chronologisch Geordnet* 19 vols. (Frankfurt a. M.: S. Fischer, 1952–1987). (Referred to as GW).

7. Gustave Le Bon, *The Crowd: A Study of the Popular Mind* (New York: The Viking Press, 1960), p. 83.

8. SE 20: 274; GW 17: 49–53

9. Theodor Reik, *Jewish Wit* (New York: Gamut Press, 1962), p. 12.

10. William James, *The Principles of Psychology*. 2 vols. (New York: Henry Holt, 1890), 2: 678.

11. Sigmund Freud, 'Briefe an Arthur Schnitzler', *Neue Rundschau* 66 (1955): 100.

the Jews' must be understood as part of the quest of the scientific psychology of the late nineteenth century.[12] For Freud this sense of the psyche of the Jew had not only to do with mental construction of the Jew but also with the Jews emotional construction. Here he would have found substantial support in the work of William McDougall, whose study of *The Group Mind* (1920) played a central role in shaping Freud's own argument about the psychology of the masses.[13] McDougall sees the fusing of the Hebrew tribes into a nation as 'having played a vital part in its consolidation, implanted and fostered as it was by a succession of great teachers, the prophets ... The national self-consciousness thus formed has continued to be not only one factor, but almost the only factor or condition, of the continued existence of the Jewish people as a people, or at any rate the one fundamental condition on which all the others are founded – their exclusive religion, their objection to intermarriage with outsiders, their hope of a future restoration of the fortunes of the nation, and so forth'.[14] Jewish self-consciousness leads to the establishment of institutions which preserve this 'common mental construction'. It is this sense of common purpose, for McDougall, but not necessarily for Freud, within the sphere of the political, which defines the Jew. Central, however, is that all aspects of the Jewish mind including all of the affective components, have their root in this 'common mental construction'.

When Freud comments to his fellow 'brothers' in the B'nai B'rith about their common mental construction, he is also in a very specific way evoking the presence of the Jewish body. Freud's major association with Jews in the 1870s and 1880s is when he joins (and helps form) a new lodge of the B'nai B'rith in Vienna.[15] B'nai B'rith means 'sons of the Covenant'. While the name was selected as a replacement for the title 'Bundes-Brüder' a German-Jewish lodge founded in New York in 1843 the name evokes, for *fin-de-siècle* Viennese Jews, a direct association with the image of circumcision. As Theodor Reik commented in 1915: 'the bond which the primordial fathers of the Jews concluded with their god is represented ... as a glorified and emended account of an initiation ceremony. The connection of the B'rith with circumcision is just as little an accident as the covenant meal in which the worshippers of Jahve identified themselves with him; and the giving of the law – B'rith can also signify law – which stands in such an

12. Philip Rieff, *Freud: The Mind of the Moralist* (New York: The Viking Press, 1959), p. 261.
13. SE 18: 83–5, 96–7.
14. William McDougall, *The Group Mind* (Cambridge: Cambridge University Press, 1920), pp. 159–60.
15. *B'nai B'rith : Zwi Perez Chajes Loge, 1895–1975* (Vienna: B'nai B'rith , 1976) and H. Knoepfmacher, 'Sigmund Freud and the B'nai B'rith', *Journal of the American Psychoanalytic Association* 27(1979): 441–9.

intimate relationship to the concluding of the covenant (Sinai) should be set side by side with the procedures of the puberty rites.'[16] The sense of 'common mental construction' is associated closely with the special form of the Jew's body and the ritual bonding which it signifies. Central to this is the act of circumcision. And this is the salient marker of the male Jewish body in *fin-de siècle* medicine.

There was a general assumption in Europe of the time that there was a 'Jewish mind' which transcended conversion or adaption.[17] And this was usually understood as being a fault. Ludwig Wittgenstein could comment about Jews such as Freud that 'even the greatest of Jewish thinkers is no more than talented. (Myself, for instance). I think there is some truth to my idea that I really only think reproductively ... Can one take the case of Freud and Breuer as an example of Jewish reproductiveness?'[18] The Jewish mind has no true originality. The Jewish mind is prosaic, as Freud wrote to Emil Fluss in the 1870s:

> How well I can imagine your feelings. To leave the native soil, dearly-beloved relatives, the most beautiful surroundings – ruins close by – I must stop or I'll be as sad as you – and you yourself know best what you are leaving behind. ... Oh Emil why are you a prosaic Jew? Journeymen imbued with Christian-Germanic fervor have composed beautiful lyrical poetry in similar circumstances.[19]

This view echoes the negative interpretation of the 'common mental construction' of the Jew as expressed in much of the anthropological and cultural debates of the late nineteenth century.

Such views of the Jews are statements about their pathology. And Freud concurs on a very basic level with the notion that the Jewish mind set is pathological. In his lecture on 'anxiety' (1917) he evoked the Lamarckian model of the inheritance of acquired characteristics in order to argue that the 'core' of anxiety '... is the repetition of some particular significant experience. This experience could only be a very early impression of a very general nature, placed in the prehistory of the individual but of the species.'[20] Or, one might add, in the prehistory of the race. Freud goes on to see this 'affective state ... constructed in the same way as a hysterical attack and, like it, would

---

16. Theodor Reik, 'Die Pubertätsriten der Wilden: über einige übereinstimmungen im Seelenleben der Wilden und der Neurotiker', *Imago* 6 (1915–16): 125–144, 189–222; translation from Theodor Reik, *Ritual: Psycho-Analytic Studies*, trans. Douglas Bryan (London: Hogarth Press, 1931), pp. 91–166, here pp. 156–57.
17. See the discussion of this concept, without any reference to the psychological or medical literature, in Steven Beller, *Vienna and the Jews 1867–1938: A Cultural History* (Cambridge: Cambridge University Press, 1989), pp. 73–83.
18. Ludwig Wittgenstein, *Culture and Value*, ed. G. H. von Wright and Heikki Nyman (Oxford: Blackwell, 1980), pp. 18–19.
19. 'Freud, Some Early Unpublished Letters', trans. Ilse Scheier, *International Journal of Psychoanalysis*, 426.
20. SE 16: 396.

be the precipitate of a reminiscence.'[21] The anxiety of the Jew is analogous to but not identical with the suffering of the hysteric. The male Eastern Jew is the quintessential hysteric for the medical science of the *fin de siècle*. It is the psychopathology of the Jew which is impressed through the experience of the collective on the individual. The roots of this view lie deep in the theories of ethno-psychology as formulated by two Jews, the psychologist Moritz Lazarus and his brother-in-law, the philologist Heymann Steinthal in the 1860s. In the opening issue of their journal for ethno-psychology and linguistics, *Zeitschrift für Völkerpsychologie und Sprachwissenschaft* (note the link of mind and language) they outlined the assumptions about the knowability of the mind.[22] For Lazarus and Steinthal their object of study was the 'psychology of human beings in groups (Gemeinschaft)'. Unlike in other fields of psychology of the time, where laboratory and clinical work was demanded to define the arena of study, ethnopsychology depended on historical and cultural/ethnological data. Their work was highly medicalised: Lazarus had studied physiology with the materialist Johannes Müller and co-founded the Medical-Psychological Society with the Berlin neurologist Wilhelm Griesinger in 1867. While they wish to separate their psychology from materialistic physiology, they are bound by the scientific rhetoric of the materialistic arguments about inheritance. They subscribe to a Lamarckian theory of mnemonic inheritance in the construction of the mind. The great laboratory psychologist Wilhelm Wundt remained the great proponent of their views of universal mental creations well into the twentieth century.[23] And Freud makes extensive use of Wundts explication of these views in his *Psychopathology of Everyday Life* (1901) and *Totem and Taboo* (1913).[24] The

21. SE 16: 396.
22. Moritz Lazarus and Heymann Steinthal, 'Einleitende Gedanken über Völkerpsychologie', *Zeitschrift für Völkerpsychologie und Sprachwissenschaft* 1 (1860): 1–73. See in this context their letters: *Moritz Lazarus and Heymann Steinthal: Die Begründer der Völkerpsychologie in ihren Briefen*, ed. Ingrid Belke. 2 vols. (Tübingen: Mohr 1971–1986). On the relationship to the medicine of the late nineteenth century see Heinz-Peter Schmiedebach, 'Die Völkerpsychologie von Moritz Lazarus (1824–1903) und ihre Beziehung zur naturwissenschaftlichen Psychiatrie', *XXX Congrès International d'Histoire de la Médecine*, 1986 (Düsseldorf: N.p., 1988), pp. 311–21.
23. Wilhelm Wundt, *Elements of Folk Psychology: Outlines of a Psychological History of the Development of Mankind*, trans. Edward Leroy Schaub (London: George Allen & Unwin, 1916), p. 2.
24. On Freud and Wundt see Christfried Tögel, 'Freud und Wundt: Von der Hypnose bis zur Völkerpsychologie', in Bernd Nitzsche, ed., *Freud und die akademische Psychologie: Beiträge zu einer historischen Kontroverse* (Munich: Psychologie Verlags Union, 1989), pp. 97–106. For the reciprocal influence see Tilman J. Elliger, *S. Freud und die akademische Psychologie: Ein Beitrag zur Rezeptionsgeschichte der Psychoanalyse in der deutschen Psychologie (1895–1945)* (Weinheim: Deutscher Studien Verlag, 1986) and Carl Eduard Scheidt, *Die Rezeption der Psychoanalyse in der deutschsprachigen Philosophie vor 1940* (Frankfurt a. M.: Suhrkamp, 1986).

psychology of the individual, as one of Freud's other sources, the Princeton psychologist James Mark Baldwin commented, recapitulates the history of the 'race experience'. One can expect general analogies to hold between nervous development and mental development, one of which is the deduction of race history epoches from individual history epoches through the repetition of phylogenesis in ontogenesis, called in biology 'Recapitulation'.[25] The history of the human race was to be found in the development of the individual. But 'racial memory' has a very different connotation for a Jewish reader of Wundt and Baldwin.

Freud, like the ethno-psychologists, needed to separate the idea of the psyche from the body, needed to eliminate the image of the fixed, immutable racial composition which determines all thoughts and all actions. For all of these thinkers, the psyche was separate from – and yet still part of the body. For it seemed to be impossible, even within the needs of such thinkers to avoid the pitfalls of race, of ever truly separating the mind from the body.

Freud dismisses the Germanic *Weltanschauung* as a 'specifically German concept, the translation of which into foreign languages might well raise difficulties'.[26] It is not the rigid paradigm of knowing which appeals to Freud, but rather the acceptance of the 'scientific model', which, while it accepts the 'uniformity of explanation of the universe' only 'does so as a programme, the fulfillment of which is relegated to the future'. It is the scientific mode of seeing the world which is not too Germanic but rather allows the Jew to see the world as a scientist.[27] By the mid-1930s Freud can shrug his shoulders at the Nazi burning of his books, sensing that this action represents the German response to his own 'common mental construction': '"They told me", he said, "that psychoanalysis is alien to their *Weltanschauung*, and I suppose it is." He said this with no emotion and little interest, as though talking about the affairs of some complete stranger.'[28] It is Freud the positivist which dominates in his comprehension of the mindset of the Jews.

These groups are called by Lazarus and Steinthal 'peoples' (*Völker*) but they stress that these groups are constituted by the individuals which comprise them and are not fixed biological 'races'.[29] 'Human

25. James Mark Baldwin, *Mental Development in the Child and the Race* (New York: The Macmillan Company, 1898), pp. 14–15. See SE 7: 173.
26. SE 22: 158.
27. Jacques Le Rider, 'Freud zwischen Aufklärung und Gegenaufklärung', in Jochen Schmidt, ed., *Aufklärung und Gegenaufklärung in der europäischen Literatur, Philosophie und Politik von der Antike bis zur Gegenwart* (Darmstadt: Wissenschaftliche Buchgesellschaft, 1989), pp. 475–496.
28. Cited in Theodor Reik, *From Thirty Years with Freud*, trans. Richard Winston (New York: Farrar & Rinehart, 1940), p. 30.
29. Lazarus and Steinthal, 'Einleitende Gedanken', 5.

beings', as Lazarus observes, 'are the creation of history; everything in us, about us, is the result of history; we do not speak a word, we do not think an idea, there is neither feeling nor emotion, which is not in a complicated manner dependent on historical determinants'.[30] The standards for definition of a people are fluid and change from group to group. Thus the standards for being French are different than those for being German.[31] Even though a 'people is a purely subjective construction' it reflects itself in 'a common consciousness of many with the consciousness of the group'.[32] This 'common consciousness' exists initially because of the 'same origin' and the 'proximity of the dwellings' of the members of the group.[33] And 'with the relationship through birth, the similarity of physiognomy, especially the form of the body, is present.'[34] For them this 'objective' fact of biological similarity lays the groundwork for the 'subjective' nature of the mental construction of a people.[35] But the biological underpinnings of this argument are clear: the Irish eat potatoes as a reflex of being in Ireland, which makes them Irish, and they are Irish because they eat potatoes.[36] Could one not argue that Jews are Jews because they circumcise their male infants and they circumcise their male infants because they are Jews. The place where these acquired characteristics is localized is not the body, but within the language of the *Volk.* Lazarus and Steinthal are constituting a definition of group identification which is rooted in a biological (and, therefore, for them observable and demonstrable) relationship but which self-consciously builds upon this basic identity a sense of group cohesion. This is an answer to the argument about 'race' constructing the mentality of the group. Here it is the group which is constituted based on the biological accidents of birth and dwelling, not the inborn identity of blood. And yet it is the observable, biological which structures their argument.

Freud sees the construction of the mentality of a group as a reflex of biology tempered by the social context in which the individual finds himself. In *Civilization and Its Discontents* (1930) Freud comments on the subjectivity of happiness: 'No matter how much we may shrink with horror from certain situations – of a galley-slave in antiquity, of a peasant during the Thirty Years' War, of a victim of the Holy Inquisition, of a Jew awaiting a pogrom – it is nevertheless impossible for us to feel our way into such people – to divine the changes which

---

30. Moritz Lazarus, 'Über das Verhältnis des Einzelnen zur Gesammtheit', *Zeitschrift für Völkerpsychologie und Sprachwissenschaft* 2 (1862): 437.
31. Lazarus and Steinthal, Einleitende Gedanken, 35.
32. Ibid., 35–36.
33. Ibid., 37.
34. Ibid., 37
35. Ibid., 38.
36. Ibid., 39.

original obtuseness of mind, a gradual stupefying process, the cessation of expectations, and cruder or more refined methods of narcotization have produced upon their receptivity to sensations of pleasure and unpleasure.'[37] Freud places himself and the reader (the 'us') separate from the victim.[38] This works in terms of the historical images he evokes from antiquity, the seventeenth century, the sixteenth century, but the image of the pogrom, while obliquely 'historical' in that they reflect Russia at the *fin de siècle,* are also quite immediate to Freud. His view that this mindset could be constructed at such times of stress separates himself out from what was occurring during his own experience, even while he wrote *Civilization and Its Discontents.*

But Freud, as in his earlier review of Forel, rejected in print traditional definitions of 'race' as a category within the discourse of science. During his analysis of Smiley Blanton he commented that 'My background as a Jew helped me to stand being criticized, being isolated, working alone ... All this was of help to me in discovering analysis. But that psychoanalysis itself is a Jewish product seems to me nonsense. As a scientific work, it is neither Jewish nor Catholic nor Gentile.'[39] He wrote in a birthday greeting to Ernest Jones in 1929:

> The first piece of work that it fell to psycho-analysis to perform was the discovery of the instincts that are common to all men living today – and not only to those living today but to those of ancient and of prehistoric times. It called for no great effort, therefore, for psychoanalysis to ignore the differences that arise among the inhabitants of the earth owing to the multiplicity of races, languages, and countries.[40]

And this to an individual with whom he felt a 'racial strangeness' *(Rassenfremdheit)* upon first meeting in 1908.[41] And to whom he first commented during this meeting him, that 'from the shape of my head I could not be English and must be Welsh. It astonished me, first because it is uncommon for anyone on the Continent to know of the existence of my native country, and then because I had suspected my dolichocephalic skull might as well be Teutonic as Celtic.'[42] Jones' response to Freud's remark is couched in the lan-

---

37. SE 21: 89.
38. In this context see Dagmar Barnouw, 'Modernism in Vienna: Freud and a Normative Poetics of the Self', *Modern Austrian Literature* 22 (1989): 327–44 on the question of Freud's construction of fictions of the self.
39. Blanton, p. 43.
40. SE 21: 249.
41. William McGuire and Wolfgang Sauerländer, eds. *Sigmund Freud-C. G. Jung, Briefwechsel* (Frankfurt a.M.: Fischer, 1974), p. 71; William McGuire ed., *The Freud/ Jung Letters: The Correspondence between Sigmund Freud and C. G. Jung,* trans. Ralph Mannheim and R. F. C. Hull (Princeton: Princeton University Pres, 1974), p. 145.
42. Jones, *The Life and Work of Sigmund Freud,* 2: 42–43. See also the description of this meeting in his autobiography: Ernest Jones, *Free Associations: Memories of a Psycho-Analyst* (London: Hogarth Press, 1959), p. 166.

guage of racial biology. These use of these categories was simply assumed and was in no way questioned.

What seems to be a contradictory view evinces Freud's complicated resistance to and restructuring of the idea of a group mentality. His conviction of the compatibility of both neutral science and ethnocentric perception is found in a letter written on June 8, 1913 to one of his most trusted Jewish followers, the Hungarian psychoanalyst Sándor Ferenczi:

> Certainly there are great differences between the Jewish and the Aryan spirit. We can observe that every day. Hence, there would assuredly be here and there differences in outlook on art and life. But there should not be such a thing as Aryan or Jewish science. Results in science must be identical, though the presentation of them may vary.[43]

This difference in 'spirit' is present and yet undefined. Many opponents of political anti-Semitism at the *fin de siècle* acknowledged that there were '… indeed, many scientific Jews, but I see nowhere a Jewish science', to quote Anatole Leroy-Beaulieu.[44] Yet it was clear that Freud understood that his own identification as a Jew both provided the 'ground' for the new science of psychoanalysis as well as limiting access of this new science to the claims of a 'neutral science'. In 1910 he had confronted his Viennese (read: Jewish) colleagues at the second Psychoanalytic Congress and stated the case bluntly: 'Most of you are Jews, and therefore you are incompetent to win friends for the new teaching. Jews must be content with the modest role of preparing the ground. It is absolutely essential that I should form ties in the world of general science. … The Swiss will save us …'[45] But the Swiss, at least C. G. Jung if not Eugen Bleuler, certainly did not see psychoanalysis as anything but a 'Jewish science'. Freud recognized this when he commented to Smiley Blanton in 1930 that he had tried to place Jung at the head of the psychoanalytic movement 'because there was a danger that people would consider psychoanalysis as primarily Jewish'.[46] Or to Abraham Kardiner that he hated the idea that psychoanalysis would founder because it would go down in history as a 'Jewish science'.[47] Psychoanalysis had to be freed, but could not be freed from the Jewish mind which, at least in Freud's view, constructed it.

43. Jones, *The Life and Work of Sigmund Freud*, 2: 168.
44. Anatole Leroy-Beaulieu, *Israel Among the Nations: A Study of the Jews and Anti-semitism*, trans. Frances Hellman (New York: G. P. Putnams Sons, 1895), p. 51.
45. Fritz Wittels, *Sigmund Freud: His Personality, His Teaching, and His School*, trans. Eden and Ceder Paul (London: George Allen & Unwin Ltd., 1924), p. 140. This translation corrected many errors (listed by Freud) in the original German.
46. Blanton, p. 43.
47. A. Kardiner, *My Analysis with Freud: Reminiscences* (New York: W. W. Norton, 1977), p. 70.

In a 1936 letter (written in English) on the death of his friend and early British supporter Montague David Eder, Freud evoked that 'common mental construction' which sets the Jew apart: 'We were both Jews and knew of each other that we carried that miraculous thing in common, which inaccessible to any analysis so far makes the Jew.'[48] He uses this rhetoric often in his exchanges with Jews. He can write to Karl Abraham on May 3 1908 of their common 'racial identification' (*Rassenverwandtschaft*) as opposed to the 'Aryan' views of Carl Gustav Jung.[49] Freud's letter reflects his anxiety about the labelling of psychoanalysis as a 'Jewish national affair'.[50] As he later wrote to Jones, science should be beyond such designations, but evidently is not. Both Freud and Abraham saw a grain of truth in this charge, a grain rooted in the way Jews were assumed to see the world:

> ... I find it easier to go along with you rather than with Jung. I, too, have always felt this intellectual kinship. After all, our Talmudic way of thinking cannot disappear just like that. Some days ago a small paragraph in Jokes strangely attracted me. When I looked at it more closely, I found that, in the technique of apposition and in its whole structure, it was completely Talmudic.[51]

Now Freud's response does not deny this but rather places this 'shared mental construction' into the following terms: 'May I say that it is consanguineous Jewish traits (*verwandte, jüdische Züge*) that attract me to you? We understand each other.'[52] Abraham's claim is that the Jews in psychoanalysis share a common discourse and he evokes, in a positive manner, the traditional negative label of 'Talmudic' for this approach. Abraham and Freud both are accepting (and giving a positive value) to the charge of the Jews possessing a secret or hidden language, which is manifested in the manner by which Jews use (or rather, abuse) language. This is the charge, which we have already seen widely stated, that Jews *mauschel*, that they speak differently from all others.

In 1912, when the break with Jung is clear, Freud in a letter to Ferenczi despairs of yoking 'Jews and *goyim* in the service of psychoanalysis ...' for 'they separate themselves like oil and water'.[53] How

48. *Sigmund Freud, Briefe 1873–1939*, ed., Ernst und Lucie Freud (Frankfurt a. M.: Fischer, 1960), p. 443.
49. *Sigmund Freud-Karl Abraham, Briefe 1907–1926*, ed. Hilda C. Abraham and Ernst L. Freud (Frankfurt a. M.: S. Fischer, 1980), p. 47.
50. On the context of this exchange see Peter Homans, *The Ability to Mourn: Disillusionment and the Social Origins of Psychoanalysis* (Chicago: The University of Chicago Press, 1989), pp. 35–41.
51. Abraham to Freud, 11 May 1908, Freud-Abraham, pp. 48–49.
52. Freud-Abraham, p. 57.
53. Freud to Ferenczi, July 28, 1912, Freud collection, The Library of Congress; cited in Peter Gay, *Freud: A Life for Our Time* (New York, Norton, 1988), p. 231.

Freud experiences the 'goyim', that is Jung, can be seen in a letter to Otto Rank a month later when the 'Jews and goyim' become 'Jews and anti-Semites'.[54] In writing to Jung's former mistress Sabina Spielrein in August, 1913 Freud commented that: 'We are and remain Jews. The others will only exploit us and will never understand or appreciate us.'[55] Or in writing to Theodor Reik in 1914 about his critique of the Lutheran pastor-psychoanalyst Oskar Pfisters theological understanding of psychoanalysis that Reiks comment is 'too good for those goyim'.[56] Not only are Jews different in terms of their mentality from Aryans but this is an unbridgeable difference. Jews are unknowable to Aryans.

In Freud's comments on the 'resistances to psychoanalysis', he writes in 1926 that 'the question may be raised whether the personality of the present writer as a Jew who has never sought to disguise the fact that he is a Jew may not have had a share in provoking the antipathy of his environment to psychoanalysis ... Nor is it perhaps entirely a matter of chance that the first advocate of psychoanalysis was a Jew. To profess belief in this new theory called for a certain degree of readiness to accept a situation of solitary opposition – a situation with which no one is more familiar than a Jew.'[57] Even though Freud expresses both pride and fear that psychoanalysis will become identified as a Jewish undertaking, he also writes to the Italian psychiatrist Enrico Morselli'[58] in 1926 that, 'while he does not know whether his thesis that psychoanalysis as a direct product of the Jewish mind is correct, I would however not be ashamed if it were. Although long alienated from the religion of my ancestors, I have a feeling of solidarity with my people ( *Volk*) and think with pleasure of that fact that you are a student of a man of my race ( *Stammesgenossen*), the great Lombroso.[59]

It is not Judaism as a religion (which is 'of great significance to me as a subject of scientific interest') with which Freud identifies in a public letter in 1925, but rather the 'strong feeling of solidarity

54. Freud to Rank, August 18, 192, Rank collection, Columbia University Library; cited in Gay, *Freud*, p. 231.
55. Aldo Carotenuto, *A Secret Symmetry: Sabina Spielrein between Jung and Freud*, trans. by Arno Pomerans, John Shepley, Krishna Winston (New York: Pantheon, 1982), pp.120–21.
56. Theodor Reik, *Jewish Wit* (New York: Gamut Press, 1962), p. 33.
57. SE 19: 222.
58. Morselli was the author of *La psicanalisi: studii ed appunti critici* (Turin: Bocca, 1926) which argued that psychoanalysis was a Jewish discovery because of the predisposition of the Jewish to theoretical solutions for material problems. See also his essay 'la psicologia etnica e la scienza eugenistica', *International Eugenics Congress-1912*, 2 vols (London: Eugenics Education Society, 1912), 1: 58–62. On Morselli see Patrizia Guanieri, *Individualit à difformi: la psichiatria antropologica di Enrico Morselli* (Milan: F. Angeli, 1986).
59. Freud, *Briefe*, p. 380.

with my fellow-people (*mit meinem Volk*)'.[60] In his response to the greetings of the Chief Rabbi of Vienna of the occasion of his seventy-fifth birthday, Freud stresses the communal, psychological identity of the Jew:

> Your words aroused a special echo in me, which I do not need to explain to you. In some place in my soul, in a very hidden corner, I am a fanatical Jew. I am very much astonished to discover myself in such in spite of all efforts to be unprejudiced and impartial. What can I do against my age?[61]

Indeed the 1934 preface to the Hebrew edition of *Totem and Taboo* stated the case for a secular, racial (or at least ethnopsychological) definition of the Jew quite clearly:

> No reader of [the Hebrew version] of this book will find it easy to put himself in the emotional position of an author who is ignorant of the language of holy writ, who is completely estranged from the religion of his fathers – as well as from every other religion – and who cannot take a share in nationalist ideals, but who has yet never repudiated his people, who feels that he is in his essential nature (*Eigenart*) a Jew and who has no desire to alter that nature. If the question were put to him: 'Since you have abandoned all these common characteristics (*Gemeinsamkeiten*) of your countrymen (*Volksgenossen*), what is left to you that is Jewish?' he would reply: 'A very great deal, and probably its very essence. He could not express that essence in words; but some day, no doubt, it will become accessible to the scientific mind'.[62]

It is not only the Jew who is unknowable within the pantheon of Freud's scientific world.

## The Transmutation of the Rhetoric of Race into the Construction of Gender

Freud's comments on the unknowability of the Jew are parallel to his claims about unknowability of the feminine. For as the scientist does not know what the essence of the Jew is so too does the scientist not know about the essence of female sexuality, even to its developmental structure: 'Unfortunately we can describe this state of things only as it affects the male child; the corresponding processes in the little girl are not known to us.'[63] This Freud wrote in 1923. It was part of a generally accepted view, echoed by *fin-de siècle* sexologists, such as Paul Näcke, that 'a man can never penetrate (*eindringen*) into the psychology of the

60. SE 19: 291; GW 14: 556.
61. Josef Philip Hes, 'A Note On An As Yet Unpublished Letter by Sigmund Freud', *Jewish Social Studies* 48 (1986): 322.
62. SE 13: xv; GW 14: 569.
63. SE 19: 142.

female and vice-versa.'[64] But Freud sees the unknowability of the female as a one-sided limitation. It is only the feminine which can not be known. Freud's comment echoes his earlier view, in the *Three Essays on the Theory of Sexuality* (1905) that 'the significance of the factor of sexual overvaluation can best be studied in men, for their erotic life alone has become accessible to research. That of women partly owing to the stunting effect of civilized conditions *(Kulturverkümmerung)* and partly owing to their conventional secretiveness *(konventionelle Verschwiegenheit)* and insincerity *(Unaufrichigkeit)* is still veiled in an impenetrable obscurity *(undurchdringliches Dunkel).*[65] The pejorative tone of this description parallels the anti-Semitic rhetoric of the hidden nature of the Jew and the Jews mentality widely circulated at the *fin de siècle*, including in the medical literature of the age.

The language which Freud uses about the scientific unknowability of the essence of what makes a Jew a Jew is parallel to that which he uses concerning the essence of the feminine.[66] The rhetoric which Freud employs in all of these categories is taken from the biology of race, with all of its evocation of hidden essences and unknown forces shaping the actions of an individual. What can be known is only the essence of the self: 'In consequence of unfavorable circumstances, both of an external and an internal nature, the following observations apply chiefly to the sexual development of one sex only – that is, of males.[67] But is the Jewish male truly a male, or has Freud constructed a definition of gender, here the male, which would include himself within a category from which Jewish males are excluded. The assumption of the knowability of the self, as one can glean from Freud's own remarks, is not extended to the essence of the Jew, only to the essence of the male. The unknowability of the Jew, the hidden nature of the Jewish mind replicated the discourse about the Jewish body and its diseased and different nature.

The problem of the knowability of the Other and the self provides the rhetoric at the heart of one of the most complex and debated

64. Paul Näcke, 'Über Kontrast-Träume und speziell sexuelle Kontrast-Träume', *Archiv für Kriminal-Anthropologie und Kriminalistik* 28 (1907): 1–19, here, 13. See SE 5: 396.
65. SE 7: 151; GW 5: 50.
66. Sigmund Diamond, 'Sigmund Freud, His Jewishness, and Scientific Method: the Seen and the Unseen as Evidence', *Journal of the History of Ideas* 43 (1982): 613–34. I would also evoke here the work of Jean-François Lyotard on Heidegger and the Jews in which Lyotard speaks of Heideggers refusal to speak of the Shoah as a form of the refusal to remember which is closely tied to the role which the Jews play in the cultural world of Christianity as the ultimate object of projection. The Jew, caught up in such a system of representation, has but little choice: his essence, which incorporates the horrors projected on to him and which is embodied (quite literally) in his physical being, must forget what he is. Jean-François Lyotard, *Heidegger et 'les juifs'* (Paris: Galilée, 1988).
67. SE 9:211.

aspects of Freudian theory, Freud's reading of the meanings of male and female anatomy.[68] In 1926 Freud (in his essay on lay analysis) referred (in English) to female sexuality as the 'dark continent' of the human psyche: 'But we need not feel ashamed of this distinction; after all, the sexual life of adult women is a "dark continent" for psychology. But we have learnt that girls feel deeply their lack of a sexual organ that is equal in value to the male one; they regard themselves on that account as inferior, and this "envy for the penis" is the origin of a whole number of characteristic feminine reactions.'[69] Elsewhere I have sketched the implications of this phrase in terms of the medicalization of the black female body during the nineteenth century.[70] But note Freud's vocabulary concerning the sense of inferiority attributed to the woman because of her 'envy for the penis'. The question of the womans attribution of meaning to the female genitalia, specifically the clitoris, is raised by Freud in this context: 'Women possess as part of their genitals a small organ similar to the male one; and this small organ, the clitoris, actually plays the same part in childhood and during the years before sexual intercourse as the large organ in men.'[71] The view that the clitoris is a truncated penis is generally rejected in contemporary psychoanalytic theory. To date the only explanation for this view has been found in the arguments about homologous structures of the genitalia.[72] But little attention has been given to what Freud could have understood within this generally accepted model.

The image of the clitoris as a 'truncated penis', as a less than intact penis, reflects the popular *fin-de siècle* Viennese view of the relationship between the body of the male Jew and the body of the woman. This clitoris was known in Viennese slang of the *fin de siècle* simply as the 'Jew' *(Jud)*.[73] The phrase used 'for a woman to masturbate' is 'to play with the Jew'. The 'small organ' of the woman becomes the *pars par toto* for the Jew with his circumcised, shortened organ. This pejorative synthesis of both bodies because of their 'defective' sexual organs reflects the *fin-de siècle* Viennese definition of the male as neither female nor Jewish.

68. See the detailed overview of the psychoanalytic debates concerning penis envy in Shahla Chehrazi, 'Female Psychology: A Review', *Journal of the American Psychoanalytic Association* 34 (1986): 141–162.

69. SE 20: 212

70. *Difference and Pathology*, pp. 76–108.

71. SE 15: 155.

72. See, for example, F. D. F. Souchay, *De l'Homologie sexuelle chez l'homme* (Paris: Rignoux, 1855). This topic is central to the argument in Thomas Laqueur, *Making Sex: Body and Gender from the Greeks to Freud* (Cambridge, MA: Harvard University Press, 1990).

73. Karl Reiskel, 'Idioticon viennense eroticum', *Anthropophyteia* 2 (1905): 1–13, here, 9. Freud makes reference to this volume in SE10: 215, n. 1.

But the clitoris, the 'Jew', becomes a sign of masculinity for Freud. As late as his essay on female sexuality (1931), Freud stressed the need for female sexuality to develop from the early masturbatory emphasis on the masculine genital zone, the clitoris, to the adult sexuality of vaginal intercourse. The clitoris, 'the Jew', is the sign of the masculine which must be abandoned if and when the female is to mature into an adult woman.[74] The 'Jew' is the male hidden within the body of the female for Freud. But it is the definition of the masculine aspect of the woman which must be transcended if she is to define herself antithetically to the male.

The analogy of the body and mind of the Jew to the body and mind of the woman was a natural one for the *fin de siècle*. Within German high and medical culture this image of the nature of the woman was already present. The entire medical vocabulary applied to the body of the female stressed her physical and mental inferiority to the male. And the terms used were precisely parallel to the discourse about the Jews. Thus the female, as Elaine Showalter has so brilliantly shown, is understood as at great risk for mental illness.[75] But the female, like the Jew, also is marked by her smell. The female like the Jew is atavistic in her body and her mind. Cesare Lombroso, the founder of modern forensic anthropology and himself an Italian Jew, provided a reading of the origin of the sense of shame in the 'primitive'. He remarked that in the Romance languages the term for shame is taken from the root *putere*, which he interpreted as indicating that the origin of the sense of shame lies in the disgust for body smells. This he 'proves' by observing that prostitutes show a 'primitive pseudo-shame', a fear of being repulsive to the male, since they are loath to having their genitalia inspected when they are menstruating. But the association between odour and difference also points quite directly to the image of the source of pollution. The smell of the menses is equated with the stench of ordure, both human and animal, in the public health model of disease which still clung to the popular understanding of illness during the late nineteenth century. Edwin Chadwick, the greatest of the early Victorian crusaders for public sanitation (who built upon the theoretical work of German writers such as E. B. C Heberstreit) perceived disease as the result of putrefaction of effluvia. For Chadwick 'all smell is disease'.[76] The link between public sanitation and the image of the corrupting female (and her excreta) is through the agency of smell. As much as

74. SE 21: 232–3.
75. Elaine Showalter, *The Female Malady: Women, Madness, and English Culture, 1830–1980* (New York: Pantheon, 1985).
76. John M. Eyler, *Victorian Social Medicine: The Ideas and Methods of William Farr* (Baltimore: The Johns Hopkins University Press, 1979), p. 100.

is said about the nature of the female, about her body, so too is there the claim that science can never truly capture her essence which is beyond the understanding of the male. In the later philosophical works of Arthur Schopenhauer as well in their medicalisation in the work of Freud's contemporary, Paul Julius Möbius, the rhetoric of female inferiority was coupled with the charge of unknowability.[77] The ultimate distance between the 'neutral' scientific observer and the object observed was the claim that the object could not share in the same perceptual strategies as the observer. Whether Jew or woman was not germane; the central category was the difference of the objects ability to comprehend the world.

In the course of his work of the centrality of human sexuality, Sigmund Freud redefined sexuality so as to diminish the stress on sexual anatomy, on the association with the sexuality of the 'normal adult'. While sexuality comes to be defined against the idea of the degenerate, it no longer was possible to recognize the 'male' or the 'female' on first glance. Sexuality was now part of the mental structure of all human beings. And the bisexual nature of all human beings destroyed any specificity as to the meaning of sexual anatomy. Each human being reflected the qualities of mind which were on the spectrum from the purely 'masculine' to the purely 'feminine':

> In the first place sexuality is divorced from its too close connection with the genitals and is regarded as a more comprehensive bodily function, having pleasure as its goal and only secondarily coming to serve the ends of reproduction. In the second place the sexual impulses are regarded as including all of those merely affectionate and friendly impulses to which usage applies the exceedingly ambiguous word 'love'. I do not, however, consider that these extensions are innovations but rather restorations; they signify the removal of inexpedient limitations of the concept into which we had allowed ourselves to be led. The detaching of sexuality from the genitals has the advantage of allowing us to bring the sexual activities of children and of perverts into the same scope as those of normal adults. The sexual activities of children have hitherto been entirely neglected, and though those of perverts have been recognized, it has been with moral indignation and without understanding.[78]

By eliminating reproduction as the goal of the sexual, Freud destroyed the argument that Jewish sexual practices (circumcision or endogenous marriage) were at the root of the pathology of the Jews.

77. On the image of the woman in *fin-de siècle* medicine see Lilian Berna-Simons, *Weibliche Identität und Sexualität: das Bild der Weiblichkeit im 19. Jahrhundert und in Sigmund Freud* (Frankfurt a. M.: Materialis Verlag, 1984); on Möbius see, Francis Schiller, *A Möbius Strip. fin-de siècle Neuropsychiatry and Paul Möbius* (Berkeley: University of California Press, 1982). Freud distances himself from Möbius' biological work on femininity. He rather sees the limitations present within the feminine as a reflex of the suppression of female sexuality in Western culture. (See SE 9: 198–99 for Freud's rebuttal of Möbius.)
78. SE 20:38.

But if we were to substitute the word 'Jew' for the word 'pervert' in this passage, we would find a restating of the need to incorporate the liminal into the universal of the sexual. 'Jews' and 'perverts' are virtually interchangeable categories at the *fin de siècle.* This phantasm of knowing on the part of the 'neutral' observer, as we shall see, is also attributed to the unknowability of the Jew. At about the same time Freud commented on the unknowability of the Jew he also complained, as well as demanded, to his friend and analysand Marie Bonaparte, Princess of Greece, that he did not know what women wanted?[79] All of these comments point toward the unknowability of the female body as that 'object' (in a Freudian sense) which is different from the self. But it also places the Jew – in its slang sense of the clitoris – into the body of the female. But, of course, the essence of the Jewish body is both too well known to be hidden and too well hidden to be known. It is both 'canny' and 'uncanny' simultaneously.

Freud's contradictions about the meaning and function of race and racial identity and his assumption that race is a category vitiated by the new science of psychoanalysis is a central theme of this chapter.[80] The very idea of the Jew within the science which formed Freud and other Jewish physicians of the *fin de siècle,* which defined the high medical science of his day, is present in images, metaphors and deep structures of his own theory. It was the case that the image of the male Jew was 'feminised' during the course of Western (read: Christian) history. Indeed, in accepting the view that the Jews are a single race, the Elberfeld physician Heinrich Singer, commented in 1904 'that in general it is clear in examining the body of the Jew, that the Jew most approaches the body type of the female.'[81] Singer's views echo the older anthropological view, such as that of the Jewish ethnologist Adolf Jellinek, who stated quite directly that: 'In the examination of the various races it is clear that some are more masculine, others more feminine. Among the latter the Jews belong, as one of those tribes which are both more feminine and have come to represent (*repräsentieren*) the feminine among other peoples. A juxtaposition of the Jew and the woman will persuade the reader of the truth of the ethnographic thesis.' Jellinek's physiological proof is the Jews voice: 'Even though I disavow any physiological comparison, let me note that bass voices are much rarer than baritone voices among the

79. Cited in Jones, *The Life and Work of Sigmund Freud,* 2: 468. See William G. Niederland, 'The Source of Freud's Question about What Women Want', *American Journal of Psychiatry* 146 (1989): 409–10.
80. See Jacques Le Rider, *Modernité Viennoise et Crises de l'Identité* (Paris: Presses Universitaires de France, 1990), pp. 197–222.
81. Heinrich Singer, *Allgemeine und spezielle Krankheitslehre der Juden* (Leipzig: Benno Konegen, 1904), p. 9.

Jews.'[82] The association of the image of the Jew (here read: male Jew) with that of the woman (including the Jewish woman) is one of the most powerful images to be embedded in the arguments about race. And it can be found quite directly in the attacks on Freud and psychoanalysis. In responding to Felix von Luschan's attack on the new science of psychoanalysis in 1916, coming from one of the greatest 'experts' on the nature of the Jew, Freud can only express himself in a letter to Sandor Ferenczi in racial terms that an 'old Jew is tougher than a noble Prussian Teuton'.[83] Luschan's attack on Freud, Wilhelm Fliess and Hermann Swaboda sees them as a pseudo-religious collectivity parallel to Christian Science. He employed a phrase coined by Konrad Rieger for all of these pseudoscientific undertakings: 'Old Woman-Psychology' (*Altweiber-Psychologie*).[84]

When we turn to Sigmund Freud's internalisation of the image of his own difference, it is the relationship between ideas of race and ideas of gender in the *fin de siècle* which frames Freud's answer. It is through the analysis of the theory in terms of its own critical presuppositions that the repression and projection of the the image of the Jew can be found in psychoanalytic theory – not within a theory of race (as is later to be found in the work of C. G. Jung) but within Freud's representation of the image of gender.

Drawing on earlier work published in 1925 and 1931, Freud wrote about the role of the scientist in resolving the question of gender in his comprehensive *New Introductory Lectures on Psychoanalysis* (1933 [1932]):

> Today's lecture, too, should have no place in an introduction; but it may serve to give you an example of a detailed piece of analytic work, and I can say two things to recommend it. It brings forward nothing but observed facts, almost without any speculative additions, and it deals with a subject which has a claim on your interest second almost to no other. Throughout history people have knocked their heads against the riddle of the nature of femininity
>> Häupter in Hieroglyphenmützen,
>> Häupter in Turban und schwarzem Barett, Perückenhäupter und tausend andre
>> Arme, schwitzende Menschenhäupter ...
> [Heads in hieroglyphic bonnets,/Heads in turbans and black birettas,/ Heads in wigs and thousand other/ Wretched, sweating heads of humans ...]
> Nor will you have escaped worrying over this problem – those of you who are men; to those of you who are women this will not apply – you are yourselves the problem. When you meet a human being, the first distinction you make is 'male or female'? and you are accustomed to make

82. Adolf Jellinek, *Der jüdische Stamm: Ethnographische Studien* (Vienna: Herzfeld und Bauer, 1869), pp. 89–90.
83. Jones, *The Life and Work of Sigmund Freud*, 2: 119; see also, 2: 398–99.
84. Felix von Luschan, 'Altweiber-Psychologie', *Deutsche medizinische Wochenschrift* 42 (January 6, 1916), p. 20.

the distinction with unhesitating certainty. Anatomical science shares your certainty at one point and not much further.[85]

This argument can be read as part of a rhetoric of race. First, let me translate this problem, which Freud articulates within the rhetoric of gender science, into the rhetoric of racial science: 'There is an inherent biological difference between Jews and Aryans and this has a central role in defining you (my listener) and your culture.' The 'you' which the 'I' is addressing is clearly the Aryan reader, for the Jewish reader is understood as but part of the problem. The Aryan is the observer; the Jew the observed. Upon seeing someone on the street the first distinction 'we' (the speaker and his listener as Aryans) make is to ask: 'Jew or Aryan?' and that distinction can be made with certainty based on inherent assumptions about differences in anatomy. Indeed, according to a contemporary guidebook, in Vienna the first question one asks about anyone seen on the street is: 'Is he a Jew?'[86] This biological distinction can be clearly and easily 'seen' even through the mask of clothing or the veneer of civilization. The young American-Jewish psychoanalyst Abraham Kardiner recounted his rejection by a young woman he met at a masked ball in Vienna once they unmasked and it was clear that he was a Jew.[87] But it was not merely social rejection which could follow. The threat of what it meant to be seen as a Jew was also articulated on the streets of Vienna. Martin Freud, Sigmund Freud's eldest son, notes 'walking with [his aunt Dolfi, his fathers youngest sister, who died in Theresienstadt] one day in Vienna when we passed an ordinary kind of man, probably a Gentile, who, as far as I knew, had taken no notice of us. I put it down to a pathological phobia, or Dolfi's stupidity, when she gripped my arm in terror and whispered: "Did you hear what that man said? He called me a dirty stinking Jewess and said it was time we were all killed."'[88]

The false assumption in Freud's text is that the uniformity of the identity of all 'males', as opposed to all 'females', can be made in terms of the form of their genitalia. Freud continues his argument to show that this physiological determinant is central in any discussion of the nature of sexual difference. He identifies himself as a male in this text, quoting a male author, Heinrich Heine, who represented the Jew as the diseased feminine in *fin-de siècle* culture, in the context of the impossibility of knowing the truth about the 'dark continent' of

85. SE 22: 113.
86. Ludwig Hirschfeld, *Was nicht im Baedeker steht: Wien und Budapest* (Munich: R. Piper, 1927), p. 56.
87. Kardiner, 92.
88. Martin Freud, *Glory Reflected: Sigmund Freud Man and Father* (London: Angus and Robertson, 1957), p. 16.

the feminine.[89] For the anti-Semitic 'Aryan' reader Heine's references would evoke quite a different set of associations than they have in the original text. Heine was (and remains) the primary Jewish writer in the German cultural sphere. Readers finally attuned to Heine's Jewishness would have associated the oriental turbans, Egyptian hieroglyphs, the sweat of ghetto poverty, the wigs of the shaved heads of orthodox Jewish brides, as hidden signs of racial, not merely sexual difference. Here is a Jew (Freud) citing a Jew (Heine) about an essentially Jewish focus, human sexuality. Freud can short-circuit this association only by constructing an image of the male to which he, Heine, and his male, Aryan listeners can all belong. In his lecture on 'femininity', Freud's argument continues – he challenges the seeming dichotomy between the 'male' and the 'female' and constructs a universal continuum between these two poles. The distinction between 'male' and 'female', like the biological distinction between Jew and Aryan, is dissolved as the seemingly fixed borders are shown to be transitory. Freud's desire to abandon such rigid distinctions in terms of a biology of gender mirrors the acculturated Jews desire to abandon them in terms of the biology of race.

The voice in Freud's text is that of a male and a participant in the central discourse about gender science of the scientific thought-collective. In my racial rereading, the voice would become that of the Aryan and part of the Aryan thought-collective. The fantasy of Freud's identification with the aggressor in my retelling of this passage as a passage about race seems to be vitiated when Freud transforms the problem of the relationship between the subject and the object into a question of sexual identity. The 'male' is the 'worrier' (read: subject) and the 'female' is the 'problem' (read: object). But this assumes that Freud's definition of the male body as uniform and constant in the norm within his *fin-de siècle* scientific thought-collective. The Jewish male body is different, is marked, in the act of ritual circumcision and in many other ways. It is not that the anatomy of the genitalia create two independent (and antagonistic) categories, but that there were three such categories – the male Jew's genitalia were understood as a marker of difference. Freud's need to distance the challenges to the special nature of the Jew's body through his creation of a universal 'male' body transmute categories of race into categories of gender. The power of these constructs is such that the fact that they are a reaction formation is obscured and they are accepted as the basis for the discussion of ideas of masculine and feminine gender as primary categories of Freud's system.

89. See the discussion of 'The Jewish Reader: Freud reads Heine reads Freud', in Sander L. Gilman, *The Jew's Body* (New York: Routledge, 1991), pp. 150–168.

# MYTHS OF FEMALE SEXUALITY*

*Sara Cooper*

I would like, in this chapter, to address two aspects of female sexuality. First, the archetypal level which encompasses ahistorical and universal myths and second, present-day beliefs and experiences as they are determined by their historical and social context. I do not intend to address the political dimension; the fact that most of the writing about female sexuality was, until very recently, done by men. Nor will I explore other aspects of the power of the patriarchy, where the suppression of women's sexuality has been used as an attempt to keep the penis down; to control male sexual desire supposedly in the interests of the preservation of civilisation.

By sexuality I mean libido in its widest sense, sexual energy as it is manifested in genitality, in sensuality and pleasure, in relatedness and in the various forms of love.

Archetypal elements of the female are conveyed in myths by two seeming opposites; the virgin, pure, untouched and untouchable, and the whore, the depraved, uncontainedly sexual figure whose cult is connected with fertility. These aspects appear in varying manifestations throughout history and across the globe. However, I would like to focus on the Kabbalistic figure of the *Matronit*, who could be termed a Hebrew Goddess. Raphael Patai suggests in his book called *The Hebrew Goddess* that in the popular mythical view, she would have been seen as a discrete divinity as opposed to the scholarly mystical view which would have seen her in more abstract philosophical terms as a manifestation of certain divine qualities.

He tells us that the Ancient Near Eastern Goddess, whose name varies according to the culture from Innana to Ishtar to Anath, is

* This chapter is based on a lecture delivered at the Leo Baeck College on 17 November 1993.

seen as being at the same time virginal and maternal, promiscuous and bloodthirsty. He says that the *Matronit* encompasses these same four qualities. He gives detailed evidence of popular cults connected with goddess figures existing side by side with more generally known and accepted manifestations of the Hebrew tradition.[1]

It seems as if the ancient thinker could conceive of a goddess, or in some cultures pantheon of goddesses who could include multiple and even seemingly contradictory facets. In modern rational thinking we have polarised these aspects. In Christian thought this split is epitomised by Mary Madonna and Mary Magdalen (the virgin and the whore) and it is clear that the Virgin Mary has many characteristics in common with an earlier goddess, who is conceptualised as the mother of, or sometimes the consort of God.

I would like to demonstrate the way in which psychoanalytic theory too, has split these aspects of the goddess so that Freud presents a model of female sexuality based on the concept of absence, on lack. This may be an inevitable reflection of the attitudes contained in the society and culture of his time, but nevertheless it apparently denies the existence of the depraved and sex-loving goddess who, I would like to suggest, is an integral and essential part of the female psyche.

His view is that the woman is the one who 'lacks' from a psychosexual perspective. She lacks a penis which, according to Freud, is conceptualised in infantile fantasy as the major organ of sexual pleasure, the active genital. It is important to remember that what we are talking about is internal fantasy, not biology, not that women don't possess adequate genitalia. Nevertheless, our experience of the world must be shaped by our internal fantasy. Psychology, biology and culture are inextricably linked.

He is saying that if the vagina cannot be seen, it cannot be known by the child. The girl's clitoris must be experienced as inferior to the penis because it is smaller. The clitoris must be superseded at puberty by the vagina which becomes the leading erotogenic zone. It is a theoretical framework where reproduction is the goal, sexuality is geared towards the meeting of penis and vagina. One of Freud's most important discoveries is that of infantile sexuality, expressed as polymorphous perversity, where every part of the body is potentially erotogenic. The aim is pleasure, rather than joining with an object; that is another human being. However, according to Freud, this diversity must be subsumed in adulthood to reproduction and, I quote, 'the pursuit of pleasure comes under the sway of the reproductive function.'[2]

1. Raphael Patai *The Hebrew Goddess* (Wayne State University Press, Detroit, 1990), 136.
2. Sigmund Freud *Three Essays on Sexuality, II Infantile Sexuality* (Pelican Edition, London), 116.

Alongside this version, where female equals absence of active desire, goes the radical theory of bisexuality where we are all seen as containing both masculine and feminine elements. The feminine is seen as the passive and masochistic component of both men and women. Yet Freud goes even further in shaking our preconceptions in his lecture 'Femininity' where he advises us against making 'active' coincide with 'masculine' and 'passive' with 'feminine'. Speaking of our tendency to do this, he says 'I advise you against it. It seems to me to serve no useful purpose and adds nothing to our knowledge.'[3] Here I think we see the struggle in Freud between the biologist and Victorian gentleman, who at the extreme appears to describe female sexuality as essentially absent or passive, and Freud the radical thinker, who recognises the danger of such straitjacketing and puts into question accepted forms of gender categorisation.

One aspect of female sexuality which is not touched on by Freud is its unlimited potential, that is the capacity of the woman for multiple orgasms. The recognition of this potential is a direct contradiction of the conceptualisation of the woman as the one who lacks. Her sexuality is not trammelled by the physical limitations suffered by the penis. She does not need an erection without which he is impotent. There is no ejaculation, which usually marks the climactic terminating a particular sexual encounter for a man. Here we come back to the whore, the potentially insatiable aspect of the goddess which is also linked to fertility and abundance, infinitely taking and giving pleasure. Perhaps the Freudian notion of the woman's lack could be seen as a defence against the recognition of her infinite and unbridled sexual potential.

The nature of female sexuality is fundamentally subversive. It serves nothing except the desire of the woman. It may, and hopefully does, add to male pleasure, but this is not a prerequisite. Female orgasm is not necessary for the process of reproduction while male ejaculation clearly is. When we explore Freud's notion of civilisation, we find that the ultimate purpose of Eros is reproduction. This could be seen as a reflection of the Jewish value system. Onan's sin (Genesis 38:4-10) is not masturbation per se, but the spilling of the seed, that is disobeying the command to procreate. All the laws of *Nidah*, ritual purity, are geared towards sexual intercourse at the best time for conception. As Shuttle and Redgrove point out in *The Wise Wound*, it is often during menstruation, the forbidden time according to a taboo common to many cultures, that women's pleasure can be greatest.[4]

3. Sigmund Freud *New Introductory Lectures on Psychoanalysis. Lecture 33. Femininity* (Pelican Edition, London), 148.
4. Penelope Shuttle and Peter Redgrove *The Wise Wound: Menstruation and Everywoman* (Penguin Edition, London), 90.

This subversive aspect of the goddess has been split off into the archetypal figure of Lilith. She is, according to *Aggadah* (Jewish folklore) the precursor to Eve, a she-demon who is anti-reproduction, a killer of babies. Her sexuality is an expression of her power. She refuses to lie beneath Adam, only on top. She is a marginal figure, originating in Sumeria and outlawed by mainstream Jewish tradition.

Historically, this subversive aspect of female sexuality has been repressed. Sexuality was linked to potential pregnancy. It is only in modern times that the link between sexuality and reproduction has been weakened so that sexuality is placed in a radically new context. In fact it is only in the nineteenth century that the term sexuality is used in its modern sense as the quality of being sexual.

In his book *The Transformation of Intimacy* Anthony Giddens has coined the term 'plastic sexuality' to represent the infinite malleability of sexual possibilities. He traces the changes in our views of love and relationships from the eighteenth century onward and shows how changes in the structure of society have altered our *Weltanschauung*. To summarise his argument, 'Modernity is associated with the socialisation of the natural world.'[5] Thus, what was 'natural' is, in our post-industrial society, determined by social structures and systems. For example the birth process is increasingly determined by social choices, governed by the availability of contraception and by medical knowledge regarding fertility and potential health risks to mother and child. At its extreme, conception can be a totally artificial process carried out in the laboratory by A.I.D. and I.V.F. (Artificial Insemination by Donor and In Vitro Fertilisation). This scenario may sound reminiscent of that described by Huxley in *Brave New World*. Its potential effect is to divorce sexuality from reproduction. Again I quote from Giddens, 'Reproduction was once part of nature and heterosexuality was inevitably its focal point. Once sexuality has become an "integral" component of social relations ... heterosexuality is no longer a standard by which everything else is judged'.[6]

The logical conclusion of Giddens's hypothesis is that there can no longer be a firm and clearly delineated notion of what is normal and what is perverse. If reproduction is no longer the main aim of sexual relations, what we are left with is the Pleasure Principle and infantile polymorphous perversity. Why prioritise one erogenous zone above another? As the song says 'anything goes'. This is epitomised by a popular youth culture which endorses cross dressing, a

---

5. Anthony Giddens *The Transformation of Intimacy: Sexuality, Love and Eroticism in Modern Societies* (Polity, Cambridge) 34.
6. Ibid.

practice no longer confined to 'gay' circles, as well as the multifarious sexual antics of Madonna, the pop star. Sexual and gender expression appear to be matters of free choice.

The problem with this account is that it is only addressing the superficial cultural manifestations of sexuality. The place of reproduction in our social relationships has altered. There is greater freedom than in the previous century in the ways in which sexuality can be talked about and acted out, more flexibility about choice and number of partners. However, the nature of human beings as reproductive animals who mate with the opposite sex remains constant. Artificial insemination is still a very minor and marginal phenomenon. We are biologically and psychologically determined by our genitalia and our hormones to a large extent. Western society as we know it is still organised around the nuclear family. The existence of alternative forms, such as one-parent families and step families simply complicates the issue; it does not fundamentally change it. Our internal worlds revolve around our relationship to the parental couple and the problem of resolving our feelings of love and hate towards them. It is within this context, the Oedipus complex, that we define our identities.

Nevertheless, the contemporary cultural climate which Giddens describes is of comparative sexual openness and freedom and I would like to explore the effects of this on female sexuality. Gone is the rule of the phallus, the woman is apparently no longer expected to do her master's bidding or lie back and think of England. Sex is no longer automatically linked to pregnancy. There is far greater flexibility about the definition of acceptable sexual practices and about what can be openly talked about. The depraved aspect of the goddess has been liberated. Lilith has her day. She no longer has to lie beneath Adam, nor to bear his children.

I think that this is an enormously important force in women's lives and have been fascinated by the number of women I have encountered in my work as a psychotherapist who have gained sexual enjoyment and freedom by encounters with someone other than their spouse or regular partner. It seems to me to be vitally important that this subversive, sexually insatiable aspect of the goddess is now being acknowledged.

But what of the other aspects? The goddess I have described embodies a potential wholeness, a reconciliation of the opposites. Jung teaches us that whatever aspect of an archetype is split off and denied will become part of the shadow, haunting us in a negative form, reminding us that we ignore it at our peril.

Let us return then to the virgin, the opposite pole to the whore. This figure contains archetypal representations of different aspects of womanhood. She has been used to epitomise absence of female desire as in the Freudian notion. This is often manifested by women today as a passive seductiveness and refusal to take responsibility for their own desire (woman as victim). Alternatively, identification with the virgin can place women in the trap of splitting off and discarding their sexuality, equating it with all that is evil, leaving them with no legitimate context in which their sexual desires can be expressed. Indeed in Judaism the *yetzer ha-ra*, the 'evil inclination', is also the sexual inclination. This attitude has prevailed in Christianity and, to some extent, in Judaism, for centuries.

However, the virgin also represents the female mystery, the untouched and hidden part of ourselves, rather than a more literal notion of virginity. If we accept this metaphorical image, then it is possible to conceptualise the woman as both virginal and promiscuous. There is some essential quality withheld, hidden as the vagina is hidden, a fundamental solitude and aloofness. At the same time there can be an enjoyment of the hungrily rapacious aspect of the feminine. Similarly the woman can be both compassionate and motherly as well as being the ruthless, bloodthirsty and aggressive warrior. This aggressive aspect of the feminine is one which we can no longer disown if we reject the notion of women as simply passive victims.

These opposites can be difficult to reconcile and it is often this difficulty which brings women into therapy. It is possibly unsurprising that a large proportion of my psychotherapy practice comprises young women in their late twenties and early thirties. It is at this point that the longing for a stable relationship, and with it motherhood, has become a pressing issue for many of those with whom I have worked and a conflict has ensued with the warrior, the aggressively independent career woman or (in some cases) artist. In other women there has been a conflict between the mother and the whore, where motherhood is experienced as in opposition to sexuality, or else is used as a defence against it. In my experience this is a defence particularly prevalent amongst Jewish women for whom motherhood can become an all-encompassing identity.

On the other hand inhabiting only the whore can be a denial of the maternal. Lilith, who seems to be an archetypal embodiment of female sexual voraciousness and freedom, is also the killer of babies. Her sexual freedom was seen as antithetical to the demands of motherhood, where nurturing and selflessness are central. Similarly, what could be seen as the modern equivalent to Lilith, the notion of 'plastic sexuality' has demoted reproduction and with it parenthood. As I have said, it offers the omnipotent fantasy that we can supersede nature and biology. I would like to suggest that this is a defence against recognition of the power of the mother. We deny this power in order not to have to face its corollary, our own help-lessness as infants.

I would like to give one example of conflicts engendered in the attempt to reconcile the previously split apart aspects of the goddess. The problem of bringing together the mother and the whore can be illustrated by the following description of a young woman. She has always played the field sexually while denying a deep longing for a settled relationship and children. Her fear has been that in having children she would get in touch with the helplessness which she felt as a child when she was left with a grandmother who had little inter-est in her and left her to her own devices. Thus, the avoidance of motherhood was linked to the feelings about her own childhood which she feared would arise if she became a mother. Sexuality was divorced from maternal feelings and it is only now that it is becom-ing possible for her to experience both, within a stable relationship.

In conclusion, I believe that the concept of the goddess which I have outlined embodies some central aspects of femininity and in particular, female sexuality. This mythical figure allows for sexual freedom and exploration while also acknowledging the importance of the secret and private aspect of the self. It recognises the conflict-ing images of the compassionate and tender mother and the ruthless and bloodthirsty warrior and reminds us of the timeless struggle to reconcile these aspects, which is the task of individuation, the attempt to achieve wholeness.

# WHAT IS SPECIAL ABOUT JEWISH WOMEN'S SEXUALITY?*

*Sheila Ernst*

## Introduction

While I was writing this chapter an inordinate amount of attention was paid in the media to the case of a young man, a nice young man, a student who was being accused of what might be called date rape by a fellow student. The young man had had intercourse with the young woman after a party; she was drunk and had apparently agreed to kiss him but claimed that she was unconscious when he actually penetrated her. This case followed another in which a Scottish solicitor was found guilty of raping his partner after a Highland Ball.

Media interest in these cases both forms and reflects public interest in the question of whether or not our sense of so-called normal heterosexual behaviour is changing; until recently male sexuality was seen as a force which, once unleashed, was unstoppable, while female sexuality could be used in a dangerous and seductive way to entice a man to the point where he is out of control and cannot be held responsible for his actions. A feminist perspective argues that men and women have sexual desires and that both should take responsibility for how they express them without imposing their desires on another person. This might sound straightforward enough but is deeply challenging to many men and women. This is why some American campuses have introduced the notion that every heterosexual initiative by a man has to be given active permission by

* This chapter is based on a lecture delivered at the Leo Baeck College on 27 October 1993.

the woman simply to counteract previous practice and assumptions. The first case I mentioned was interesting to the public because it showed a protesting woman in a ridiculous light, being too drunk to know who she had ended up in bed with, later making a public spectacle of herself, and thereby allowing those people who want to reinforce the status quo of the relationship between the sexes to dismiss her protest as part of a general view in which women like that only get what they ask for. Thus in popular opinion the framework of a male sexuality which is active and irrepressible and female sexuality which is passive and dangerous can be, temporarily, reinstated.

The answers to certain basic questions provide the framework within which such debates take place. What are masculinity and femininity; what if any, relationship do these terms have to the person's biology or physiology; are there unalterable aspects of maleness and femaleness and how they are produced which are true for all people at all times or are these relative qualities which are formed through our experience? Why is men's sexual behaviour seen in terms of power and desire, while women's is seen in terms of being potentially abused, or having the power to say yes and no, to seduce rather than to initiate? How are the relations of domination established, maintained and replicated? Is this the way sexual relations have to be? The subject of this chapter goes further in asking whether there are specific ways in which Jewish culture and religion have affected our understanding of Jewish women's sexuality. Many of these questions have been addressed within psychoanalysis and I will be drawing on the psychoanalytic literature to show how such issues have been debated.

## Psychoanalysis and Femininity

The issue of female sexuality was at the centre of psychoanalytic controversy from the early days. Freud's somewhat limited and phallocentric view of human nature was soon challenged by psychoanalysts, mainly, but not exclusively women. It has been argued that Freud's view of women was based on his inability to analyse his relationship with his mother and particularly the way in which his family's Jewish heritage impacted upon that key relationship. This is important for us in two ways: firstly it helps us to re-read Freud and develop his ideas and secondly, it shows how sexuality cannot simply be understood as a universal subject but rather one which has to be understood within its context. I will be looking at some of the subsequent developments of ideas about female sexuality within psychoanalysis including recent feminist thinking. I shall examine how this has been done by subsequent different groups of psychoanalytic thinkers, including the more recent feminist ones; I will be looking at the particular development of Jewish women's sexuality within the inevitable framework of the holocaust and its profound and prolonged effects. I will suggest that the sexual development of a daughter of survivors has been affected and will go on to argue that some similar if less extreme processes could be at work for many other Jewish women and that this may be helpful in understanding aspects of Jewish women's sexuality. I should emphasise at this point that any case material will have been altered carefully in order to preserve anonymity.

Psychoanalytic thinking about gender and sexuality attempts to understand what the relationship is between the difference in male and female anatomy and the ways in which we grow up, firstly to know ourselves as having a gender, being male or female, and secondly, the varied and complex ways in which we might express ourselves sexually. Within psychoanalysis there is a wide range of views from those who see the relationship between masculinity and femininity as being very closely linked to basic biological functions to those who see sexuality as constructed only through the social medium of language.

Freud himself faced his readers with the problematic nature of gender: 'It is important to understand clearly that the concepts of "masculine" and "feminine" whose meanings seem so unambiguous to ordinary people are amongst the most confused that occur in science.' (Freud, 1915, p.219)

Freud encompassed the duality involved here between the implications of the anatomical differences between men and women being inescapable and the other and equally significant view that we are not born man or woman but only acquire a gendered identity slowly and partially; that each of us is a mixture of both masculine and feminine traits.

The initial problem with Freud's thinking about women's sexuality was that it was described in terms of what a woman didn't have and what a boy did have. For Freud, both the girl and the boy became aware of the difference between masculine and feminine when they recognised their genital difference. The boy saw that while he and his father had a penis, mother did not; he became anxious lest he should lose his penis. The girl recognised her femininity when she saw her lack of a penis and, realising that her mother also had no penis, was angry and disappointed with the mother and turned to the father hoping that she might gain what she lacked at least through her relationship with father and later with other men. Boys were described as fearing castration while the girl's response was seen in terms of her envy of the penis. Freud recognised that these discoveries were complex and painful and that each individual would come to terms with his or her own difference in an individual way.

Freud's views on the development of female sexuality were almost immediately challenged and throughout the 1920s and into the 1930s debates rage about whether it was really only the woman who lacked something or whether this was just a cover for something else that Freud could not face, namely that men might find women threatening and enviable because they were able to produce babies and feed them. Characterising the debate in this way can make Freud seem absurdly flatfooted. I think that what gets missed is that Freud was trying to look at the question of how we distinguish the sexes in a psychosexual way and that he acknowledged how difficult a task this was; that somehow as soon as you thought you had something clearly distinguished between male and female the distinction seems to fade away; the biological and psychological processes do not overlap, they are out of focus. Mitchell, 1974, suggests that the opponents of Freud easily became preoccupied with the question of what has each sex got of value that belongs to it alone. This may seem a slightly obscure distinction but I think it is an important one; if we start making generalisations about how all women are passive and have a difficulty in expressing their aggression and their sexuality we are immediately brought up against the problem of how we can incorporate into this picture, for instance, Jane who is by far the most active and aggressive member of one of my therapy groups. Are we left saying that Jane is somehow not really a woman, not feminine, or would it be both more interesting and more helpful to Jane to ask questions about what her psychic development and her object relating in the group might be able to tell us about her femininity and her sexuality, and what the connections might be between how she experiences her sexuality in relation to her early family dynamics.

## The Impact of Freud's Jewishness on His View of Women's Sexuality

Given that Freud was such a radical thinker within the context of turn of the century Vienna there are two aspects of his theoretical work which seem to show him in another light; one is the question of what has been called 'the real event' or the discovery that he made that many of his patients were not just abused in fantasy by their parents but that in reality the incest taboo was broken, and the way in which he later dismissed the reality of these events preferring to explain them in terms of fantasy. The second and the more significant for our present discussion is his determination to conceptualise the development of female sexuality entirely in terms of, or in relation to, masculine sexuality. Moreover he seemed to be only able to see his patient's transferences onto him as a powerful father rather than noting, as we would do nowadays, the maternal transferences. This is often explained away as being to do with the *Zeitgeist* but this seems implausible given how challenging his work as a whole was to contemporary thought and customs.

In a fascinating book on this subject Estelle Roith, 1987, argues that Freud's perception of women and femininity, which he took to be universalisable, was in fact the product of his difficulties in confronting the issues surrounding his relationship with his own mother, which were very much a part of the Jewish background from which he came. Roith suggests that Freud's conception of women's sexuality is consistent with what would have been the prevalent views of women in the Galician community from which his parents came. She then goes on to show how these views lead to a particularly fixated relationship between mother and son. She suggests that Freud's relative silence and idealisation of his relationship with his mother could be seen as supporting the view that his relationship with his mother fell into this pattern. She also points out that it was not until after his mother's death that he was able to develop some of his ideas about women's sexuality and to acknowledge his own difficulties with the subject.

Roith highlights some of the differences between Christian and Jewish perceptions of sexuality. While for the Christian there is a profound conflict between the spiritual and the bodily leading to the idea of romantic and often chaste love, within Eastern European Judaism sexual needs were seen as potentially dangerous unless gratified, but were in no sense focused on as the site of a high passion; rather, sexuality was seen as something compulsory which must be clearly regulated so that the men in particular could get on with the things which were seen as being of a much higher calling and value, namely prayer and study. Women were clearly placed as being outside the realm of prayer but as standing in a position between culture and nature. They were responsible for sexuality and the home, but they were also defined as having unclean bodily functions. Thus in a way women had large areas of responsibility and were often, as Amalie Freud was, powerful figures but with power of a kind that was never legitimated. Since marriage was really seen as a convenient arrangement or way of controlling sex, whatever romance there was in life for a mother was likely to come from her children and, of course, particularly her sons.

It is precisely the intense ambivalence of this mother-son relationship which Roith suggests that Freud ignores; thus he makes

Oedipus central to his theory but leaves Jocasta, the incestuous
mother, out of the picture. Perhaps, Roith suggests, Freud created an
image of a powerful father with whom he was in desperate rivalry to
protect himself from the recognition that he might still have some
profound identifications with his mother. In addition, he did not
recognise the phase of the boy's idealised love for his father which
later theorists have seen to be a crucial part of the boy's developing
sense of himself as male. This picture of the Jewish family in which
the parent's relationship is diminished and the relationship between
mother and particularly her sons, is heightened and sexualised, was
immortalised in Roth's 1971 novel *Portnoy's Complaint.*

> The mother greets her son, 'Well how's my lover?'
> 'If I'm her lover who is he? The schmegeggy she lives with.' responds
> the son.

Roith's re-reading of Freud in relation to his Jewish background
and the place of women within it serves to remind us that psychoanalytic thinking is culturally relative and that to understand more
about Jewish women's gender identity and sexuality we must look at
the interrelationship between the internal and external worlds. Much
work has been done, looking at ways of understanding women's psychological development, taking into account the connections
between women's less powerful position in society, her idealised yet
denigrated role as bearer and carer for the next generation and the
ways in which she uses her body as a site for expressing many conflicting feelings for which she has no other obvious outlet.

## The Gender Conundrum Within Psychoanalytic Thinking

Psychoanalytic psychotherapy, in the main, has moved on from the
days when in one of Freud's famous cases, Dora, he could not bring
himself to see that Dora was far more preoccupied with the adult
females in her life than with the males. Work done by the object
relations psychoanalysts on the early mother-infant relationship
paved the way for the greater understanding of the mother-daughter
relationship and its significance throughout the life of the woman. In
a sense Freud had already begun his work when, following the studies of several women analysts, and the death of his mother, he was
able in the early 1930s to take up the topic of femininity again and
to acknowledge that the so-called pre-Oedipal phase of the daughter's relationship to her mother was far more significant than he had
at first thought and that there was much about femininity which he
had not understood.

The focus of recent work has been on the kind of mothering that the daughter receives and the effect that this may have on her future capacity to develop as an autonomous individual. Some important ideas and approaches to therapy with women have emerged from this line of thinking; although in the external world it may appear that women are dependent, emotionally speaking, women have very little experience of being able to be dependent; they are mothered by deprived mothers who themselves, far from being able fully to respond to their girl children, may find their demands too painfully evocative of their own deprivation; thus in turn the mother may unconsciously demand mothering from her daughter rather than vice versa. (See Eichenbaum and Orbach, 1985) The significant emotional relationship for the woman will clearly be the bond with mother and the relationship with a man is often seen as being a heterosexual substitute for mother rather than a real change of object. For Chodorow 1978, for instance, women's psychology is to be understood in terms of it preparing her to become a mother. But interestingly enough, as O'Connor and Ryan 1993, point out in their new book about female homosexuality, what is absent from much of this work is any significant mention of homo-erotic feelings between women. While the importance of women's emotional relationships with one another is extolled, and a new vision of woman's identity being established through connectedness rather than autonomy is proposed, the dimension of sexuality and sexual feelings between women is minimised.

Where is women's sexuality? It is no accident that women's sexuality as such seems to have almost disappeared from the discussion. As we saw to start off with, we can look at sexuality from the perspective of women trying to control men's lasciviousness. We can develop ways of working with women who have been sexually traumatised by being abused as children; in the majority of cases this being men abusing girls or young women. We can understand how women use their bodies by bingeing on food, losing any accurate sense of body image and developing a thick layer of fat around them which may contain many contradictory messages including some about their sexuality. The binge may destroy the woman's immediate feelings, particularly if they are painful or conflictful; the fat may, for example, be saying 'I am a married woman and I must put up a barrier between myself and other men for fear that I might be tempted'. It may also be saying 'This fat binds me to you mother and it shows me that we are still as one even if we do live hundreds of miles away from each other.' Equally the young woman refusing to eat may be saying 'This is my life not yours and I'll control what goes into me not you.' Similarly the body may be used to get pregnant as a way of saying things that cannot otherwise be said and this is particularly true when the woman decides to have an abortion. Whatever the practical reasons she may be saying: 'Look I can abort this baby part of myself.' Women's bodies are used as objects within society; women themselves may use their bodies to express complex contradictory and painful emotional states of mind; yet it is still difficult to talk about how women may express their own sexuality.

We have already looked in some detail at what might make it problematic for men to acknowledge women's sexuality as a powerful force, rather than as something secondary and responding to men's desire. In particular we have looked at what it was about Freud's Jewishness and the Jewish conceptions of men and women and sexuality which might have affected his views on women's sexuality.

The problem for us now is twofold; that the cultural representation of sexuality is phallic with no way of conceptualising women's desire or sexual subjectivity and that it is when we come to talk about women's sexuality or to question this way of looking at it, that we have to face something unpalatable in ourselves. The simplest way I can put it is to say that it faces women with a dilemma; either we continue to accept conceptualisations of female sexuality which form part of the patriarchal culture in which in some sense women will always be defined by what they are not; coming back to the Freudian lack. Thus men have the desire and women respond or don't respond or are really concerned with intimacy and not sheer sexuality. Or if women are really to become the subjects of their own sexual lives; i.e. being the desirers and not just the desired or the rejected, then we may also have to take back certain other aspects of ourselves which we have projected into masculinity. Moreover we might really then have to take on board the meaning of Freud's comments on the bisexuality of all people. 'I am accustoming myself to regarding every sexual act as a process in which four individuals are involved.' (Freud, 1899) Jane Flax, 1993, in a paper criticising this aspect of feminist psychoanalysis points out that it serves to perpetuate the idea that the daughters can continue to try to be good and to please mother thus perpetuating a fantasy of the continuation of a safe childhood in which mother will protect her. 'By denying our own pleasures and expressions of aggression, assertion and control, we represent ourselves as innocent victims outside circuits of power.'

What is striking is that whereas certain other aspects of a woman's life may be open for her to change, making herself more active, when it comes to sexuality many women find (both heterosexual and lesbian) that they are drawn back to fantasies of an idealised love relationship in which they will find themselves through submission to the other. While Freud sees this as the outcome of 'anatomical imperatives' (i.e. the lack of the penis etc.) more recent object-relations theory sees things somewhat differently. Jessica Benjamin 1986, has argued that women's retreat from active sexuality can be explained in terms of the problems and failures of her early identifications and her difficulties in the process of individuating herself.

To understand this quite different way of seeing things we must go back a step or two. You will remember that Freud thought that the awareness of gender developed at the point at which both girl and boy noticed the presence or absence of the penis; Stoller, 1968 suggested that children developed a sense of core gender identity (defined as conscious or unconscious knowledge of belonging to one sex rather than the other) by the time they were about eighteen-months to two-years old. Stoller approached this problem in a more empirical way, by looking at the experience of children whose anatomy was different from their core gender identity. From these studies he concluded that the child's sense of being gendered did not simply come from anatomical awareness but was also developed through interaction with others treating the child as a boy or as a girl. The important point here is that the formation of gender identity is seen as being an interactive process based not on an inevitable anatomical recognition but a complex social awareness and internalisation of how masculinity and femininity are seen. Incidentally this also allows us to make important distinctions between different cultures' perceptions of gender.

We are now in a position to try to reframe our understanding of women's psychosexual development and why it may be so difficult for women to perceive themselves as desiring subjects rather than desired objects. The roots of the problem lie in the process of the child's separating and individuating from her primary object, the mother. When the child emerges from early infancy and his/her fantasy of having omnipotent control over the mother/caretaker, the child needs the mother's recognition and confirmation of what he/she can do in the outside world to, in a sense, compensate. The loss of infantile power becomes bearable because the child's increased capabilities offer a compensation for this loss. Moreover, recognising what the child can do in the world is also a validation of the child's desire to do, be and relate in an active sense. The mother may have difficulty in providing sufficient recognition at this stage for two reasons which are inextricably connected. She herself is desexualised, 'is not articulated as a sexual subject; she is the woman without desire.' Also she has been the primary caretaker and is not seen as representing any kind of entry into the world. The important points to note here are that firstly mothers do not have to be desexualised; secondly they do not have to be so clearly defined as not being connected with the world. (Here we may ponder on the significance of the role of Jewish women in Central and Eastern European countries where, on the one hand, fathers provided the connection with God and the spiritual dimension, but mothers often had far more connections in the worldly world.) The girl has another difficulty to face; unlike the boy she cannot identify as the boy can, with the father representing desire and a recognition of her separate identity. While the boy repudiates his relationship with mother through identifying with father and being recognised by him and having an ideal love relationship with him (which brings all kinds of difficulties for boys and men) the girl needs to maintain her identity with mother; in order to reach her own capacity for desire she may turn to an idealising love for a male figure who represents desire. It is not the girl's lack of a penis or phallus which is at stake but rather the girl's need for an ideal identificatory love relationship with someone who represents desire and agency. 'Women are often drawn into relationships of submission because they seek a second chance for ideal love; a chance to reconstitute the father-daughter identification in which their own desire and subjectivity can finally be recognised.' (Benjamin, 1986, p. 129) In other words, the woman repeats the girl's search for a powerful ideal figure who can, as it were, replace her desiring self and thus return it to her.

## Jewish Women's Sexuality: The Influence of the Holocaust

I now want to return to the more specific topic of Jewish women's gender identity and sexuality and look at it in relation to the experience of Jewish women post-Holocaust. I believe that the effect of the Holocaust upon the survivors, the children of survivors and on all Jews has been profound. Howard Cooper and Paul Morrison in their 1991 book about British Jewry point out that since the Holocaust the Jewish preoccupation with survival has taken on a new meaning which cannot fail to affect the lives of all Jews. A similar point is made by Dinora Pines, 1993, a psychoanalyst, writing about her work with women who survived the camps and the second generation of women whose parents were directly affected by the Holocaust.

> I have come to realise that here, more than in any other paper I have previously written, I have been engaged not only in the rediscovery of my patients' Holocaust history and its impact on their lives, but also – as for all analysts of my generation – in the rediscovery of my own. Thus I too am deeply affected by the guilt of the survivor. The sense of psychic continuity that is important to us all was brutally broken through in my patients' lives, but also to some degree in my own. It is as though an

unquiet grave for our murdered forebears, a hole in family tradition as a result of twentieth-century European history, cannot be repaired by the normal process of mourning. (p. 223)

Looking at what has been learned from psychotherapeutic work with these women will shed more light on the particularity of many other Jewish women's sexuality.

Second-generation Holocaust survivors often come to psychotherapy because their capacity or will to live as opposed to merely survive is severely impaired. Inevitably this will be linked to sexuality and its expression. For women this may take many outward forms; one woman may have many casual sexual relationships with both men and women; another has married and had children but feels she cannot love them 'properly'; a third has had very few sexual encounters and no ongoing relationships. It seems that for each woman in a different way their parents had been unable to process their own traumatic experiences and had, therefore, been unable to provide a containing environment within which the girl's inner self could develop. Dina Wardi suggests that in each survivor's family at least one child is designated to be the family's memorial candle; to remain in a state of psychological preoccupation with the parents' trauma at the expense of their own personal development. She suggests that the daughter is deprived of belonging to a line of women and that often the mother herself expresses very little sexuality or femininity. It is as if the daughter experiences an exaggerated version of what many daughters encounter in seeing their mothers as de-sexualised; but these survivor mothers do not even allow themselves to be sexual objects. Since the connection the child has to the mother is again exaggeratedly undifferentiated, the daughter is unconsciously aware of the heavy weight of her mother's experience and her repressed sexuality. Wardi suggests that unconsciously the daughter may be preoccupied with what has happened to the mother's sexuality during the period when she was in a concentration camp or in hiding, asking herself questions like, 'How did she manage when her periods started? What kind of indescribable experiences did she have?' Perhaps the most difficult questions of all concern whether the mother used her sexuality in order to survive. Wardi points out that in a sense the relationship between the woman camp inmate and the German SS officer was an extreme form of the dominant-submissive relationship which can excite both men and women. Wardi describes it thus:

Occasionally the figure of the SS officer aroused mixed feelings ... a threatening frightening figure, an omnipotent tyrant, capable of humiliating his victims thoroughly ... but at the same time his abundant masculinity attracts and seduces women and hidden in his power is a spark of hope for survival ... the tyrant will save the beautiful girl who finds favour in his eyes and she is the one who will serve as the victim for satisfying his desires. (p. 199)

The girl or young woman who carries such material for her whole family, usually without any conscious awareness of what is burdening her, is not able to go through even the usual tortuous process of separating from mother. This can be made more difficult when the father in such a family turns to his daughter for an emotional closeness he cannot get from his wife. Wardi suggests that these daughters will fear that psychic separation might be like the kinds of death and loss suffered by the parents in the Holocaust. She thinks that the 'memorial candle' daughters actually need to begin to find out and to imagine what the parents' experience might have been in order to begin to distinguish themselves from their parents. I suggest that from these most traumatised patients' experience we can learn something more about what is particular about Jewish women's sexuality.

## Conclusion

Traditionally Jewish women are seen as sexual and being responsible for sexuality within family and community life. We have seen that this is not highly valued, rather it is seen as necessary, although at times unclean and unsavoury. It is a very different way of looking at sex and love from that of the Christian tradition with its distinction between mothers, madonnas and whores. Within traditional Judaism sexuality is seen as a necessary if not highly valued aspect of life. Moreover, in the often perilous situations in which Jews lived for centuries there must have been a history of Jewish women using their sexuality to help them survive. In contemporary Western-European influenced societies Jewish women struggle to connect their own historical and cultural sense of their sexuality with the predominating view of women as sexual objects. Perhaps to understand the many different positions that Jewish women have taken up, ranging from an extreme preoccupation with exterior presentation, looks and clothes to those who have 'returned' to Hasidic practice, to those who have been active feminists, we need to look at these women and see how the Holocaust history and their own particular family history have impacted upon their psychological development and their sexuality.

# References

Benjamin, J. (1986) 'The Alienation of Desire: Women's Masochism and Ideal Love' in J.L.Alpert ed. *Psychoanalysis and Women: Contemporary Reappraisals.* New Jersey, The Analytic Press.

Chodorow, N. (1978) *The Reproduction of Mothering: Psychoanalysis and the Sociology of Gender.* Berkeley, California University Press.

Cooper, H. and Morrison, P. (1991) *A Sense of Belonging: Dilemmas of British Jewish Identity.* London, Weidenfeld and Nicholson in association with Channel Four Television Company Limited.

Eichenbaum, L. and Orbach, S. (1983) *Understanding Women.* Harmondsworth, Penguin.

Flax, J. (1993) 'Mothers and Daughters Revisited' in J. van Mens-Verhulst, K. Schreurs and L. Woertman, *Daughtering and Mothering.* London and New York, Routledge.

Freud, S., (1899) 'Complete Letters of Sigmund Freud to Wilhelm Fliess 1887–1904' *Standard Edition of the Complete Psychological Works of Sigmund Freud, SE1.*

Freud, S., (1905) *Three Essays on the Theory of Sexuality SE7*

Mitchell, J. (1974) *Psychoanalysis and Feminism.* Harmondsworth, Penguin.

O'Connor, N. and Ryan, J. (1993) *Wild Desires and Mistaken Identities.* London, Virago.

Pines, D. (1993) *A Woman's Unconscious Use of Her Body.* London, Virago

Roith, E. (1987) *The Riddle of Freud.* London and New York, Tavistock.

Roth, P. (1971) *Portnoy's Complaint.* London, Corgi Transworld Publishers.

Stoller, R. (1968) *Sex and Gender.* London, Hogarth.

Wardi, D. (1992) *Memorial Candles: Children of the Holocaust.* London and New York, Routledge.

# TRADITION AND MODERNITY

# JEWISH SEXUAL ATTITUDES
# IN EASTERN EUROPE 1850–1920

*John Cooper*

When we attempt to analyse the sexual attitudes prevailing among
the Jews in Eastern Europe prior to the First World War, we come
across a paradox. It has been argued by Mark Zborowski and Elizabeth Herzog that whereas the fine folks belonging to the religious
sections of the community adhered to a system of strict morals and
arranged marriages, underpinned by marriage contracts specifying a
fixed dowry, the poor married for love. A similar class-motivated
argument was advanced by Ruth Rubin, who was of the opinion that
'playing at love', the concept of romantic attraction, had existed
among the lower strata in Eastern Europe from the early nineteenth
century.[1] Yet at the same time, there was the growth among the Jews
of a flourishing sexual industry which drew into its ranks both religious girls and their more secularised sisters. In Buenos Aires there
was a sumptuous synagogue for the East European prostitutes and
their protectors; in London the girls boycotted Christian rescue
homes because of fear of conversion and their objection to eating
non-kosher meat; often the prostitutes refused to work on the High
Holidays; and in Rio in 1910, pimps marched through the street to
dedicate a new Torah scroll for their synagogue.[2] I hope in this paper
to go beyond these popular stereotypes by showing that the period

1. Mark Zborowski and Elizabeth Herzog, *Life is with People. The Culture of the Shtetl*
(New York, Schocken Books 1978), pp. 270–71. Ruth Rubin, *Voices of a People. The
Story of Yiddish Folksong.* Philadelphia, (Jewish Publication Society of America 1979),
p. 72 (hereafter cited as Rubin, *Folksong*).
2. Edward J. Bristow, *Prostitution and Prejudice. The Jewish Fight Against White Slavery
1870–1939.* (Oxford, Clarendon Press 1982), pp. 140–41 (hereafter cited as Bristow,
White Slavery).

from 1850 to 1918 was one of rapid social change accelerated by the mass migration from Eastern Europe from the 1880s onwards and the dislocation in family life caused by the impact of the First World War. If the stereotype was untrue for the large cities, such as Warsaw and Vilna, it was not an accurate depiction of life in the smaller towns, where the idea of romantic love and new views on morality cut across the religious divide.

Maurice Fishberg argued in 1911 that where Jews were not affected by the modern way of life

> ... the chastity of the women is much superior, the family ties are much stronger, and girls only rarely go wrong. In the small towns in Russia, Poland and Galicia one rarely hears of a Jewish child born out of wedlock. Unmarried women seldom associate, even socially, with men before marriage. The absence of alcoholism, particularly among Jewesses, who never drink, is another factor in keeping the sexes apart. But in the large cities in Eastern Europe, where the separation of the sexes is not so strict, illegitimacy is frequently encountered. In Western Europe it is more frequent for the same reason.[3]

Nevertheless, this tells us little about the chastity of Jewish males, particularly the industrial working class, which expanded rapidly from the 1890s and began, in part, to frequent brothels.

Moreover, the sexual code of morals in Eastern Europe was not as simple as Fishberg leads us to believe. If one sifts the evidence in Chaim Aronson's autobiography which deals with the mid-nineteenth century, a more nuanced picture of small-town life emerges. Aronson was an orthodox teacher and clockmaker from Lithuania, who educated himself in German literature, while remaining loyal to the religious practice of his people. He was married three times, often through tortuous negotiations conducted through a traditional matchmaker or *shatkhn*, each time receiving a dowry of two hundred roubles or more plus maintenance for three years. His first, short-lived marriage ended in divorce, despite the birth of a son, because his wife's parents failed to pay the promised dowry. He confessed that 'I continued to live with my wife, whose name was Bathsheba, for seven months, sleeping in the same bed, without touching her, nor did she attempt to arouse me, for she had been brought up in a small town'. No doubt this point is of wider application in showing that wives from small towns did not usually take the sexual initiative in bed.[4]

3. Maurice Fishberg, *The Jews. A Study of Race and Environment.* (New York, The Walter Scott Publishing Co. 1911), p. 243. Arthur Ruppin, *The Jews in the Modern World.* (London, Macmilllan and Co. 1934), pp. 81–82.
4. Norman Marsden, *A Jewish Life Under the Tsars. The Autobiography of Chaim Aronson, 1825–1888,* (New Jersey Allanheld, Osmun 1983), p. 109 (hereafter cited as Aronson, *Autobiography*).

His next marriage was again of brief duration, but this time came to an end when his wife died shortly after a miscarriage. She was of a somewhat melancholy disposition following her divorce from her previous husband, whom she loathed. When the couple first met, Aronson was badly dressed and somewhat bedraggled in appearance, so that her father allowed her to question Aronson and to have the final say as to whether or not she wished to marry him. So much for generalisations about modest maidens complying with the wishes of authoritarian fathers, when it came to choice of marriage partner.

> My [second] wife, who was a wise woman, appreciated my personal qualities which she often compared with those of the guests she received at the hotel, whose sole wit was to pass crude remarks about her. When, on occasion, we made love, she began to tell me what she had heard them say, I would quickly stop her saying that I did not wish to hear such language from so beautiful a soul, that it was unbecoming to her and only suitable for carters and drunkards.

This observation, that Aronson had to restrain his wife from repeating crude remarks while love-making, casts a different light on the attitudes of Jewish girls from small towns; they were not quite as innocent as the current stereotype assumes. Further, when Aronson was working as a teacher, he had occasion to rebuke a father over his daughter's conduct. 'Do you know that these maturing girls are all wayward, to a lesser or greater extent? I, however, am a man and not a boy', a remark which seems to indicate a certain sexual precociousness and deviousness on the part of the girls.[5]

After his divorce from his first wife, Aronson was briefly engaged to a girl of sixteen, with whom he was left alone in the house, apart from the company of some younger sisters, when her family had to go and stay out in the fields for a few days at a time during the week, as it was the sowing season.

> My fiancée began to speak more often with me, and sometimes in the evenings, after her sisters had retired to bed, she remained with me in my bedroom ... During that second week, I began to fall in love with my bride, and she returned my affection. Every night we delighted in our love for each other, although she would not permit intercourse, saying wisely: 'If I let you take my virginity, you might cease to love me and suspect me of behaving wantonly with other men' ... She of course had no way of knowing that it is my nature to be constant, and that if she had given herself to me, I would have been faithful to her for ever ...

What Aronson seems to be implying is that they were involved in 'heavy petting' and that he as an engaged man was willing to go 'the whole way' until restrained by his fiancée. Rumours, however, reached Aronson that she was having a secret affair with a shepherd,

5. Aronson, *Autobiography* pp. 139, 142 and 160.

which seemed to be confirmed, when he caught them together, and the engagement was broken off.[6]

After the demise of his second wife, Aronson was engaged but unhappy. It was, therefore, suggested that he should shelve this attachment and become engaged to a wealthy bride from the town of Vilklomir, with the chance of securing a dowry of five hundred roubles. Fortunately he forwent this opportunity. 'Later I discovered that it was true that the people were wealthy, and their daughter was pretty and diligent – but she was immodest and wanton'.[7] Again, Isaac Meir Dik claimed that Jewish women who sold goods in the market, instead of staying at home, were an easy prey for seducers.[8]

It was not only the girls from religious homes who infringed the past norms of expected sexual propriety, but a fair number of the youths at *yeshiva*, some from households of modest means, others from rich families, either secretly read revolutionary literature or indulged their sexual appetites. When Aronson was attending the *yeshiva* at Vilna as a young man, another student approached him, saying

> You know, I also spend a few Sabbaths at the tailor's house, and I found out that his only son has been stealing his possessions in order to have enough money to indulge his frivolous desires in the company of a band of loose-living young wastrels who can always lay their hands on as much money as they want, whether by stealing or as a gift from their fathers. On the period of the full moon they hold a festive gathering during which they disappear from home for a couple of days to indulge in drink and lust until their money gives out. Now, this tailor's son stole from his father some silver spoons and religious articles, and hid them ... Later, the son sold some of the books which the father had bought for his teacher ...[9]

After this, Aronson was approached to become the treasurer of a White Society, a band of dissolute youths at the *yeshiva*. It was explained to him that the youths arranged '"a celebration: they leave home for a few days, or for so long as they are able to be absent without their families worrying over them, and indulge in wild celebrations outside the city ... Look they have saved money, so they go to the houses where they can eat the best foods and drink the best wines and spirits and also have beautiful girls for their amusement ..." I could not ... understand why rich youths, who enjoyed the best that their loving parents could give them, should behave so madly ...' On another occasion, Aronson was called at nine o'clock one morning to the attic room of a *yeshiva* student. ' ... I saw three or four young men there, with their phylacteries and prayer-shawls lying unused and unwrapped on the

6. Aronson, *Autobiography* pp. 114–16.
7. Aronson, *Autobiography* pp. 139 and 142.
8. David Biale, 'Eros and Enlightenment: Love Against Marriage in the East European Jewish Enlightenment' *Polin* vol.1 1986 pp. 60 and 66 (hereafter cited as Biale, *Love*).
9. Aronson, *Autobiography* p. 71.

table. Beside a wooden bed in a corner stood a tall, dark skinned young girl about twenty years old: she was dressing herself in front of them, while they watched and joked'.[10] All these experiences of the wild youths from Vilna were a far cry from the diatribes of the *maskilim* against early marriage and the sad stories of their inability to perform adequately sexually, Guenzburg even confessing his impotence, when he was rushed into marriage as a young adolescent.[11] None the less, the tales of this other group of sexually mature youths leading a care-free existence in Vilna can be duplicated for other large cities.

With the gradual abandonment of early marriages from the mid-nineteenth century and the spread of secular literature, the idea of romantic love spread more widely among the East European Jews. Whereas in 1867 43 per cent of the Jewish bridegrooms and 61 per cent of the brides were under the age of twenty, by 1897 teenage marriages had dwindled significantly, the percentage of such unions dropping to 5.8 per cent and 27.7 per cent.[12]

Aronson wrote letters to one fiancée with such florid phrases culled from German literature, that when the contents became more widely disseminated, they started the whole town gossiping. Israel Kosover (1859–1929) successfully wooed his future wife, who was sophisticated and immersed in popular novels, with romantic phrases taken from the *Song of Songs.*[13] According to Yehuda Leib Cahan, in 1912 young persons gathered in basements and other places on the Sabbath to dance and sing. 'And mostly love songs ... and love affairs went on in secret, hidden, on the bypaths and sideroads where young lovers went strolling together, just as is described in the very songs they sang'. In these Yiddish love songs high-spirited and independent maidens played at love, mothers worried about their daughters staying out late at night with their lovers, and daughters appealed to their mothers to allow them to marry the poor man of their choice. 'Beloved, devoted mother, Don't try to change my mind. Quench the fire that is within me ...' With the spread of industrialisation from the 1870s, the young girls bemoaned being 'chained to the needle and wheel', and some sang sad dirges of being jilted by their lovers for a prettier girl. 'I have gambled away my life mother dear, for I am about to give birth', was the admission in one song.[14]

A.S. Sachs, in his intimate portrait of a small Lithuanian town prior to the First World War, discerned three classes of Jewish girls.

10. Aronson, *Autobiography* pp. 86 and 95.
11. Biale, *Love* pp. 54–56.
12. Rubin, *Folksong* p.72 and Biale, *Love* p. 51.
13. Aronson, *Autobiography* p. 116. Israel Kasovich, *The Days of Our Years.* (New York: Jordon Publishing Co., 1929).
14. Rubin, *Folksong* pp. 72–85.

First the modest maiden, who would dutifully bow to her parents wishes and marry the bridegroom of their choice in an arranged marriage. Yet this generalisation was partially contradicted by Aronson, while the Yiddish love songs speak of the resistance of girls and young Talmudic students to their parents' proposed choice, if a romantic attachment had to be abandoned.[15] Sachs contended that 'The Jewish maiden of the small town had no social life ... She had heard that in the great centres, in Riga, in Vilna, and in other such "loose-living" cities, young fellows and girls met and danced together. She had heard many other strange goings-on; but she did not envy these girls'.[16] I would suggest that the concept of the free, 'loose-living' maiden in the big cities must have had some knock-on effect elsewhere, whereby the small-town girls were rendered less compliant and more determined to marry a man, who conformed somewhat to their idealised dreams.

Secondly, Sachs explained that there was a class of 'talked about' girls. 'Some loved to dress up on week days, to giggle loudly over everything, to look too much into the mirror, to run out into the street dishevelled and to the very spot where gathered the unmarried apprentices and store clerks, who were very fond of immodest tales, suggestive stories and spicy jokes'. Further, 'The girls would make a pretence at upbraiding the young fellows for their loose talk, curse them that they should bite off their tongues. But at the same time they would open their eyes and cast roguish glances at the merry fellows, who knew full well that the girls were really not much offended.' Sometimes the engagements of these girls were broken off and the marriage contracts returned, when the bridegroom's family discovered that the girl had a reputation for being 'talked about'. Despite everything, these girls came from traditional families, which shows that the concept of romantic love was swiftly permeating these families in the small towns. Below these girls in public esteem, were the daughters of poor widows, such as water-carriers and washerwomen, who were neglected by the community, and as a result, became dissolute and open to the opportunities available as prostitutes.[17]

Russian government statistics for 1889 showed that Jewish madams controlled seventy per cent of the brothels, some 203 out of 289 licensed houses, in the Pale of Settlement in Poland and European Russia, which mushroomed with industrialisation in the late nineteenth century. In Warsaw, sixteen out of the nineteen licensed houses in the contracting licensed sector were run by Jews, while in

15. Rubin, *Folksong* pp. 78–80.
16. A. Sachs, *Worlds That Passed* Philadelphia, (Jewish Publication Society of America 1943) pp. 46–48 (hereafter cited as Sachs, *Worlds*).
17. Sachs, *Worlds* pp. 48–49.

the Kherson province which embraced Odessa, thirty out of the thirty-six licensed brothels were controlled by Jews. Yankele Adler, who came from a traditional family and was later a star of the Yiddish theatre, was a member of a juvenile gang in Odessa in the 1870s. 'These were the famous young sports and toughs who came out at night sporting their fancy vests and canes, looking for a wedding brawl, and a chance to turn the town upside down. Sons of rich fathers, petty commission men, more sinister types, too, dabbling in prostitution and blackmail.' In 1910 Jews ran all fourteen tolerated houses in Minsk, at which Jewish workers used to spend much of their earnings at weekends during the 1890s, until the Jewish socialist party, the Bund, began to recruit them.[18] While it is clear that there were many Jewish prostitutes in the brothels of Poland, the extent to which Jewish workers frequented them has not been established, although the increasing politicalisation of the workers by the Bund, particularly in Warsaw, sharpened their antipathy to the brothel owners.[19]

In 1913 a Jewish gang which specialised in procuring girls, mostly servants and women from dressmaking establishments, for brothels at Vilna, Minsk and Riga were arrested, and from this we can surmise the background of the girls who were recruited for these houses. At the same time, orthodox girls were vulnerable to the wiles of pimps, partly because Jewish education for girls was often sketchy, and partly because their elementary sexual knowledge was so deficient.[20] As we have seen, many of these girls remained religious or at least traditional, even when they went overseas to the bawdy houses of Argentina and Brazil.

During the second half of the nineteenth century and the years leading up to the First World War, there was a constant migration of Jews in Eastern Europe from the small towns to the larger industrial centres, where greater opportunities for employment abounded, but in migrating they often lost their small-town innocence. As a girl of fourteen, Chaia Sonia Luria went to work as a servant in Kharkov, where she was seduced by a tailor some twelve years her senior, who later married her. Coming from an orthodox family and retaining their values, Chaia Luria's guilt over this incident continued to haunt her.[21] Of even more importance than the internal Jewish migration was the massive flow of immigrant families to the West, to Germany,

18. Bristow, *White Slavery* pp.54–56. Lulla Rosenfeld, *Bright Star of Exile. Jacob Adler and the Yiddish Theatre* (London, Barrie & Jenkins 1978), pp. 13–14.
19. Bristow, *White Slavery* pp. 58–62.
20. Bristow, *White Slavery* pp. 51 and 57.
21. Rubin, *Folksong* p. 81 Don Gussow, *Chaia Sonia* New York, (Bantam Books 1981) pp. 13–14, 192–93.

France, Britain and the United States, anywhere to escape from the poverty and dearth of employment in Poland and Russia. Both in the old Country and in the United States, this time of upheaval frequently led to wives being deserted by their husbands, either because of another woman or because their dowries were deemed to be insufficient. If settlement in a new country meant greater exposure to Western values and modernisation, the disintegration of some of these migrant families was not accidental, as some of these new values had already been imbibed in the *shtetl* or larger city. 'His wife grows sickly', wrote one observer of the American scene. 'His wages are too low to allow him any fun. He fights with his wife ... There are gay young girls out there, and carefree bachelors. The anarchists preach free love; the freethinkers guarantee there is no ... punishment in the afterlife. He becomes a missing husband'.[22]

Prior to the First World War both traditional Jews from the wealthy middle class, and their more assimilated brethren from the Austro-Hungarian Empire which included a part of Poland, flocked to the spas of Karlsbad and Marienbad. Here mothers brought their daughters to meet suitable suitors and marriages were arranged with the help of gentlemen who called themselves international matchmakers. Couples or individuals came to drink the mineral waters and take a cure for some physical or mental ailment, and individuals came to dally in a cafe, play cards and flirt and to seduce other men's wives.[23] Also popular with the Jewish upper middle class were the sanatoria, to which young Jewish girls were sent if they were suffering from a neurosis or were to be weaned off an unsuitable lover. Helene Deutsch stated that 'They [girls] are sent to sanatoria where instead of real psychiatric treatment they are given hydro-electric therapy. Flirtations with doctors and affairs with other patients spoil these girls for life'.[24]

Jewish family life in Eastern Europe at the time of the First World War was fragile, wives were sometimes deserted and children were abandoned. It was likely that Chaim Weizmann lived with Sophia Getzova after their engagement. Even in rabbinic hasidic families, the bridegrooms agreed to be vetted by their future wives. One such wife, before the engagement was finalised, asked her old-fashioned husband-to-be brutal questions and poked fun at his replies.[25] Dur-

22. Irving Howe, *The Immigrant Jews of New York* (London, Routledge & Kegan Paul 1976), pp. 179–80.
23. Sholom Aleichem, *Marienbad* translated by Aliza Shevrin. (New York, Perigree Books 1982.)
24. Paul Roazen, *Helene Deutsch* (New York, New American Library 1986) p. 117.
25. Jehuda Reinharz, *Chaim Weizmann* (New York, Oxford University Press 1985) p. 69. Isaac Bashevis Singer, *In My Father's Court* (Harmondsworth, Penguin Books 1980), p. 82.

ing the war the uprooting of the population and the dispersal of families, the sudden deaths of husbands and fathers in battle, the disintegration of families as a result of starvation and disease – all further undermined Jewish family life in Eastern Europe. A rabbi complained about the situation in postwar Poland. 'Jewish daughters in the company of soldiers! ... What will become of them? Drinking and dancing and playing cards and what not, and the parents seem to encourage them for the sake of the piece of bread they may get'.[26] Similarly Chaim Grade's mother could 'not understand these modern girls: What do they see in the pleasure-seeking young fellows of today? The young men of former times, say the girls, were savages with their beards and earlocks ... But what's the use of the modern young men's playing at love, kissing and caressing their fiancées before the wedding, if afterwards they look for other women?'[27] What I would suggest is that Jewish family life re-constituted itself in a new form in the West between the two world wars.

26. Boris D. Bogen, *Born A Jew.* (New York, The Macmillan Company 1930), p. 195.
27. Chaim Grade, *My Mother's Sabbath Days. A Memoir.* (New York, Schocken Books 1987), p. 123.

# SEXUAL BEHAVIOUR AMONG ULTRA-ORTHODOX JEWS
## A Review of Laws and Guidelines*

*Hannah Rockman*

## Introduction

This paper was originally written to offer guidelines to non-Jewish therapists working with ultra-orthodox Jews. It examines the relationships,
attitudes, laws and guidelines regarding sexuality within this community.
The largest and most influential group in this community are the
Hasidim. Hasidism, a religious revitalisation movement, originated
in the eighteenth century among East European Jews. The movement which attracted a large number of adherents, called 'Hasidim',
has been maintained until this day. One prominent feature of this
group is the authority of the *Rebbe* in all matters, be they social, political, religious or spiritual (Ben-Dor, 1983).

It is rare for the members of such a closed community to seek
advice for their personal problems from 'outsiders', thus little is
known about the laws and attitudes governing their intimate lives.

Throughout the *Halakhah* (Jewish law) the view is held that a loving
companionship between husband and wife is a virtue and a duty, *mitzvah*, sanctified by the Creator. 'It is not good that man should be alone'
– man's inner capacity for goodness can never be realised unless he has
a mate upon whom to shower his selfless affection (Lamm, 1980).

Marriage and the problems related to it form a significant part of
the entire Talmudic literature (the compendium of Rabbinic debates

---

* This chapter is based on an article published in *The British Journal of Sexual and
Marital Therapy*, vol. 8, 3, 1993.

on Jewish law). Over one sixth of the Talmud itself, one whole 'order', is devoted to such matters as marriage, divorce, and women's rights. Of special importance are the sexual aspects of marriage, to which the Talmud devotes a full tractate, called *Niddah* (Lamm, 1980). Under the wedding canopy itself, among the seven blessings recited, one blesses God for creating man in His image and forming him so as to perpetuate himself. According to the Torah, God imprinted His dual nature in man without considering it an inner contradiction. 'And God created the man in His image... male and female created He them. And God blessed them, and God said unto them to be fruitful and multiply ...' (Genesis 1:27-28). The divine image and sexuality are not antonyms. To be spiritual and beget children are not conflicting aspects of man's life (Lamm, 1977).

According to the sages, the Torah presents man and woman together as comprising the image of the Divine. Therefore, when husband and wife are intimate, a man can see himself as being filled with the male aspect of the Divine, making an intimate connection with the female aspect. Similarly a woman can see herself as receiving the male aspect. They can both realise that through their union they are creating an 'image of God'. Thus, it is also significant that there is no encouragement of celibacy in the Jewish tradition, mystical or otherwise. Moses himself was married as were virtually all the prophets and the sages. Sex is not seen as a weakening of the flesh or as a necessary evil, but as a means of drawing close to God on a most intimate level (Kaplan, 1985).

However, despite this emphasis on the virtues of being a couple, the process has to occur within an explicit and restricted framework. 'Romantic love' is not encouraged and is seen by some as an American misconception based on watching 'too many movies'. Further, it is an irrational idea which, if one is not careful, will lead to foolish and even sinful behaviour. It can also be a tool used by scheming girls to lure unsuspecting young men to marriage (Stopler, 1967).

There are several general guidelines as to what is considered appropriate. Although the details of these rules will be presented later in this paper, the following are considered axioms and propositions for sexual conduct and its place in society in general.

- Sexual relations may take place only between a man and a woman.
- Sexual relations and marriage are not permitted with someone outside the circle of the Jewish people or inside the circle of close relatives established by the Bible and the Sages.
- Sexual relations are a *mitzvah*, a religious duty, within a properly covenanted marriage in accordance with Jewish law. Outside of that covenant, premarital sexual relations are not condoned and extra-marital relations are considered crimes.

- Sexual relations within marriage must accord with the laws of family purity with respect to the wife's menstrual cycle.

The 'synchrony' required of sexual partners reflects a possible imperfection in God's creation. However some Jewish scholars interpret this as evidence of the difference between animal and human sexual behaviour. Furthermore, to achieve genuine satisfaction one is forced to express his/her humanity. 'Sex exposes us to failure and success and in all this it confronts us with the theme of human communication instead of mere animal copulation' (Lamm, 1980).

If Jewish scholars do not perceive people as animalistic they by no means see them as angelic. Judaism therefore frowns on celibacy. As recorded in the Talmud, one scholar chose to remain celibate in order to study the Torah and was severely chastised for it.

Finally, Jewish law maintains that the sex act ordained by the Bible as the right of the wife, must be accompanied by closeness, *kiruv*, and joy, *simchah*. Both of these require a meaningful permanent relationship and sanctification which raises the physiological act of sex onto a higher, more spiritual plane (Lamm, 1980).

The Jewish conception of marriage counselling is founded on the policy of *shalom bayit*, (marital harmony, literally 'peace in the home'). Although the Torah promotes this cause, and the *Halakhah* recognises the role of third parties in achieving this, there are limitations which have to be taken into account when advising orthodox couples in these matters. These *halakhic* limitations take two forms: a) the types of relationships for which marriage counselling is sanctioned and b) what techniques are acceptable with the religious law.

The relationships which are not halakhically sanctioned include the following:

1. that between a *cohen* (descendant of a priestly family) and a divorcee, a woman who has had premarital sex or one who is born out of a forbidden relationship with a *cohen.*
2. any of the incestuous relationships enumerated in the Torah;
3. a mixed religion relationship;
4. that between an adulteress, her husband and the man with whom she committed adultery; and
5. that between a Jew and a *mamzer* (a person born as a result of one of the forbidden unions.)

The question then arises of whether, if the therapist discovers that the couple in therapy are in a 'forbidden relationship', therapy should be terminated. There are three options. The first is to terminate therapy so that the counsellor, if Jewish, does not aid another Jew in committing a sin. The second option is not to do anything that can be construed as active encouragement of the relationship but just to act as a sounding board. The third option is to rebuke the couple in order to prevent them from sinning any further.

In all events it is recommended that the counsellor seeks *halakhic* guidance. The *halakhic* prohibitions to be kept in mind when counselling the couple about their sexual problems are forbidden thoughts and destruction of the seed.

The first prohibition relates to any thoughts which may lead to sexual arousal and possible emission of seed at night or coveting one's neighbour's wife/husband. The thoughts are often considered worse than the actual sin. As for therapy which involves ejaculation, it can be considered acceptable if in the long run this would help with the *mitzvah* of procreation. The use of surrogate partner or transsexual surgery is not acceptable (Schindler, 1983).

## Sexual Relations Within Marriage

One purpose of marriage is the avoidance of illicit sexual relations. The Talmud says 'He who reaches the age of twenty and has not married, spends all his days in sin. Sin actually? Say better in the thought of sin.' Once married the husband is exempt from work and any other external obligation (for the first year) so that he 'shall rejoice in his wife whom he has taken'.

The Bible conceives of sex within marriage as the woman's right and the man's duty. Jewish law goes as far as to say that if either partner refuses to participate in conjugal relations the person is considered rebellious and the other spouse can sue for divorce.

One may not have intercourse while either intoxicated or sluggish or in mourning, nor when one's wife is asleep nor by using coercion of any sort. One may not have sex if the partners are not committed to each other and are thinking of separating or even if they have had a disagreement and have not resolved it by nightfall.

The initiation of desire will be the man's role, though the wife may hint of her desire by dressing nicely and speaking softly. It is considered immodest on her part to be open about her desire (Lamm, 1980).

Before discussing sexual etiquette and law, the issue of timing has to be examined as physical contact can only commence after the time of *niddah*.

### The Laws of *Niddah*

According to the Torah's definition, a woman has the status of *niddah* from the time that she has her period until she immerses in the *mikveh* (ritual bath) seven days after the last day of her period.

There are clear guidelines regarding the size, shape and colour of the blood stain as to whether it can be considered to be menstrual blood or not. The stain has to be larger than the size of a barley kernel and have an oblong shape. This is to distinguish from a stain made by a squashed louse, a common pest in the days the Talmud was written. The colour has to be a shade of brown or red. Any other colour does not qualify as an indicator of menstruation onset (Eliyahu, 1986).

The Torah states (Leviticus 15:19), 'when a woman has a discharge of blood ... she shall be a *niddah* for seven days'. The word *niddah* comes from the word *nadad,* meaning 'removed' or 'separated'. This indicates that a women must forgo all physical contact with her husband. The Jews in Ethiopia went as far as to go to a special hut for the week of menstruation at the edge of the village.

Sexual intercourse between a man and a woman in the status of *niddah* is considered a most serious sin. 'If a man lies with a woman who is *niddah,* and uncovers her nakedness ... both of them shall be cut off from their people' (Leviticus 20:18).

This is the same penalty that is imposed on people committing incest with their siblings and those violating *Yom Kippur* or eating bread on Passover (Kaplan, 1982).

Moreover, if a woman senses that she has begun to menstruate during intercourse, she must inform her husband and the act must be terminated. However, the man should not withdraw while his penis is still erect as he may gain further pleasure. Rather, he must think holy thoughts until his erection subsides and only then separate from his wife. If this mistake occurs more than three times, thanks to the wife's miscalculation, she is forbidden to engage in sexual relations with her husband ever again and must be given a divorce or undergo special examination to discover the cause of this unpredictable bleeding (Eliyahu, 1986).

The state of *niddah* is considered 'unclean'. This is associated with humanity's expulsion from the garden of Eden. Menstruation is seen as a result of sin when God punished Eve in saying 'I will increase your anguish in pregnancy – with anguish you shall bear children ...' (Genesis 3:16).

As a result of the covenant of circumcision, Abraham and his children were elevated from the fallen state resulting from the expulsion from Eden. Consequently, the sexual act of the Jew enters the realm of the holy and can not be participated in by people who are considered unclean (Kaplan, 1982).

This also explains the purification of a *niddah.* Since *niddah* is associated with the expulsion from Eden, its purification must involve something that re-establishes the connection with Eden, namely, the waters of the *mikveh*. The *mikveh* is seen as representing a womb. Thus an individual emerging from it is as if born anew and leaves all uncleanliness behind. On another level the *mikveh* represents a grave. This is because when a person is submerged in water for those few moments without drawing a breath, it is as if she were in a state of non-life and when she emerges she is like one reborn. Both these analogies explain why the *mikveh* has to consist of pure water (as in the womb) and be built directly into the ground (as is a grave) (Kaplan, 1982).

The laws of *niddah* are seen to have two basic functions. First, the state of *niddah* represents the imperfection of man's reproductive process and therefore precludes sexual contact until this is removed through immersion in the *mikveh*. Conversely, it represents one of the best cures known for this imperfection which then brings about the best possible sexual relationship (Kaplan, 1982).

Not only does the Torah prohibit sexual relations with a woman in the *niddah* state, it forbids hugging and kissing. A rabbinic injunction forbids even touch. The Talmud equates sharing intimacy with a *niddah* with sharing intimacy with another man's wife.

There are four categories of prohibitions related to conduct between man and wife during this period:

    a. behaviours forbidden because of the Torah command 'do not come close ...';
    b. actions that may lead to sexual relations;
    c. signs of affection which may lead to the transgression of the command above;
    d. situations that may arouse a man and may cause him to 'let his seed go to waste'.

The prohibited behaviours are specified further in another twelve detailed rulings:

### Frivolous behaviour

Included in this category is the prohibition against smelling one's wife's perfume, lighting a cigarette for each other, cooling each other with a fan and acting in flippant and gay manner lest these behaviours lead to sexual arousal and emission of seed.

### Touch and the passing of articles from one to another

The husband is also prohibited from touching his wife's clothes while she is wearing them. If a *niddah* offers her husband an article, he should not tell her 'you are *niddah*' and refuse to accept it. Rather he should accept it with an attitude of displeasure, allowing her to place or drop it into his hand while taking care not to touch her.

There is a disagreement among halakhic authorities on whether a husband or wife may blow a feather or an insect off each other's clothing. In practice most authorities discourage such actions.

## Eating together at the same table

The Talmud states that a couple should not eat at the same table unless a clear distinction between the two is made. This distinction can be an object that is not usually on the table, placed between them or, if the use of place mats is customary, then one may eat without them as a form of distinction.

## Eating one's wife's leftovers

A husband may not eat or drink his wife's leftovers in her presence because this is considered to be a sign of affection. In contrast, the wife may eat the leftovers from her husband's plate even in his presence. A husband and wife may eat from the same serving plate as long as they transfer the food to their individual plate before eating it.

## Lying or sitting on one's wife's bed

The husband should not sit or lie in his wife's bed even outside her presence lest he become aroused.

## Sitting together on a bench

Two reasons are given for this prohibition. The first is that it is customary for lovers to sit together in such a manner and particularly when one rocks the bench and thus moves the other, a possibility of intimacy may arise. Second, it is possible that they may touch when the chair rocks.

It is therefore not advised to take journeys alone at this time in case the couple has to share a car seat.

## Sleeping together in one bed

As obvious from the above, a double bed may not be used while the wife is in *niddah*. It is advisable that the husband give his wife the choice of where to sleep.

## Seeing one's wife's 'nakedness'

While the wife is in *niddah*, a husband should not look at the parts of her body that are normally covered. However, he may gaze at her clothed and take pleasure in doing so. Since relations will be permitted at a later date, it is considered that mere gazing will not arouse him.

Among the areas that are normally covered are the woman's arms and calves. She must cover her hair at all times even when sleeping. The sages taught that a woman's voice is considered 'nakedness', as implied by the verse in the *Song of Songs:* 'your voice is sweet and your appearance attractive'. A husband may not, therefore, listen to his wife singing during her period.

### Serving food and drink

When in *niddah* a wife may continue with all household chores. However, as serving food and drink may arouse intimate feelings, it is advised that she refrain from doing so, or else serve in a matter that is different from her usual manner (e.g. carrying the cup with her left hand).

### Preparing a bed for one's husband

This prohibition applies only to spreading the sheets and blankets, as this action may arouse intimacy. Harder tasks such as straightening of a mattress are considered hard labour and unlikely to lead to arousal.

### Caring for each other when sick

The Torah teaches that prohibitions may be relaxed where there is danger to life. Hence if there is no one else to take care of the husband the wife may do so. Moreover, if he is mortally ill it is unlikely that he will have a strong sexual urge and thus she may care for him even when this involves much physical contact.

The husband may take care of his ill wife while she is in *niddah* if no one else is available; however, contact should be minimal e.g. if taking her pulse, he should attempt to do so by interposing a thin cloth between his hand and her wrist (Eliyahu, 1986; Abramov, 1988).

Once menstruation has ended (this is determined by the insertion of a special cloth into the vagina and asserting that there is not blood on it), the woman has to wait seven (clean) days and then go to the *mikveh*. Only on her return may the couple resume sexual or any physical contact.

## Laws and Guidelines Regarding the Sexual Act

Consummation of the marriage is accomplished even if penetration is only partial and no bleeding occurs. If bleeding does occur then bride and groom must separate as in the time of *niddah*. The difference here is that the bride needs only to count four days before the counting of the seven 'clean' days. The reason for this separation is to ensure that hymenial bleeding is not mistaken for menstrual blood. This gradual initiation into married life is considered positive for the couple as it enables them to form a bond and build up some intimacy before they resume the sexual side of their relationship. One of the problems presented before counsellors and doctors arises from the fact that both partners are virgins and may have difficulties consummating the marriage (personal interview with Dr Ebbing).

As mentioned earlier, it is the man's obligation to his wife to engage in sexual relations. There are times when this is particularly encouraged. These include the night she returns from the *mikveh*, before going on a long journey and when the husband is conscious of his wife's desire. However, the sages also defined the required frequency of sexual relations according to the man's occupation. Workers who are employed in other cities yet sleep at home are obligated once a week; donkey drivers – once a week; camel drivers – once a month; sailors – once every six months and Torah scholars – once a week, preferably on the Sabbath. In this manner both partners are deriving pleasure from the Sabbath.

The sages stated that a husband should prepare for sexual relations by showing his wife extra affection and love before nightfall, speaking to her of love and embracing her. Though in a more modest way, a woman should also take part in the process of preparation: 'A man requests sexual relations and a woman does so with her heart'. The Talmud relates how Rabbi Chisda, one of the pious saints of the Talmud, personally instructed his daughters how to prepare for sexual relations. He told them,

> Do not eat vegetables that cause bad breath, do not eat foods that will cause you to expel gas, do not drink beer at night ... When he wants to hold the pearl [a euphemism for the breast] with one hand and the little fish [vagina] in the other hand, offer the pearl to him, but don't offer the little fish to him until he is aroused. Then offer it to him.

Before engaging in sex a person must create an environment fit for holiness. The couple are encouraged to spend time studying relevant texts together. One such text is the *Iggeret Ha-qodesh* authored by the Ramban who writes,

> When you feel that it is fitting that you engage in sexual relations, you should make an effort that your wife's thoughts become one with yours. You should not arouse your desire hurriedly. Rather work to appease your wife and enter her in a manner of love and will, so that she will give seed first (in Eliyahu, 1986).

When a couple approach the act they should not talk about other matters, so that they do not distract their thoughts from the act. It is thought that conversation unrelated to sexual matters or love will have an adverse effect on the children born of that union (Eliyahu, 1986).

## The Direction

The Talmud states that the bed be placed between north and south. The most desired position for the man to lie in is with his head fac-

ing north. If that is not possible, his head should be pointing south
and if that is impossible to the west.

## The Position

The desired position for sexual relations is with the man on top of the
woman and the woman on her back facing the man (the so-called mis-
sionary position). There are several reasons for this. Among them are:

1. Each person faces the place from which they were created (the
   man from the ground and the woman from the man).
2. There is a belief that labour pains experienced when giving
   birth to a girl are lengthier than those felt when giving birth to
   a boy. This is because a girl's face is turned upward as in sexual
   relations and a boy is born facing the ground.
3. The man above and the woman below is the way of the world.

A man may kiss and caress any part of his wife's body. Though
not *Halakhah*, according to the principle of *middat hasidim* (a personal
piety that goes beyond the letter of the law) he may not kiss or even
look at her genitals. This would be transgressing the prohibition 'Do
not make your souls disgusting'.

If for some reason the couple cannot engage in sex in the desired
position and wish to use another position as a regular alternative, a
rabbinical authority must be consulted (Eliyahu, 1986).

Among the basic principles of modesty is not to carry out or
engage in sexual relations in a lit room. This applies to any source of
light including moon, sun and electric light. If the couple cannot control their desire during the day and decide to engage in sex, they are
required to darken the room 'in case the very nakedness of his wife
might cause him to consider his wife loathsome' (Eliyahu, 1986).

Although the couple are required to darken the room and keep
themselves covered for the sake of modesty, they are expected to
remove all their clothing. The Talmud explains that as an expression
of love and closeness sexual relations should be carried out while
both parties are naked. If one of the pair consistently objects to this,
his or her behaviour can be considered grounds for divorce. However, if both consent to the other being partially clothed, this is
acceptable. For example, it is considered that if she so wishes, a
woman may only lift her dress above her breasts (Eliyahu, 1986). All
religious articles in the room must have a double covering and only
one of those may be transparent. Any sacred books must be removed.

No sexual relations may take place for at least ten minutes after
either partner has been to the toilet. The husband must wash his
hands the ritual three times before and after sex.

One should not have sex when satiated or hungry. Thus, the middle of the night is considered an optimal time when the food has been digested properly but hunger has not set in (Blumenkrantz, 1984).

A husband may not engage in sex if he is experiencing an early morning erection. He must wait until the erection subsides and if he is then aroused anew he may proceed with sexual activity.

A person who is weak because of illness, giving blood or before or after strenuous physical activity should not engage in sexual intercourse. Of course, the wife's consent must be sought for this form of abstinence (Eliyahu, 1986).

## Appropriate Times

The days on which sexual relations are forbidden are the fast days of *Yom Kippur* and *Tisha B'Av*, the ninth day of the month of Av, which is the day the temple was destroyed. However, on other fast days, if the woman had immersed herself in the *mikveh* or makes it clear that her desire is aroused, sexual relations may be permitted. One who has not fulfilled the commandment of procreation may engage in relations during forbidden dates too (Eliyahu, 1986).

There are certain situations when it is considered immodest to engage in the sexual act. These include doing so in public places or gardens. A couple may not engage in sex in front of other persons, including children who have learned to talk. If an infant is sleeping at the foot of the bed the negative effects may be averted by placing a hand on the child. If the couple are guests at another's home they may not have sex unless they bring their own sheets or towel so that they do not stain their host's sheets. They must also make sure the room is locked and that their actions will not be overheard by their hosts.

The most appropriate time for sexual relations is on the Sabbath night and the nights of other holy festivals. A person should not engage in sexual relations at times of communal distress such as famine or war, as that is one way a person separates himself from the suffering of his people. This rule also applies to times of mourning (Eliyahu, 1986).

## Following the Sexual Act

After the husband ejaculates he should remain within his wife so as not to accidently spill any semen and so that his wife feels his love for her continues after intercourse is completed (Eliyahu, 1986). As mentioned above, once they have separated they are required to wash their hands and the man is expected to wipe away traces of semen with a wet cloth, except on the Sabbath when he should use a dry cloth. The following day he should immerse himself in the *mikveh* (Eliyahu, 1986).

## Additional Rules Regarding Male Sexuality

It is forbidden to discharge semen in vain. Any discharge of semen other then into a woman, with regard to the rules stated above, is considered to be 'in vain'. This includes practising coitus interruptus and masturbation. It is stated in the Talmud that the offender incurs the punishment of 'death by heaven' as these actions are considered the equivalent of murder. A man is forbidden to bring on an erection except in preparation for intercourse. This refers to sexual thoughts or affectionate behaviour towards one's wife that may lead to arousal outside the time of intercourse. It is considered a matter of piety to avoid holding one's own member while urinating. While bathing it is preferable to hold one's genitals through a cloth.

To avoid nocturnal emission men are advised to do the following:

1. eat a light supper;
2. avoid obscene talk and lies;
3. not share a bed with another man;
4. sleep on one's back;
5. not ride bareback on a horse;
6. avoid listening to 'evil' talk; and
7. refrain from looking at pictures of women (Blumenkrantz, 1984).

Male homosexuality is prohibited and is considered a crime. Female homosexuality, though forbidden, is not a crime. According to Judaism there is no such thing as a 'homosexual', only a Jew who engages in homosexual activity. Hence 'homosexual' is a not a noun but an adjective describing one's activity.

The implication of this is that the person engaging in this activity remains a fully fledged member of the community who, like the adulterer, or the Sabbath defiler, is obligated to change his ways or seek a 'cure'. The community should help him with this and not punish him or stigmatise him (Freundel, 1986).

## Birth Control

Technically, two commandments are focal when considering the question of birth control. First, the duty to have children. The acceptable minimum being at least one child of each sex. Second the prohibition against wasting seed.

When consulting rabbinical authority, several questions are posed before a decision can be made.

1. What is the reason for wanting birth control? If the woman's mental or physical health are at risk then birth control may be an option.
2. What means will be used? Mechanical and chemical means are less satisfactory than oral contraception as they are directly destroying the seed. The 'wasting of seed' refers to the male, thus contraception for the man is ruled out.
3. How many children do the couple have and what is their gender? (Blumenkrantz, 1984)

However, a couple is discouraged from making the decision on their own and a rabbi is most often consulted on the matter (Eliyahu, 1986).

## Conclusion

As illustrated above, it is obvious that the Hasidic or ultra-orthodox way of life is a strict and highly structured one. Hasidic couples are not inclined to seek out public social agencies or discuss their marital problems. Counselling is mostly sought through the *Rebbe* whose advice is followed diligently. Hasidic families do not talk about sex openly. This is understandable as the primary function of sex is for procreation. There is no exposure to this subject during childhood. Religious modesty requires separation of the sexes from an early age and thus, little is given in the way of sex education at home or at school.

In adolescence, sexual experimentation is strictly prohibited and sex is reserved for marital life only. This often leads to a lack of communication between the couple regarding sexual matters, and lack of knowledge, which will not be exposed because of the secrecy that surrounds the issue (Schindler, 1983).

The model of marriage is clear and well defined. There are prescribed roles. The husband has the authority in family decisions and is expected to be the bread-winner and overall supervision in religious matters. The freedom of the wife is limited. She is not expected to pursue a career but to spend her time and effort in bearing and bringing up children (Schindler, 1983).

It is essential that any therapist counselling this population does not try to disrupt this balance by interjecting his or her own opinion.

In working with Hasidic couples one should also be cautious in recommending modern therapeutic techniques to enhance sexual functioning. For example the squeeze technique, for premature ejaculation, would be prohibited by Jewish law and special advice would need to be sought. Solutions need to be found within the framework of Jewish law and, if need be, with the guidance of religious leaders.

*Note*

Interviews were held with Dr Ebbing of North Manchester and various members of the orthodox Jewish community in Manchester.

# References

Abramov, T. and Touger, M. (1988) *Secret of Jewish Femininity*. Michigan, MI, Targum Press.

Ben-Dor, S. (1983) 'Letting the therapist talk it through: a case study of Hasidic psychotherapy', *Journal of Psychology and Judaism* 8, pp. 63-70.

Blumenkrantz, A. (1984) *Gefen Porioh*. New York, Simcha Graphic Associates.

Eliyahu, M. (1986) *The Paths of Purity*. New York, Sucath David.

Freundel, B. (1986) 'Homosexuality and Judaism' *The Journal of Halacha*, 6, pp. 71-88.

Kaplan, A. (1982) *Waters of Eden: The mystery of the mikveh*. New York, NCSY.

Lamm, M. (1980) *The Jewish Way in Love and Marriage*. New York, Harper and Row.

Schindler, R. (1983) 'Counselling Hasidic couples: the cultural dimension' *Journal of Psychology and Judaism* 8, pp. 53-61.

Stopler, P. (1967) *Responsible Jewish Adulthood*. New York, NCSY.

Wikler, M. (1982) 'Another look at the diagnosis and treatment of orthodox Jewish family problems' *Journal of Psychology and Judaism* pp. 43-53.

# HASIDIC ATTITUDES TOWARDS
# SEXUALITY*

*Eduardo Pitchon*

One cannot hope to understand the Hasidic attitude towards sexuality, unless one places it within the wider context of the Hasidic world view. I would like to make it clear from the start that I am no expert in Hasidism, nor indeed am I a Hasid. The only qualifications that enable me to tackle this work are rather nebulous. I have, over the years, been blessed with the good fortune of having made some friendships with certain Hasids and their families, and in the way that one thing leads to another, my interest in them deepened. I then decided to offer a psychological service to the Hasidic community. My main role there is as adviser to four Hasidic schools, two for boys and two for girls. It follows that my views will be affected by my role and function in the community.

This paper touches on three aspects: the first part is concerned with my understanding of the Hasidic community; in the second part, I will explore the Jewish ideal of sexuality; finally, in the last part, I will look at how these apply in the daily life of the Hasidic community.

While the identity of the secular Western person is composed of a multitude of streams that reflect the complexity and contradictions of the society in which we live, the Hasidic identity is radically different. It depends on tightly knit communities which comprise a different world. In London, this world is called 'Stamford Hill'. This is a place where Jewish Hasidic and non-Hasidic groups converge. They all live together, yet separated by their own regional identities. There are numerous Hasidic groups such as the *Belz*, the *Bobov*, the

---

* This chapter is based on a lecture delivered at the Leo Baeck College, 8 December 1993.

*Satmar*, the *Gur*, the *Ritzhin*, the *Yerushalmi*, and the *Lubavitch*. Their names indicate where each of these groups originated from, which was usually some small town in Eastern Europe or Russia. In the unfolding of history, the Jewish communities in this part of the world were forced to emigrate, and were scattered around the globe. In spite of this, the Hasids managed to hold on to their regional identities, and endeavoured to keep their traditions alive.

What is a Hasid? I will quote at some length a definition given by Simon Glustrom in his book, *The Language of Judaism*, which I found quite enlightening:

> *Hasid* – a pious man. Coming from the word *Hesed* (lovingkindness), the Hasid was most highly regarded in the Jewish tradition. If any word in Hebrew approximates the word *saint*, it is the *Hasid*. He is placed on an even higher scale of virtue than the *Tzaddik* – the righteous man – because of his godly nature. ...& Unlike the man who seeks merely to observe the law, the Hasid is anxious to go beyond the requirements of the law. He does not wait until he is asked to perform a mitzvah. He says, 'Mine is thine, and thine is thine.' He is hard to anger and easy to pacify.
>
> In time, the term Hasid, like *Tzaddik*, came to be associated with a sect of Jews. Their way of life was called Hasidism. The Hasidim in some ways patterned their lives after the original type of Hasid. They too prayed with deep religious fervour, not confining their prayers to appointed times. Among their devotees, they encouraged humility and love for all God's creation. They often went beyond the confines of religious law to experience an extra measure of spirituality. As their movement became more highly developed, however, their mystical beliefs, their emphasis on miracles, their unquestioning devotion to their leadership, created a different emphasis, far removed from the way of life espoused by the original Hasid.
>
> With all the luxuries and pleasures that are offered to modern man, and with the secular demands that require his attention, it becomes exceedingly difficult to pattern one's life in the image of the original Hasid. Yet, one cannot help but admire his religious devotion, and appreciate his spiritual goals. Even if this generation of Jews can keep a vivid picture of the Hasid in mind as it deals with its own day-to-day problems, and if it learns the value of self-control or goes beyond the requirements of the law in its religious enthusiasm, it shall have paid lasting tribute to the Hasid in Jewish tradition.

The question that arises is how Hasids manage to retain their identity in the modern society. Many do it by insulating themselves from the wider world as much as possible. This insularity was best explained to me by a perceptive Hasid: 'The communities are like delicate tropical plants; in order to survive in this climate, they have to live in a glass house. God forbid that anyone should start throwing stones!' However, it is important to understand that the Hasidic communities have an international dimension, because they are in touch with other Hasidic communities in other parts of the world, and they often support each other in a variety of ways.

This will suffice as a good background. In discussing the Jewish ideal of sexuality, it is useful to consider the words of Rabbi Hershel: 'Life passes on in proximity to the sacred, and it is this proximity that endows existence with its ultimate significance. In our relationship to the immediate, we touch upon the most distant. Even the satisfaction of physical needs can be a sacred act. Perhaps the essential message of Judaism is that in doing the finite we might perceive the infinite.'

In the Hasidic world, sexuality is perceived as sacred and conceived of in the context of marriage, and with the possibility of procreation. Then in essence it is never separate from a spiritual dimension which always includes God's will. This concept not only represents an ideal in the community; it is also part of the collective psyche.

This could well differ from a purely secular consciousness where either no spiritual dimension is present or there is a wavering between the two polarities. These quite profound differences create different types of conflict and have significant implications when we come to understand how a society organizes itself. In a purely secular consciousness, the concept of sexuality may be studied and understood from a variety of points of view, but if the concept is a sacred one, all other points of view must be subsumed under the sacred or spiritual one which joins man to God.

This brings me back to Rabbi Herschel's view that life passes on in proximity to the sacred. If, as he says, this proximity endows existence with ultimate significance, it follows that it also endows sexuality with its ultimate significance.

Here the *Zohar* provides some explanation of the idea that sexuality expresses a mystery which is referred to by Gershom Scholem in the book, *Major Trends in Jewish Mysticism*:

> In so far as the Zohar shows a positive attitude towards the function of sexual life, within the limits ordained by divine law, it may be said to represent a genuine Jewish outlook. Chastity is indeed one of the highest moral values in Judaism: Joseph, who by his chastity has 'upheld the covenant' is regarded by the *Midrash* and the *Kabbalah* as the prototype of the righteous man, the true *Tzaddik*. But at no time was sexual asceticism accorded the dignity of religious value, and the mystics make no exception. Too deeply was the first commandment of the Torah, 'Be fruitful and multiply' impressed upon their minds.

This injunction to procreate is understood as a commandment to be carried out, and has a particular poignancy for the post-War Jewish consciousness, a poignancy which is never far from the Hasid's mind. This sexuality connotes not only a biological function, or the union between man and wife which reflects the union between the *King* and the *Shekhinah*, but it also fulfils a commandment. This is why asceticism is not an ideal within Judaism and the Hasid shares this view. Thus, within lawful limits, the attitude to sexuality is a positive one for the Hasid. Sexuality is therefore understood as an expression of love, a reflection of the divine, a union by which means a commandment can be fulfilled.

Those who hold a purely secular view can argue about the truth value of the sacred view and vice versa. In this work, I am more concerned to understand how these concepts are experienced by the individual and his community.

In the next section, I would like to highlight aspects of the sexual ideals in Jewish law which Hasids take seriously, and which they try to live up to. I will discuss briefly the education of boys and girls, the meeting process known as *shidduch,* and the *onah* or time of conjugality between man and wife.

Boys and girls are separated into single sex schools from the earliest age, and their education is not exactly parallel. The teachers and parents form part of a close-knit community; consensus is considerable, and the educational styles of the schools place the main emphasis on religious education. What a man is, what a woman is, and their duties and responsibilities towards each other, towards the children they may raise and towards the community, are central to this type of education.

Just as boys and girls are protected from the earliest age from contact with each other except in a family context, children are also protected from the influence of television. The male and female ideals currently present in our society do not form part of their world of meaning. It may come as a surprise to some to discover that while material success is not rated very highly, sexual success in the sense of conjugal happiness and mutual satisfaction is highly valued. Hasidim have clear ideas about providing the best facilitating framework for this to take place.

As a first step, I would like to discuss the initial painstaking efforts that precede the first meeting of a young man and a young woman, which is part of the process of *shidduch.* A girl is considered of marriageable age from about eighteen or nineteen. A boy is thought to be ready for marriage by the age of twenty-two or twenty-three. At this stage it is likely that the girl will have completed two years of study at a girls' seminar, and the boy will have completed about six years of *Yeshiva* education.

Parents may choose to go to a match-maker, whose success is partly dependent on his extensive first-hand knowledge of the young people of the community. The role of match-maker can be either a formally recognised one or a more informal one. Depending on what the family values are, extensive preliminary enquiries are made into the prospective partner's family, character, vocation, habits, capacity for study or material circumstances. The fact that transatlantic matches are often made is a reflection of the fact that young people in these communities travel far more widely than is generally realised, and often carry out their post-secondary school studies abroad, in countries such as France, Australia, the United States, Canada, etc.

The reticence which has been cultivated regarding the opposite sex also means that young men and women are usually strangers when they first meet. The preliminary enquiries are crucial because they serve to prevent embarassing objections which may arise, once a face to face encounter has taken place between the young couple.

The first meeting is a highly charged affair. This is due to the fact that in principle both should be ready to choose each other for marriage. Meetings prior to a decision are comparatively few, perhaps two or three. The young people do not engage in any physical contact; instead, they actually interview each other quite thoroughly. Despite these strictures, as one rabbi put it, 'The enquiries are for history, the meetings for chemistry.'

Once the decision has been made, an engagement takes place in the presence of their families and friends. It is thought advisable that the marriage should take place soon after this, preferably within about three months. During this time, the young people are encouraged to meet and to continue to get to know each other, while maintaining the ideals of modesty which preclude physical contact. In all cases, the head is supposed to rule the heart. When the young people marry, they are expected to have a period of time together, and the young man does not go to work at this stage. Both partners would have received instruction as to their sexual duties and responsibilities.

This leads to a consideration of the concept of *onah*, the lawful time of conjugality, when sexual communication is positively encouraged. Viewed in the simplest way, according to Jewish law, having sexual relations (within the right framework) is considered to be a woman's *right* and a man's *duty*. Sexual enjoyment and satisfaction are valued highly within this context. This is why it is said that when a man and his wife engage in a lawful sexual act, the *Shekhinah* is with them. The *Shekhinah* is understood as the Divine Presence, and thus the sexual act becomes holy. Husband and wife are enjoined to procreate, to enjoy each other, and to strive for each other's enjoyment.

It is a fact that people often fall short of this ideal. Equally, everyone in the community has a friend who acts as a counsellor or *Mashpiah*. Any problem can be discussed with the *Mashpiah*. This is an indication of the great care that is taken to try to uphold particular values in the community.

According to Jewish law, sexual relations between a man and his wife alternate between periods of abstinence and periods of conjugal intimacy. A five day period of the menstrual cycle followed by a seven day period of further abstinence ends when the woman goes to the ritual bath, the *mikveh*. The time of conjugal intimacy is then allowed until the onset of the woman's next menstrual cycle, when the period of abstinence begins again. It may be that relatively few studies exist within the broader scientific community of the advantages or disadvantages of this pattern. However, no such study could be concluded without evaluating the ethics and ideals of the community in question. My point here is that it is not only a matter of examining what one might call the conditioning of the community; the vantage point from which an enquiry is conducted is also subject to conditioning, and this conditioning may take a different form.

By conditioning, I am referring to the assumptions which are present in every society, and which are the result of particular belief systems. As an example, Western economics rely on an assumption of growth as an aim in itself, and this is leading to destructive impacts on the environment. The belief in the desirability of growth is in conflict here with the ethical ideal of conservation. When an investigator examines a community with a value system different from his own, he is not entirely objective because he too relies on assumptions which are part of his own conditioning. Currently in Western society, the provider / customer model has led to considerations of educational and medical providers and their customers who 'consume' certain services. The relationship between a teacher and a student is much more than a provider / customer relationship in societies as yet unaffected by this model. The teacher has responsibility for the transmission of values and tries to help the student develop his character. He does not merely provide facts and information.

This model also affects our understanding of sexuality in subtle ways. If we care to view ourselves primarily as providers and customers, then we begin to think of sex as an end in itself, an item we have to get. We may develop the idea that we have to shop around for the best sex. Current preoccupations such as the 'multiple orgasm' widely discussed in popular literature are a reflection of this tendency. Quality is reduced to quantity. There are communities with a different world view where this type of preoccupation is not an issue. This is why it is important that the investigator should become aware of the assumptions he has incorporated which are the result of his own belief system. This belief system, in turn, is a product of the society in which he lives. Too often psychotherapeutic practitioners observe the casualties: those who are considered deviants in the communities. While it is fair to say that certain problems can be understood in considerable depth, simply because we all share the same condition of being human (e.g. fears of sexual inadequacy, personality shortcomings which have a bearing on our sexual behaviour), no adequate counselling can take place without a sufficient awareness of the person's cultural, ethical and religious background. It is important to discover whether there are shared concepts which can act as a common language between those within and without the community. This in turn becomes a door through which a deeper mutual understanding is attained.

I have considered briefly the role of the psychotherapeutic practitioner, because my own experience has led me to a deeper consideration of these issues. In a more secular environment, we may view ourselves as functioning in a freer system with a wide range of choices as to styles, values and ideals. Thus close-knit communities such as the Hasids may appear to us as over-regulated, or even claustrophobic. Looking from the viewpoint of those within these communities, the more secular life outside is seen as fraught with dangers of too much choice and too little guidance. Society does not appear at present to be particularly stable, and the high divorce rate bears this out.

These facts suggest that much more thought should be given to those factors that contribute to good relationships, within which a balanced sexuality plays an important role. A purely instrumental view of sexuality does not seem to lead to sexual happiness.

I would like to conclude this chapter with a brief consideration of some differences between religious and secular communities. The role of man and the role of woman are clearly defined in Hasidic communities, whereas in the broader secular world there is continual flux and an ongoing search for role models. For instance, these may be pop stars, sporting heroes, wealthy people or other 'successful' individuals. It is quite likely that the modern consciousness contains a number of conflicting role models simultaneously. While this allows for change, it also reflects a situation where people are unable to digest adequately the pace of change. Some of the resulting casualties are seen by psychotherapists in their consulting rooms every day. As part of their own training, psychotherapists have had to struggle with precisely the same issues. Equally, they have not been devoid of guidance and their ideal remains a full and balanced sexuality which is an expression of mutual love and respect. In this there is a shared ideal and it can provide the basis for mutual understanding.

# CHALLENGES TO JUDAISM
## Surrogacy and Genetic Engineering*

*Julia Neuberger*

An example of the oldest trick in the book of assisted reproduction, was Sarah, matriarch par excellence, 'giving' her handmaid Hagar to her husband Abraham as a concubine, so that Sarah might have children by her. (Genesis 16:2) The consequences of that action were not wholly happy. Hagar and Ishmael were banished into the wilderness. Jealousies were certainly in place. But that method of having a child by another person was distinctly low tech, unlike most modern fertility treatments.

Despite its roots in Torah, many Jewish authorities are extremely negative about surrogacy, arguing that it exploits women (an argument rarely used elsewhere in Jewish debate, which tends to be male dominated), and that it complicates inheritance. Yet it continues, both outside infertility clinics, with the man having sexual intercourse with the surrogate mother, and within the fertility clinic system, with artificial insemination.

Surrogacy is one form of infertility 'treatment' which is causing an outbreak of moral disquiet. On the whole that concern is being expressed at some of the higher tech in-vitro fertilisation methods. Women in their late fifties have been giving birth as a result of new technologies and stimulatory drugs. (Sarah did it without!) Black women have chosen to have white babies – to match their husband's colour, perhaps, where there is a mixed marriage, but also because they feel white children have an easier life.

*This chapter is based on material previously published in the *Jewish Chronicle*, 7 January 1994, and in *AT & T Istel Viewpoint* Spring 1994.

It may now also be possible in the future to use the aborted foetuses from women who did not want their children, to gain eggs for fertility treatment for other women who want children desperately. It would also be possible to use those eggs for research purposes, in order to look at the development of a variety of conditions, for the ultimate benefit of as yet unborn children. Those who specialise in moral outrage can be extraordinarily outraged as these advances come upon us, and the new technologies ask a series of moral questions of us which we are poorly equipped to deal with.

In the original Genesis story, it was regarded as a divine miracle that the same Sarah who went in for low-tech surrogacy, gave birth at age ninety. Meanwhile, elderly fathers have never been a cause of major disquiet, even though these days we include fathers in active parenting. Indeed, all the evidence that men's sperm counts are diminishing is material with which our traditional *halakhic* material in this field cannot cope. In Jewish tradition, it was always the woman who was infertile. A man was supposed to divorce his barren wife of ten years' standing – even if he loved her – in order to take another wife and fulfil the *mitzvah* of *'p'ru u-r'vu'*, 'Be fruitful and multiply', a *mitzvah* which applied only to men.

Similarly, in the current objections to much of the assisted conception work, there is a recurring theme about natural mothers. However, we forget, in our desire to see 'natural' mothers, that many women would die young in childbirth or shortly after until well into this century, and that it was one of the family norms to have people who were not the 'real' mothers of children bringing them up.

Yet, somehow, that seems 'natural'. Whereas what we are doing here is 'interfering' with nature. For Jews, for whom traditionally a child is a gift of God, requiring three players, mother, father and God, we are interfering with God's will, and God's design. But before condemning that outright, before seeing all this as somehow defying God's law, there are several considerations to come into play.

First, Jews have been the greatest of advocates of the wonders of medicine. With our strong life-affirming tradition, we do everything to keep alive, to invent new and better ways of healing and alleviating disease. We never ask ourselves whether we are interfering with God's design in so doing. Instead, we regard ourselves as human beings with free will, and God-given intelligence, who have been given our brains to use in all sorts of ways, particularly for the preservation of that most precious of gifts, human life itself.

If that is the case, then modern science and modern medicine, however terrifying the speed of their discoveries, are simply using what is divinely given, the human intelligence, in order to affect the lives of other human beings. We have every right to expect that intelligence to be exercised by morally responsible people for the good of others. If it is not, then it is up to other human beings to ensure that abuse does not take place.

The second critical point is the extent to which childlessness was a source of terrible misery in our history. Sarah supplied Abraham with Hagar so that *she* could have a child. Rachel said pathetically: 'Give me children, lest I die.' (Genesis 30:1) Hannah wept in the Temple so piteously that Eli the priest thought she was drunk. (1 Sam. 1:13) Jewish law allows a man to divorce a wife who is barren after ten years of childlessness. The commandment to be fruitful and multiply is taken very seriously. Within our tradition, we should understand women – and men – being so desperate to have children by whatever means they can. Assisted conception *per se* should not be anathema to the Jewish community.

Providing we are sympathetic to their motives, the extent to which we vary on what precisely should be allowed in terms of hi-tech treatment should be open for debate. Many conservative authorities are already unhappy about donor insemination, allowing only artificial insemination by the husband, on the grounds that anything else is adultery, even if no actual sexual union takes place. Meanwhile, for some authorities, egg donation, if allowed at all, would have to be from another Jewess, in order to ensure the child's Jewish status. Others would regard it as quite possible for a child of a donated egg to be Jewish, like adopted children in non-orthodox Judaism, by upbringing and intention. Meanwhile others regard the use of more than one embryo for replacement in the woman's womb, with the conscious knowledge that not all would implant, as willingly engineering the waste of life, similar to the spilling of seed in vain. There are any number of views, depending on precisely which position is taken by the individual authority.

Where the issue of aborted foetuses comes into play, the varying views on abortion itself change people's perceptions. Those who are implacably opposed to abortion in any circumstances other than the saving of the mother's life would be more negative than those who can see reasons for allowing abortion in some circumstances, a debate well documented by David Feldman in his excellent *Birth Control in Jewish Law*.

However, it is the broader questions which need to be examined, although we are not ready to come to any conclusions. Is it right to make moral decisions on the basis of the aptly named 'yuk factor', because we do not like what we see and hear? Or should we argue that moral debate rests on principles, and the question here must be whether we are providing a benefit, or doing harm, by allowing these treatments. Is it better for women in their fifties to have chil-

dren than not at all? Are they undoubtedly going to be worse mothers because of her age? Can we legislate against those rare women
who have a child naturally in their fifties? Is this a matter of personal
choice once the technology has been established?

Or take the issue of unborn foetuses as mothers. To some, this
seems to be pushing out the boundaries of science too far. To others,
it seems that at last we have a use for those unwanted creatures,
deliberately got rid of by their mothers. To still others, there is something unethical in using the foetuses of women who did not want
their children, to create others for women who desperately desire
them. Would it not be simpler to stop the abortions and give the children to those who want them? How does one tell a child that its
mother never lived? Or do we mistake this longing for children, failing to realise how important it is that the child has at least the genes
of one half of the couple that will become its parents?

We do not yet know the answers to these questions. Suffice it to
say that our tradition simply gives us some clues, about the value of
human life, about the value of the gift of children, about the feeling
that God is a participant in the creation of children. But those are
only signals. The debate is yet to be had. We must share in it, with
our respect for children, our desire for them, and our sympathy, ages
old, for women unable to have them. In the end, we believe that scientific advance is in itself a gift of God, but whether that means
allowing all the research, all the advances, to go unchecked is
another matter. For we live in an age when hardly a day goes by
without another news story about some great advance, all too often
in this field of assisted conception or genetic engineering. Some feature or other of the human personality is found to be genetically
transmitted. Recently, there were accounts of genetic predisposition
towards homosexuality, with the apparent discovery of the gene concerned. This led to the former Chief Rabbi, Lord Jakobovits, suggesting that if it were possible to genetically engineer that gene out of
future children, parents might choose to do so. The furore cased by
that view was considerable; the reaction from the gay community
was understandably hostile, and cries of 'eugenics' were heard
throughout the land.

The problem is that eugenics got its bad name with good reason.
Its history is appalling. In the 1920s, discussion of racial hygiene was
commonplace. Compulsory sterilisation of mentally ill and handi-
capped people seemed perfectly acceptable in the USA, and Marie
Stopes herself was concerned to limit the breeding of the very poor.
There was undoubtedly a sense that it was right to create the perfect
human beings – in one's own image – and to limit the breeding of
others. When the Nazis came to power they took on what had

already become a respectable view of mercy killing, as propounded by Ernst Haeckel (1834-1919), the scientist and philosopher. They set up the General Foundation for Welfare and Institutional Care, or T-4 as it came to be known, consisting of doctors and psychiatrists, and carried out 70,000 killings of men, women and children in institutions before the programme was stopped as a result of protest, largely from clergymen. That added to the Nazi attempt to eliminate certain other groups – notably Jews, gypsies, and homosexuals – with the result that the resonance of eugenics is far from happy.

Yet genetic engineering implies eugenics, of a very sophisticated kind. If we can remove or repair one gene, we might be able to prevent cystic fibrosis, for instance, a heart-rending condition leading to early death for many people. We might be able to deal with Tay-Sachs disease, a fatal disease for the children of some Jews from eastern Europe. We might also be able to do something about the genetic element in other, commonplace diseases.

For instance, evidence is growing that women are considerably more likely to develop some forms of breast cancer if their mothers or sisters have it. There is a genetic component, though its extent is unclear. Increasingly, that component can be identified. One woman in Britain recently had a double mastectomy for preventive reasons, since she was seen as being at such a high risk genetically speaking. If we were able to pinpoint more accurately those women at very high risk, we might be able to treat them preventively with more accurate targeting than at present. We could watch them very closely too, since early diagnosis leads to a better prognosis. And, if we were more accurate about our picture, we could work more directly on the women concerned to develop a form of genetic treatment to counter their increased risk, or even alter the gene so it did not carry the risk at all.

We are not there yet, but the gradual ability to screen, and increasingly to engineer, makes such possibilities more likely. All these investigations, and experiments, rely on assisted conception techniques. Embryos will have to be treated – the defective gene removed or altered – and then replaced. Few people would quarrel with doing something for people with cystic fibrosis. Still fewer would quarrel with doing something to halt the relentlessly-growing death rate from breast cancer of women in the UK and worldwide. But genetic engineering nevertheless raises a variety of ethical issues, which impinge quite considerably in the debate about assisted conception as a whole.

First amongst these is the question of creating 'perfect' human beings. Some of our talents may well be genetically transmitted – such as our degree of musicality, for instance, or our mathematical ability – as well as some of our defects. A world a century hence when genetically-transmitted diseases have all been virtually eliminated might see the genetic engineers' attention turning to creating geniuses of one sort or other. There have already been sperm banks in the USA which sell the seed of Nobel prizewinners to ambitious would-be parents, so such a picture is not entirely unrealistic. And the mixed race couple where a black woman and a white man had donor gametes for fertility treatment, and elected to produce a white baby, was thought to be another form of selecting a 'designer' baby, in some people's views.

Many of us are uneasy about some of this. The use of genetic engineering to provide healing is one thing, morally speaking. Even that requires strict legal and ethical governance, with full consent and the maintenance of confidentiality. But the creation of super-children is quite different, or children of one race rather than another, and begs many questions, including what value is put on those of us who are less than 'perfect'. William Rees-Mogg wrote in *The Times* (13 December 1993) that he would not have cared to have been part of an experiment to produce 'a pool of exceptional general talent, from which some of pre-eminent talent will come.' His reasons are mixed, but he hopes it will not happen in his lifetime.

If it is not to appear in his lifetime and ours, we must take care to regulate assisted conception, genetic engineering, and particularly gene therapy in humans. Gene therapy is now vetted after the Polkinghorne Committee considered it in depth. But even if regulations are strict in the UK, other countries will not be so demanding. Assisted conception techniques are mostly regulated in the UK by the Human Fertilisation and Embryology Authority, but are not necessarily regulated elsewhere. The combination of assisted conception and gene therapy is where abuse could take place, and also where public understanding has not yet caught up with the speed of scientific advance.

For the eugenicists may be in the ascendant in some countries where the birthrate is too high, where parents are only allowed to produce one child, where infertility treatments are growing, and where the prospect of the 'perfect' child seems remarkably attractive. But, however careful geneticists are, mistakes can happen, and it is a new field. One does not have to be a science fiction addict to fear the rogue gene, or simply the gradual breakdown of genetic material as one moves further away from Mother Nature. Strict controls are necessary, with some international force. However, so is a public debate about what is acceptable; nationally and internationally.

This has not yet happened in the field of genetic engineering, where progress has moved faster than the public ability to comprehend. In genetic screening, however, we have the beginning of a genuine public debate, as the result of work conducted by the Nuffield Commission on Bioethics, with its report published in December 1993. For the first time material has been put before the public for debate. Should insurance companies be able to require genetic screening, when it would materially affect policies? How should society deal with confidentiality? Should screening ever be required by employers? These are some of the questions with which we have to grapple, as we do in the field of the engineering itself. But there is an urgent need for the debate to move on genetic engineering, so that people can decide what kinds of interventions are acceptable, and what not, what we should try to prevent, and what not, and who, ultimately, should take control of this fascinating, but deeply disturbing, series of scientific advances.

The Jewish community, with its emphasis on life and healing, has much to contribute to this debate. But it cannot be waged on traditional orthodox-versus-reform lines. It is no longer relevant to talk about the use of donor insemination other than by husband as adultery, for it could be that it will be donor insemination by the husband, with gametes considerably changed by genetic manipulation. It may be right to argue against replacing more than one fertilised egg in in-vitro treatment of women, but when those eggs have been genetically treated to remove or alter a defective gene which would lead to appalling suffering for any ensuing child, is it still right to say only one at a time, when chances of implantation may be very low? What balance do we regard as correct between the desires of parents to have children, and preferably healthy children, in order to fulfil the *mitzvah* of being fruitful and multiplying, and the necessary research work that would have to be carried out necessitating the eventual destruction of many human fertilised eggs?

These are the debates we need to have in the Jewish community, and our traditional sources help relatively little. They take us a little way down the path, but they do not solve the challenge of dealing with instinctive revulsions by looking for benefits, and arguing against interfering with God's handiwork, when we do that all the time in our general healing and healthcare process.

These are not easy questions, and our attitudes towards assisted conception and to genetic engineering in its wake are unformed. What we have to do is be prepared to have this debate, to recognise that traditional sources may not help though traditional life affirming attitudes will, as will attitudes to childlessness, and be brave enough to come out saying that many of these advances are for the good of us all, provided we discuss them, regulate them, and learn to understand the science.

# Selected Bibliography

Bleich J.B., *Contemporary Halakhic Problems*, vol. 1 1977, Chap. V 'Medical Questions' and Chap. XV 'Abortion in Halakhic Literature'. Ktav Publishing House Inc. and Yeshiva University Press, New York/Hoboken.

Block R.A., 'The Right to Do Wrong: Reform Judaism and Abortion', pp. 3-15 *Journal of Reform Judaism*, Spring 1981.

Brickner B.,'Judaism and Abortion', Kellner, M.M. ed., *Contemporary Jewish Ethics*, 1978

Feldman D.M., *Birth Control in Jewish Law*, 1968, especially Part 5 'Abortion'. New York University Press, New York/University of London Press, London.

Freehof S.B., 'Artificial Insemination', *CCAR Yearbook* Vol. LXII, 1952, pp. 123-125.

Freehof S.B., *Reform Responsa*, 1960, pp. 217-18 'Artificial Insemination'. Hebrew Union College Press, Cincinnati.

Freehof S.B., *Contemporary Reform Responsa*, 1974, Chap. 34 'Study of Foetal Material'. Hebrew Union College Press, Cincinnati.

Freehof S.B., *Reform Responsa for our Time*, 1977, 'Fertilized Ovum Implant', p.215. Hebrew Union College Press, Cincinnati.

Guttmann A., 'Artificial Insemination', *CCAR Yearbook* Vol. LXII, 1952, pp. 125-128.

Jacobs L., *What Does Judaism Say About. . . ?*, 1973, Chaps. 'Abortion' and 'Artificial Insemination'.

Jakobovits I., *Jewish Medical Ethics*, 1959, 2nd edition 1975, Chap.14 'Controlling the Generation of Life' and Appendices 'Artificial Insemination' and 'Recent Developments in Jewish Medical Ethics'. Bloch, New York.

Klein I., 'Abortion and Jewish Tradition', Kellner, M.M. ed., *Contemporary Jewish Ethics*, 1978

Klein I., *A Guide to Jewish Religious Practice*, 1979, pp. 415-17 'Abortion' and pp. 417-18 'Artificial Insemination'. The Jewish Theological Seminary of America, New York.

Rosner F., 'The Jewish Attitude Toward Abortion' Kellner, M.M. ed., *Contemporary Jewish Ethics*, Sanhedrin Press, 1978

Siegel S., 'Fetal Experimentation' Kellner, M.M. ed., *Contemporary Jewish Ethics*, 1978

# DOWN-TO-EARTH JUDAISM:
# SEXUALITY*

## *Arthur Waskow*

What about the issues of sexual ethics that for many Jews today pose
extraordinarily puzzling and painful dilemmas in their daily lives?
Few progressive Jews – indeed, rather few Jews of almost any political and religious hue – turn to the traditional Jewish code of sexual
behaviour as an authoritative or practical guide to their own actual
behaviour. Most of us feel strongly that the tradition as it was conveyed to us does not resonate with our own values and that indeed,
for us, hardly any collective or communal ethical code could apply,
because sexual ethics depend so much on unique individual situations. So an approach paralleling what we have suggested about food
– a sort of 'Commission on Practical Jewish Sexual Ethics' – seems
laughable and neither possible nor desirable.

However, many of us do not feel we are doing so well when we
try to act totally on our own, either. Indeed, the problems many liberal and progressive Jews now face in shaping their sexual ethics is
one of the strongest pieces of evidence that a wholly individualistic
ethic, not in some sense shaped by interaction between communal
and individual needs, is destructive to individuals as well as to communities. So even here it may be useful to see whether aspects of
Jewish practice might help many of us sort out deep doubts and confusion in our sexual lives.[1]

* This chapter was first published in *Tikkun*, vol. 3., 2 March/April 1988.
1. In developing the ideas in this article I have drawn on conversations with Rabbi
   Zalman Schachter-Shalomi, founder and chair of the *P'nai Or* Religious Fellowship,
   and Phyllis Berman, president of the *P'nai Or* board. In addition, some of the ideas
   come from a pioneering article on Jewish sexual ethics in the *Second Jewish Catalog*

What is it in the tradition that we reject or profoundly question?

There are several areas in which a great deal of doubt is expressed, whether in quiet practice or in public questioning. Among these areas of doubt are:

- sexual activity by unmarried people;
- sexual activity between people of the same gender;
- sexual monogamy in marriage;
- the breadth of acceptable sexual practice in whatever kind of relationship.

We will look at each of these areas in some detail; but first let us explore why the traditional sexual ethics in these areas seem out of tune, or questionable.

For most of Jewish tradition, the link between sex and procreation was very strong – though not absolute. This connection strongly influenced rabbinic attitudes about masturbation, homosexuality, contraception, abortion, and marriage. The rabbis paid great attention to the first of all the commandments: 'Be fruitful and multiply, and fill up the earth.'

In our generation, however, it is possible to argue that the commandment has been so thoroughly fulfilled by the human race as a whole that it no longer needs to be obeyed by all human beings. The earth is filled up; we have done Your bidding; what comes next?

Since 'Be fruitful and multiply' is the command that comes at the outset of the Garden of Eden story, perhaps what comes next is Eden for grown-ups: the garden of the *Song of Songs*. The sexual ethic of the *Song of Songs* focuses not on children, marriage, or commitment, but on sensual pleasure and loving companionship. What if we were to take this as a teaching for our epoch? What if we were to look at the human race as a whole as if it had entered that period of maturity that a happily married couple enters when they no longer can (or want to) have children? They continue to connect sexually for the sake of pleasure and love – and so could the human race and the Jewish people. Without denigrating the forms of sexuality that focus on children and family, we might find the forms of sexuality that focus on pleasure more legitimate at this moment of human and Jewish history than ever before.

With this broader understanding in mind, let us turn to the specific areas in which ethical doubts and questions have arisen.

First, in regard to sexual activity by unmarried people: most Jews reject in their own practice and in theory the traditional adherence to early marriage and the traditional opposition to sexual activity by

---

by Rabbi Arthur Green, until recently president of the Reconstructionist Rabbinical College.

unmarried people. The two sentiments are connected. Few American Jews believe that early marriages are wise in our complex society, where personalities, careers, and life paths almost never jell in the teens and often not until the mid-thirties, sometimes come unjelled during the forties and fifties, and usually change again with long-lived retirements beginning in the sixties or seventies. It is hard enough to make stable lifelong marriages when one partner is changing in this way; when both are changing, it becomes extremely difficult.

There are several different conceivable responses to this situation:

1. Reverse the basic situation and restore the kind of society in which life patterns are set close to the onset of puberty and do not change much. Few American Jews believe this can be, or should be, done. The Hasidic communities, however, may be showing that for a subcommunity such a society can be created.

2. Accept the notions that first marriages will occur many years after sexual awakening and that most marriages will end while the partners are sexually active and alert – and practice celibacy for long periods of unmarried time. This is the solution that almost all American Jews have rejected. It is also, however, the solution that they identify as the 'official' position of Jewish tradition and religious authority. There are few public assertions by religious authorities or communities that this is *not* the 'correct' Jewish view, and almost no public Jewish way of honouring or celebrating sexual relationships other than marriage exists.

This chasm between the practice and the understanding of the Jewish tradition may be one of the most powerful elements driving most Jews in their pre-married, sexually active years – from sixteen to thirty-one – and in their 'postmarried' sexually active years away from Jewish life. Who wants to be part of an institution that looks with hostility or contempt on the source of much of one's most intense pleasure, joy and fulfilment?

3. Accept the fact that life patterns will change several times in any person's lifetime and that marriages will change accordingly, and greatly change our expectation of 'marriage' so that it carries fewer burdens of financial, emotional and other involvement. In other words, make it easy for sexually active people from puberty on to enter and leave marriages – make marriage a much 'lighter' contract unless children result from it. But to make marriages 'light' enough so that sixteen-year-olds or eighteen-year-olds could easily enter them, expecting to exit from them at twenty – and to enter and exit again at twenty-one, twenty-five, twenty-eight, thirty-two – would make that kind of 'marriage' so different from one that provides an adequate context for child-rearing that it is hard to imagine the two sharing the same name. (Note that many American marriages are dissolving even during the child-rearing years. Should

leaving marriages be 'light' then too? Or is the distinction one that most Jews would want to keep?)

For those Jews who try to abide by *Halakhah*, it might be easier to use the traditional labels and forms of marriage and redefine the content than to follow the paths listed above or those listed below. The Talmud, for example (*Yebamot* 37b), mentions that a few of the rabbis, when they went on what we could call lecture tours, would marry a woman one night and divorce her the next morning. In that period, of course, men were permitted to practice polygamy – so such a practice of 'light' marriage did not undermine simultaneous 'heavy' marriage – at least not in law.

4. Accept and publicly honour the fact that many unmarried people are sexually active and that there are likely to be periods of 'fluidity' in sexuality during any life path – without creating standards of ethical behaviour for unmarried sexual relationships or creating ceremonial or legal definitions of them. This is basically the pattern followed by the burgeoning *havurot* (participatory and relatively informal congregations of prayer and study). In many of them, married couples and unmarried people who are fluidly coupled and uncoupled share the same communal space. Acceptance of unmarried sexual activity has been high and public, with little effort to set standards or to deal with painful experiences except among close friends or with the help of psychotherapists who themselves use only such 'Jewish' sources as Freud, Reich, Fromm and Perls.

This solution is not as opposed to Jewish tradition as many of us suppose, for there are many references in the traditional literature that legitimate sex between unmarried people. (See, for example, in the thirteenth-century Nachmanides – No. 2 in Responsa – and in the eighteenth century Rabbi Jacob Emden, cited in Gershon Winkler, 'Sex and Religion: Friend or Foe?' in *New Menorah*, second series, No. 7, pp 1-3.) But the main definitive statement of traditional law in the last four centuries – particularly in the popular Jewish consciousness in Eastern Europe whence most of our grandparents came – ignored these permissive authorities.

5. Redefine marriage and create new Jewishly-affirmed forms of sexual relationships that are to be publicly defined with certain standards and are to be ceremonially honoured. Certain vestiges of ancient tradition might even be drawn upon for such new forms – the *pilegesh* relationship, for example, which is usually translated 'concubine' but has great openness to legal, practical and ceremonial definition.

We could imagine three different basic forms of sexual relationship:

a. Times of great fluidity, when the community might affirm only such basic norms as honesty and the avoidance of coercion, without expecting monogamy or emotional intimacy;

b. Times of commitment without great permanence, when notice of a *pilegesh* relationship is given to a face-to-face Jewish community – not to the state – and is defined by the people entering it (explicitly monogamous or not, explicitly living together or not, explicitly sharing some financial arrangements or not, etc.). In this pattern, the community joins in honouring, acting in accord with, and celebrating such arrangements, and there is an easy public form by which either of the parties may dissolve the relationship.

c. Times of marriage, which may also be partly defined by the couple through the *ketubah*, but which are expected to be more long-lasting, to be essential for child-rearing (though used also by couples who do not expect to have children), and to be dissolved only by joint agreement of the couple and by serious participation of the Jewish community as well as the civil order in arranging the terms of separation.

This last approach, it seems to me, takes the complexity of our present situation and the resources of Jewish tradition most fully into account. But it would take more than a piece of paper announcing *pilegesh* for this approach to begin functioning. Let us come back to the necessary institutional processes after we have looked at the other areas of doubt that exist in our practice of sexual ethics.

There is much less agreement about sexual relationships between men, or between women, in the Jewish world than about heterosexual relationships between unmarried people. Many American Jews – probably a majority – support guarantees for the civil and employment rights of gays and lesbians. What seems to be a growing minority is ready to assert that a gay or lesbian life path can be a fully and authentically Jewish life path. Somewhat fewer are ready to act in such ways that would allow publicly gay and lesbian Jews to become rabbis, communal Jewish leaders, members of broad-spectrum congregations, and celebrants of life-cycle transformations such as weddings.

The written texts of Jewish tradition and most of the actual practices of the majority of Jewish communities are more heavily weighted against the public acceptance of gay and lesbian life paths than they are against the acceptance of sexual relationships between unmarried heterosexuals. When we look at the most ancient texts, however, some of them may turn out to be slightly more ambiguous than we are used to assuming. For example, what are we to make of the fact that the Bible gives us no obvious prohibition against lesbian relationships? What are we to make of the Bible's celebration of David's love for Jonathan – whose 'love was more pleasing than the love of women'?

There can be no doubt that during the rabbinic era of Jewish history most communities and rabbis were strongly hostile to homosexuality on the part of men or women. Yet even in the rabbinic era,

Jewish practice may not have been so single-valued as we usually assume. During the Golden Age of Jewish culture in Spain, more than one of the greatest liturgical poets of the period, whose poems grace our traditional *Siddur*, also wrote poetry of homosexual love. Did these poems rise out of life experience, or only out of literary convention? Even if the latter, what does that say about our assumptions regarding Torah-true Jews and Judaism?

For us to think intelligently about these questions today, we must go beyond biblical texts and rabbinic rulings – even beyond our own midrashic understanding of the texts – to try to hear what may have been the hopes and fears that were at stake; to take them seriously; and then to see where we ourselves come out, trying to hold together all the values that are bespoken by Torah and Jewish life.

Two of the strongest strands of Torah are the hostility to idolatry and the importance of having children. Indeed, one of the deepest traumas of the Jewish psyche seems to have been the fear of not being able to have children – as expressed in the stories of Abraham and Sarah, Isaac and Rebekah, Jacob and Leah and Rachel. The story of slavery in Egypt focuses on the danger that children would be murdered. So do the attacks on Canaanite religion – claiming that in it, children were 'passed through the fire to Moloch'. Whether or not these descriptions are accurate, they bespeak a deep Israelite concern for producing the next generation.

In such a culture, homosexuality might have seemed a dangerous diversion from fecundity. If, as seems likely, the practice of sacred homosexuality was also part of the worship of the surrounding 'idolatrous' cultures of Canaan, then the hostility of the Israelites to homosexuality would have been doubled. As the rabbis encountered Hellenism, with its nontheistic or polytheistic philosophies, its emphasis on the body as an end in itself, and its approval of homosexuality, the Jewish hostility to homosexuality might have been intensified even further.

If these are the concerns that underlie the traditional view, then we may see the issue differently today – perhaps in a manner closer to that of the Golden Age in Spain. We too, in the era of the H-bomb, are concerned about whether there will be a next generation. But we also live in an era of a population explosion. It is clear that the human race as a whole has much more to fear from violence and environmental destruction as threats to its children than from the failure to reproduce. It is true that the Jewish people are not experiencing a population explosion, but in an era when conversion to Judaism is at an extraordinarily high level, the actual need to procreate is not so extreme, even for Jews. What is more, gay and lesbian Jews have been exploring the possibility of having children and rearing them as Jews. So the reproduction issue is not nearly so problematic for openness to homosexual practice as it once was.

As I have already suggested, we may live in an era when the sexual ethic celebrated by the *Song of Songs* – an ethic of sexual pleasure and love – comes into its own alongside the sexual ethic of family. It may seem ironic that the *Song of Songs*, one of the greatest celebrations of heterosexual sexuality in all of literature, might be taken to affirm the homosexual community's bent toward sex as pleasurable and loving rather than as procreative. But sometimes ironies bear truth. If any community of Jews in our epoch embodies the values of the *Song of Songs* (taken at its literal meaning, not allegorically), it is the community of gay and lesbian Jews. Perhaps in our epoch, then, the despised and rejected gay subcommunity may turn out to be the unexpected bearer of a newly-important teaching. As the tradition teaches, sometimes the stone that the builders rejected becomes the cornerstone of the Temple.

In this light, it is especially poignant that the sexual ethics of commitment and family have taken on new seriousness within the gay community as a result of the impact of AIDS. It is as if the two ethics, ghettoized from each other and embodied in separate communities, have now formed a more holistic sexual ethic that can incorporate the values of family, commitment, procreation, sensual pleasure, and loving companionship.

If another of the ancient Jewish objections to homosexuality was the belief that it was connected with idolatry or Hellenistic philosophy – today it seems clear that homosexual practice accords with the same range of dedication to and rejection of honesty, modesty, fidelity, intimacy, spiritual searching, holiness and God as does heterosexual practice. If multiple sexual partnerships, as reportedly practiced in certain specific gay male subcultures, seem incompatible with most Jewish values, then care must be taken both to avoid categorising all homosexuality in that subculture and to note that there exist similar heterosexual subcultures in our society as well. In other words, if the basic value at stake is some level of stability and focus in sexual relationships, then that value ought to be affirmed without regard to the sexual orientation of the partners; and it is also important to be clear about whether we will respect a 'time of fluidity' in sexual practice of the kind that we already have sketched.

Two other factors recently have come into play that have their own connections to values of Torah. One is the discovery that for some large proportion of gay men and some (perhaps smaller) proportion of lesbians, homosexuality is not a matter of choice -but of identity set either genetically or very early in life. For those who continue to accept the traditional understandings of *Halakhah*, this discovery has brought into discussion the Halakhic principle that absolves of 'sin' those who act under compulsion. At a more Aggadic level, this relatively new discovery raises the question of whether a community that has celebrated the *Song of Songs* as 'the Holy of Holies', imagined its own relationship with God as that of spouse and lover, and refused to make a virtue of heterosexual celibacy ought to be insisting that someone whose deepest sexual identity is homosexual and who cannot experience sexual pleasure with a partner of the other gender should choose a life of celibacy or of privatised, closeted, stifled sexuality rather than one of publicly affirmed homosexuality.

The other new factor is an increasing sense that gay men and lesbians are an oppressed community, 'strangers in the land' as we were strangers in the land of Egypt, fellow victims (though not in the same way) of the Nazi Holocaust, and therefore to be treated as the Torah commands that 'strangers', the excluded and oppressed, be treated: with love, respect and equality.

Once we have noted the Torah's demand that the stranger be treated with justice and love, we should also note that it may be precisely the 'strangeness' of homosexuality that is at the root of the fear and hatred that has been expressed toward it. Perhaps it is not the desire for children nor the hatred of idolatry that has been the root of the rejection of homosexuals – but rather the fear of what is different, strange, queer. ('What do they *do* in bed, anyway?') Especially the fear that 'I myself' am somewhat different, strange, queer – different from the person I have advertised myself to be. The deep fear that when I take a close look at the strange face of the stranger, it will turn out to look a great deal like the strange face in my mirror. The Torah repeats the command to love and respect the stranger thirty-six times – a hint that this command is not easy to obey. We could honestly face its difficulty, and then persevere in our perennially difficult task of embodying Torah. So in our generation it may be necessary for the Jewish community as a whole, in the light of *all* these values, to re-examine its attitudes toward gay, lesbian and heterosexual Jews. Is there a way to reaffirm the importance of raising the next generation of Jewish children without denigrating homosexual practice – indeed by affirming the right, the ability and the duty of *all* Jews to join in that work? Is there a way to develop an ethic of sexual relationships that takes into account the experience of gay and lesbian as well as heterosexual relationships, while the ethic itself addresses the quality of the relationship – not the gender of the partners? Is there a way of celebrating God as Lover and Spouse with images that work for Jews of all sexual orientations?

In my judgment it is possible and desirable to move in these directions – to re-examine ways in which all the values of Torah can be upheld, rather than upholding some (such as fecundity) while shattering others (such as free and equal participation in the community) for part of the Jewish people. On such a path, the values that seem to have been the reasons for celebrating heterosexuality do not need to be discarded. On such a path the choices do not need to be 'either/or' – but 'both/and-what-is-more'.

If this is the path that a new Jewish sexual ethic is to take, we will need to work out ways for congregations and communities to open up prayer, life-cycle celebration, *tzedakah, shalom bayit,* and other aspects of Jewish life to full and public participation by gay, lesbian, bisexual and heterosexual Jews. No matter what sexual ethic we develop about the nature, techniques and celebration of different forms of sexual relationships, it could be applied equally to sexual partnerships regardless of the gender of the partners. Homosexual marriages, homosexual *pilegesh* relationships, and homosexual 'fluid' time could all be treated in the same way as their heterosexual equivalents.

The question of what sexual ethic should operate within a marriage is another area of doubt. The asserted norm, for most Jews, continues to be sexual monogamy and fidelity for married people. But a sizeable number violate this norm in practice, and the community is certainly unclear what sanctions to apply. Should known adulterers be expelled from congregations? Denied leadership offices? Denied honours such as being called up to read Torah? Admonished privately? Treated as if their sexual behaviour were irrelevant?

The question becomes more complicated when some argue that the norm is disobeyed in practice not because people are perverse, but because the norm is untenable – at least for many couples. Should couples then make their own decisions whether their particular *ketubah* requires monogamy? Are sexual relationships outside marriage 'adultery' only if the partners entered a commitment to monogamy, and one then betrays that commitment? Or does the community as a whole have a stake in affirming that a 'marriage' should be monogamous?

A very few voices have suggested approaching the question by drawing on one of the oldest strands of Jewish sexual ethics – the openness to certain forms of polygamy. Until one-thousand years ago among Western Jews, and until a few years ago among Eastern Jews, it was legitimate, though unusual, for men to have more than one wife. Was there any wisdom in allowing this possibility? Because one of the main reasons it was abandoned was the protection of women, who were deeply unequal in status, does the reason for the prohibition of polygamy still stand, or do changes in the status of women suggest that instead the prohibition be ended and men and women both be allowed to take several mates? (For those who would like to avoid a radical break from traditional *Halakhah*, the latter decision would be a great deal harder to accomplish.) Or, since the other main reason that polygamy was forbidden to Western Jews was that it exposed them to contempt in Christian eyes, does the incredulity or ridicule that the notion provokes in many people suggest that polygamy is still viewed with contempt in the West and should still be avoided – that *de facto* adultery is less dangerous than *de jure* polygamy?

To point out how hard some of the questions about 'adultery' are, consider the following hypothetical case: a well-known leader of the Jewish community approaches his rabbi and the lay leaders of his synagogue. He has been lovingly married for many years. His wife has for several years been institutionalised with a debilitating and disabling but not fatal illness. He has cared for her with love and devoted attentiveness. Her illness has now been diagnosed as incurable. He does not wish to divorce her, for that would damage her both financially and emotionally. Yet he cannot bear to live forever lonely. He has come to love another woman and wants her to live with him and be his sexual and emotional partner. What is the view of the congregation?

Should the Jewish community force this leader to retire rather than let him carry on such a relationship, considering his high visibility in Jewish and public life? Or should he be retired simply on the ground that adultery is forbidden? Should the community tolerate his life path, provided he leads it in secret? Should it insist that he divorce his wife? Should it affirm his choices as being in accordance with Judaism under the circumstances? Or should it perhaps refuse to decide at all, and leave the whole matter to individual conscience?

Even in less agonising situations, some who assert that they do in fact live by the monogamous norm and some who assert that they have agreed to 'open', non-monogamous marriages both report enormous social pressure against their decisions. Among the monogamous, some report that in a society suffused with sexual attractions, even close-knit Jewish communities do not act fully supportive of their commitment to monogamy, but that some members of the community act both sexually seductive and politically contemptuous, as if such a commitment were old-fashioned and repressive. Some also report that when they seek emotional intimacy outside marriage, not intending to include a sexual relationship as part of the intimacy, both they and their friends find it hard to draw the lines.

As for those who assert that their marriages are 'open' and non-monogamous, some also report that their communities treat them with derision or fear, and some report that they experience intense jealousy and fear of loss. In both groups, some say ruefully that hypocrisy turns out to be more comfortable to live with than either a clear commitment to monogamy or non-monogamy in theory as well as in practice.

Finally, there is the area of doubt about specific sexual practices in any relationship, without regard to who the partner is. Here again, the tradition is more permissive in some areas than some modern Jews assume – though in other areas a great deal more restrictive than most modern Jews would accept in their life practice. For example, some of the rabbis have for centuries approved of both oral and anal sex where the partners find these the source of greatest pleasure. (See, for example, Maimonides, *Mishnah Torah Hilkhot Issurei Biah*, 21:9, cited in Winkler, *New Menorah*, Second Series, No. 7.) On the other hand, the rules of *niddah*, prohibiting sexual relations during the menstrual period (and a good many days afterward) have been a clear biblical-rabbinic tradition. Most liberal and progressive Jews see *niddah* as a regressive rejection of femaleness in that it rejects menstruation as an 'unclean' time and process; but in our generation it has been explained by Rachel Adler as a way of honouring the uncanny edge of life-and-death that is involved in menstruation's casting off of a viable egg cell, and by others as a way of creating a rhythm of separation and renewal between two sexual partners. Similarly, the opposition of much of Jewish tradition to the use of some forms of contraception has been rejected by most liberal and progressive Jews.

Discussions of *niddah*, however, have turned up suggestions of ways to affirm some of the values that may be at stake without denigrating women. When one couple who were in disagreement about the question asked for help from a feminist leader of the movement for Jewish renewal, she suggested that they explore separating sexually for the days of *Rosh Chodesh* – the new moon – rather than at the time of menstruation. In this way they could experience the rhythm of separation and return without focusing on menstruation. Others have suggested refraining from sex for just a day or two of the menstrual cycle, thus honouring its occurrence without defining it as unclean.

The more basic possibility underlying these responses is that they come not from law or judgmental sentiments, but from nurturing wisdom, seeking to reconcile deeply held values that did not need to be seen as contradictory and drawing on Jewish tradition in new ways without rigidly obeying strictures that have risen in the past. In a sense, the feminist whom the couple consulted acted as a rabbi not judging as part of a *beit din* (house of legal judgment) but as part of a *beit rachamim* or *beit chesed* (house of nurturing love) or perhaps a *beit seichel* (house of prudence). Pursuing this approach on matters of sexual ethics could be one of the most important steps that Jewish communities and congregations could take. Imagine how different attitudes toward the rich fabric of Jewish thought and practice might become, and how unnecessary the desperate loneliness of people now faced with decisions they see as utterly individual, if every synagogue and *havurah* were to create a panel of women and men noted for their practical *chesed* and *seichel* from whom a person or a couple in an agony of doubt and pain over sexual issues could choose one or a few people with whom to counsel.

We might even consider making it a matter of communal ethical agreement and obligation that before undertaking a major change in sexual relationships, congregants were required – not simply encouraged – to consult with such a *beit chesed*. Whether they followed its recommendations would be up to them. The legal obligation would go not to the content but to the process of consultation. Such an understanding suggests one way to resolve the tug between individual and communal desires.

The decision to create such *b'tei chesed* might begin in any congregation – and if it worked, would spread. Some of the other decisions I have suggested – for instance, a clear and public affirmation that there are three different 'times' or kinds of legitimate and holy sexual relationships, the clarification of *pilegesh* relationships, the clear legitimation of homosexual relationships – would require statements by authoritative individuals or groups in Jewish life. Even the clarification of the process of ending a Jewish marriage would require not only a new decision by the Reform movement to insist that a *get* or Jewish divorce is necessary along with a civil divorce to end a Jewish marriage – but a decision by *all* branches of Jewish life to issue a *get* not simply as a formula, but after serious consultation with the couple on the conditions of the end of the marriage.

[The remainder of this article addresses certain practical issues about the implementing of these ideas, together with those discussed in the previous part of the article. Questions raised by Dr Waskow specific to the topic of this book are addressed in the following critique by Rabbi Daniel Landes and in Dr Waskow's subsequent response. – Ed.]

# Judaism and Sexuality*

## Daniel Landes

Arthur Waskow's 'sexual teaching for our epoch' – the 'fluidity' of 'sensual pleasure and loving companionship' – represents the triumph of the 1980s I/It Zeitgeist. The other in a relationship is reduced to an object of desire only to be discarded as one's own 'life pattern' mysteriously changes. This is an ego-centred ethic in which the measure of all people is how they can aid or delight the self. Not surprisingly, this places 'marriage, family, and commitment', exemplified by the Adam and Eve 'procreation story', at the opposite end of the spectrum of values. Waskow embraces, instead, the *Song of Songs* as the paradigmatic promise of perpetual orgasmic bliss. In doing so he paradoxically belittles sexuality's importance as he romanticizes its nature. He fails to realise that far from being only a means toward personal fulfilment, sexuality, as an eternal and problematic dialectic between alienation and integration, is rooted in the human's essential nature.

Sexuality is at the core of human identity. In Genesis, human creation is described as both singular and dual: 'And God created Adam in His image, in the image of God He created him; male and female He created *them.'* (1:27) Reading this literally and with a view to the later emergence of Eve, one *midrash* arrives at this psychological insight: Adam was 'bisexual and double faced with each identity back to back.' The human is composed of a twofold nature – apparently whole, but actually, and tragically, unfulfilled. True sexuality is not internally focused, but rather relational, directed outward toward one who is strangely familiar but totally different: *ezer ke'negdo*, 'a helper who stands in opposition' (Genesis 2:20). Adam is split into two separate identities so that he might eventually (re)discover his other (self) with this cry: *Zot hapa'am 'etzem mei'atzamai u'basar me'bisari.* 'At this moment, essence of my essence, flesh of my flesh!'

Sexuality at its root is consciousness. The biblical term for sexual congress is *yada* – 'to know'. Adam's declaration discloses the para-

*This article was originally published in *Tikkun*, vol.3, 2 1988.

doxical consciousness of sexuality – that at the moment of integration and wholeness, it is simultaneously a fleeting *zot hapa'am* – 'at this moment'. The human must find her/himself in the other, but because it is the other, achieved unity disappears.

*Halakhah* is acutely aware of this dichotomy of sexual being. Its method is not the overcoming of separation for a constant unification. The perceived task is for the couple to live together in both realms. *Taharat ha'Mishpachah* – the rhythm of family purity rather than the bridging of the two realms radicalises their very nature. Functionally understood, *tumah* is 'physical alienation' while *tahurah* is 'potential [re]integration'. For reasons of *kedushah* ('Holiness' – literally, 'separation'), not personal abhorrence, partners uncouple and retreat and must relate to each other from within that ground of physical alienation. They cannot push aside an argument with a kiss nor can they rely upon passion to mask differences. By being friends first, and only then lovers, they re-enact primordial separation and (re)discovery.

To live such a life with a helper who stands in opposition is not simple. The story of what it takes is contained within a literal reading of the *Song of Songs*. A sensitive reader notes not only a reverie of pleasure, but also the constant separating of the Shulamite and her Beloved accompanied by painful yearnings as well as a seeming inability to overcome differences. Nonetheless, at the end of the *Song*, we witness a clear anticipation of a life together. What was the problem and whence the transformation?

The Shulamite describes herself as one who has always had to tend to the concerns of others – her mother's sons – but 'my own vineyard I have not guarded' (1:6). Accordingly, she meets her beloved only in assignations, 'under the bower' (1:16) or in the 'drinking room' (2:4). The Beloved, however, makes his offer from behind the latticework of her carefully protected life: 'Arise, my darling; my fair one, come away! ... The blossoms have appeared in the land. ... Arise my darling; my fair one, come away!' (2:10–13). Her lack of response reveals the Shulamite as one who is terrified at the prospect of replacing her present life with another. She remains hidden and silent as 'a dove in the cranny of the rocks' (2:14); distant as a 'garden locked' or a 'sealed-up spring' ( 1:12). It is not that she refuses the Beloved – it is that she wants him only on her own terms. After seeking him vainly in her dreams, she runs through the empty city at night shouting questions as to his whereabouts to the watchmen. 'Scarcely had I passed them when I found the one I love. I held him fast; I would not let him go 'till I brought him to my mother's house to the chamber of her who conceived me.' (3:4). Her pursuit is solely for the purpose of holding him within in her own safe reality. Over and over again we hear her yearning lament as to the way love should flow: 'My Beloved is to me. ...'

'The Shulamite's transformation comes at the end of the *Song* as she declares 'I am to my Beloved,' reversing the direction of love. Now she can add 'upon me is his desire' – that is, I accept his challenge. Indeed, now she urges him to 'Come my Beloved. Let us go into the open. ... Let us lodge in the villages. ...' (7:12–13). She is anxious that they join in a quest for a new reality that they shall create together. This vision is so compelling that the observer can presently see them: 'Who is she that comes up from the desert, leaning upon her beloved?' (8:5). Such a life requires a total and absolute commitment to each other only – a 'love [which] is as fierce as death' (8:6).

Society's responsibility has been to cherish, nurture, and protect these fierce relationships without intruding upon them. The *dramatis personae* of the Shulamite's brothers emerge precisely at this point to consider how that can be done: 'We have a little sister, whose breasts are not formed. What shall we do for our sister when she is spoken for? If she be a wall, we will build upon it a silver battlement; if she be a door, we will panel it in cedar.' Evidently, they are successful in their loving concern, for she can respond confidently: 'I am a wall, my breasts are like towers. So I have become in his eyes a source of peace.' (8:8–10)

Nonetheless, the pressure for sexual fluidity makes me feel that the brothers have reason to worry. Members of society are constantly threatened by those who wish to employ the cloak of morality and an emotional/physical causality to appease their own desires. Listen to Maimonides in the *Fundamentals of the Torah* (5:9):

> One who has cast his eyes upon a woman becoming sick unto death [with passion]; and the doctors said: he will not be cured unless she has relations with him – he should rather die and she should not have relations with him, even if she is single. And even to speak with her from behind a partition – this is not allowed. Rather he should die ... for the daughters of Israel are not to be [considered] *hefker* and become through these matters licentious.

The claim to sexual fluidity in this case certainly has a moral element. The lovesick man faces death; does not the Torah affirm the sanctity of rescuing life by anyone, including the unfortunate woman? Nonetheless, Jewish leadership is mandated to prevent the mixing up of moral claims and social atomization, so that its vulnerable people are not subject to abuse. *Hefker* means 'ownerless' or 'abandoned', the seldom spoken of dark flip side of autonomous being. The Jewish myth enacted in *halakhah* is that no one – and today this must be extended to the sons as well as the daughters of Israel – is to be considered *hefker*. All belong to the Jewish family and are to be protected and cherished.

What is the source of a behaviour and ideology that in search of sexual fluidity views the other as *hefker*? The Talmud (*Sanhedrin* 75a) attends to this question by answering why the man doesn't simply marry the woman: 'This would not settle his mind for as Rebbe Yitzhak said: "From the day that the Temple was destroyed, the taste of intercourse was taken away and given to transgressors as it says stolen waters are sweet and bread eaten furtively is tasty".' (Proverbs 9:17)

For the obsessed man who can consider only the object of his obsession, there is no brokenness to the world. He pantingly anticipates only the moment of pleasure. Such a man has no notion of the sacrifice demanded by marriage and family, nor does he know the sanctity of commitment. For him there is only the pleasure of the stolen water and the greedily secret eating of bread. For such people, redemption, the ultimate integration, can never emerge.

# Response to Daniel Landes*

*Arthur Waskow*

To the Editor

When I opened the March/April issue of *Tikkun,* I was surprised to find that, along with my article on Jewish sexual ethics, there was one by Rabbi Daniel Landes commenting on mine quite critically. Yet after his angry first paragraph, there came an interesting and pleasant *midrash* on the *Song of Songs* which I enjoyed, and mostly agreed with. How come, I said to myself.

Instead of flinging hand grenades via the word processor, which is what all modern Jewish intellectuals are supposed to do, I called Rabbi Landes I told him that I felt misheard.

Specifically, I felt his criticism conveyed the notion that my piece had called for pure hedonism as a Jewish sexual ethic and had used the *Song of Songs* as a prooftext for a hedonistic ethic. My own sense of what I had was that both sensual pleasure and loving companionship (the two inter-twined ethics of *The Song of Songs*) ought now to have a greater weight than before in shaping a Jewish sexual ethic,along with the traditional elements of family commitment and procreation. So I had suggested that we affirm three different 'times' or seasons of sexual practice; one of fluidity and experimentation, one of loving companionship, and one of marriage.

Rabbi Landes explained that he had focused on my suggestion for a season of 'fluidity' because he thought this would be dangerously contradictory to what I was saying were my other values. As I hear him now, he is suggesting that the learning that goes with the one could undermine the learning that is necessary for the others.

This, I agree, is an important question. It seems that his and my life experience and observation lead to different conclusions on this point. Mine is that people can grow from each of these three 'seasons' and that they do not have to be seen as either/ors, but can be shaped in the direction of both/and. But I might be so much want-

* This article was originally published in *Tikkun,* vol. 3, 5, 1988.

ing both/and to be true that I am fooling myself about the possibilities. All of us will have to draw on our own life experiences to judge.

Rabbi Landes also pointed out that I had strongly criticised Jewish tradition regarding sexual ethics and that, since he affirms the tradition strongly this may have influenced his response. I understand and honour his love for the tradition. My own self-understanding is that I criticise not the tradition as it was but the continued application of it in the same form under quite new conditions. But I understand this distinction – which to me seems an important difference – may not seem like a difference at all to someone who affirms the tradition in a different way. And I also want to honour Rabbi Landes' own creative development of the tradition in looking at the *Song of Songs* as indeed (in at least one aspect) a poem about human sexuality – since, for many who affirm Jewish tradition, it would seem scandalous to view it as anything but an allegory about the love between God and Israel.

In any case, the issues between us seem much clearer to me, and it seems more possible to pursue them as 'controversy for the sake of Heaven', as the Talmud says. For myself, a next step in doing so would be to ask Rabbi Landes what are reasonable sexual ethics flowing from his understanding of the *Song of Songs* (as well as other elements of the tradition). Would he strongly recommend early marriage in our generation? If not, does he strongly urge sexual abstinence for all who are not married? If not, what criteria would he apply to ethical sexual relationships? And so on.

Finally, some notes on this old-new method of carrying on a controversy in a Jewishly decent, Godly way. It would have been a lot easier to do without a sense of shock and hurt, at least for me, if *Tikkun* had put Rabbi Landes and me directly in touch with each other from the git-go. The result might have been more still-small-voice and less thunder and lightning; would that have been so bad? Perhaps deeper truth might have emerged between us sooner.

# 'AND THEY BOTH WILL MAKE IT ...'
## Sexuality, Spirituality and Storytelling
## in the Garden of Eden*

*Howard Cooper*

## Adam's Story

It's true: I do feel guilty now, when I look back at what happened.
Perhaps I shouldn't blame myself, but I can't help it. I feel really bad
about it. Oh, it's not what you think: it wasn't eating that fruit that
was the problem. Everyone always thinks that was our great sin, that
snack we had. We knew we shouldn't eat between meals. No, that act
of disobedience wasn't the source of our guilt. Our guilt was about
something else.

But I mustn't talk for her. Eve can tell her own story. She was
always better with words than me. I was a man of few words. Still am
really. You see, that's kind of what my guilt is about: I never could
find the words, never knew how to say what I was feeling – to either
of them, her or God. I was never any good at feelings. All I could do
was name things, things I could see and touch. I did have a sort of
gift for that, I suppose. I came up with some good ones, though I say
so myself 'Hippopotamus' – that was my idea. I liked the sounds of
language in my ears: 'rhododendron', 'aponica', 'willow'.

But feelings! I couldn't talk about them. Not to save my life. And all
the time I was bursting with unspoken things: hopes and dreams and
questions and desires and passions. Torn apart I was. Feelings pulling
me everywhere, leading me nowhere, round and round, round and
round the garden ...

* This chapter was first published in pamphlet form by the Leo Baeck College in 1990.

That bloody garden! Well that's how it feels now, now we're no longer there. Such a relief to be out of it, I can't tell you. At least now we know. We needed to know. It was our salvation, even though life is harder now. There's no denying that. Consciousness is a burden. But now at least we know how little we know. We were so innocent before. We knew – nothing.

We – but I must stop this 'we'. That's something I have learnt. I can't assume I know what's in Eve's mind. I can't speak for her. That was where the problem between us really began. I always spoke for her – I never spoke to her. Not once. It's hard to believe now, but you can read the story for yourself and you'll see. It's true. I never knew how to speak to Eve.

I know now that if I had been able to talk to her, and not for her, she would never have been so receptive to the other one. He was the one who spoke to her, not me. He could *really* talk. He had all the right words. He was so smooth, so subtle, so insidious with his clever cunning words. They slipped right inside her those words. I could never do it like that. The creep. The slimy creep – well he is now, isn't he? But he was like that then, too.

I hated him, with his coiled presence, and his twisted thinking. He was never lost for words. I envied him that ease to speak his mind. I could see how she would turn to him for real conversation, for the exchange of ideas, for discussion, for the shared intimacy of language. I was envious as hell. And I felt guilty about it. I mean, he had a right to be there too, in the garden. In fact he was there before me. I couldn't bear that guilt. It came out of my envy. It felt like something inside me, persecuting me. So I suppose in the end I turned it against him, that smooth, treacherous bastard, seducing her with his words. I'm still not free of it: the envy, or the guilt.

It's probably hard for you to imagine just how tongue-tied I was in those days. But just consider what I said the first time I ever met Eve. I'd been in this deep sleep – I don't know what came over me – and when I woke I could feel this pain, in my side. And I realised what must have happened. God had been trying to find me a companion for ages. And he made all these creatures, so many I lost count of them, myriads of animals and birds, an incessant awesome flow of natural creatures, every one different: different shapes and sizes and smells. I don't know how he did it.

And it wasn't that I was so choosy, but none of them could help me with what I needed help for – which was to be creative too. I realise it now: I was envious of that God. Such an ability to create – it was mind boggling. He could create anything, everything. He did create everything. He even created me. He took a lump of earth, *adamah*, breathed on it, breathed into it – I don't know how he did it

- and there I was: *adam*, a living soul. I could never have done that! Never in a million years.

So I admit it, I was envious of Him. He was my father and my mother. I say 'he', but it didn't feel quite like that. Perhaps I should say 'she'. She was my mother and my father. That's not quite it either. I haven't ever got the language right. That's always been my problem: finding the words to express the things that matter. Amazing that envy. God spoke – and creation began. You can't imagine how I envied God all that creative potential, that ability to create a world and feed it and sustain it. God! What you could do! But I had to hide that envy, deny it. You see, I felt so guilty about those feelings. I know it was crazy but I felt that my envy could somehow spoil your goodness.

It still feels all mixed up inside. After all, you're so good, aren't you? So creative, so powerful. I hate your power sometimes. You make me feel so small, so insignificant, so inadequate. And that's where my guilt comes back again. How can I express my hatred and my envy when I'm so dependent on you? Will you stop loving me if I tell you what I really feel? Will you punish me – again?

Perhaps it's best not to think about these things. It hurts too much. I was talking about that deep sleep, wasn't I, and waking up. And then I saw her. And she nearly took my breath away. I didn't know what to say to her. You see she reminded me of God. I wasn't expecting that. I knew I'd been made in the image and likeness of God: 'male and female' I'd been told. But I'd never understood it. How could I be male *and* female?

Well when I saw her I began to understand. I caught a glimpse of something. She was the same as me, the first creature I'd ever seen the same as me 'bone of my bone and flesh of my flesh', but she was also different from me, opposite me. Meeting her felt like meeting a part of myself, a part I did not know existed. I felt that knowing her would help me know myself in new ways. And I felt that joining with her would heal the split within me. Because immediately I saw *her* otherness, her difference, I understood that I too was divided. Male and female.

It was a terrifying moment this recognition – and a liberating one – but I was so overwhelmed by what I was feeling that I had to avoid her presence. 'This is now bone of my bones, flesh of my flesh' I stammered. Then I began again: 'This shall be called ...' It was an automatic reaction really, I was so used to naming things. But this time? I didn't know what to call her. I was an *ish*, a man, and she was so similar, and it just came out: 'This shall be called *ishah*' – I just added a syllable, an empty breath – then I felt I had to explain it: '... because out of *ish*/man has been taken ...' And I wanted to say 'you'. But I couldn't. So I ended the way I'd begun: '... because out of man has been taken this'.

Pathetic really: making her into an object, right at the beginning 'This ... this ... this' was all I could say. How I wish I'd been able to say 'you' somewhere along the line. Things might have turned out very different. We might have learnt to speak to each other. As it was I lived with a fantasy. The fantasy was that we could live without words and that all we had to do was cleave to one another and we would be one flesh. Now I know it's not so easy to overcome our separateness, our differences. But in those days we were both innocent, naked, unknowing. We weren't ashamed. There was nothing to hide, no gap between how we were and how we should be.

It was only after I'd eaten the fruit that I knew that I could never return to that innocence, that naivete. I became reflective, self-conscious, conscious of having a self It was quite a shock. Of course I hadn't realised when she gave it to me that this was *the* fruit, the one which would help us discriminate, help us understand the difference between good and evil. But the effect was immediate. After I'd eaten I suddenly saw things I'd never seen before. It was a revelation, but so painful, so shameful. And the guilt grew out of it.

First of all, I hadn't spent the time with her I should have. There was a lot to do in the garden. People don't realise it, but we'd been told we had work to do in it right from the beginning 'work it and watch it' God had said. Somehow though we never did this together. After I ate the fruit I realised for the first time how separate we had been. My eyes were opened. I felt bad about what'd been happening I had ignored her. I felt naked, exposed, ashamed. There were no excuses really.

When we sewed those fig-leaves together it was really too late. We were just covering up the fact that we had never done anything together. In that one symbolic act of mutuality, of joint enterprise, I realised, paradoxically, how alone I had been, and how alone I had left her.

And it wasn't just this lack of reciprocity, because as I said before, there was also the absence of communication. I hadn't ever listened to her. I didn't know her voice. It was the strangest thing as I realised – to my shame – that we'd never spoken to each other I had this terrible feeling that something awful was going to come out of this; something dreadful would happen out of this absence of words. And it did. As I realised that we hadn't given voice to what was going on between us I thought I heard this other voice – it wasn't hers and it wasn't mine – but it was in me and it was around me and I didn't want to hear it; I was frightened of it; I was frightened of what I was beginning to understand; I was frightened of what my life would become when I had to live with this kind of knowledge.

So I did hide. But really I knew that I couldn't hide away like that from the new awareness I'd tasted. I was like a child hiding under the bedclothes, but I felt in the grip of something I couldn't control. That's what fear does I suppose. I don't think that first hiding would have been so bad, but it was that question that made it all so much worse.

'Where are you?' It felt so sad. It reached into my heart. And I couldn't answer. I knew it wasn't the kind of question that was designed to gain information.

God knew where I was, obviously. He knew everything: that's one of the reasons I envied him so much. Oh he knew all right. But the question was for me, so that I could take responsibility for myself and move beyond the guilt.

But I couldn't do it. I couldn't take responsibility for what I'd done. Instead I hid again. This time I hid inside my answer. First of all I pretended I didn't understand: 'I heard your voice and I was frightened because I was naked and I hid myself'. Then I felt ashamed of my evasion. I was turning my life into a system of hide-outs and I felt guilty and then angry and I couldn't contain it any longer. So I did what I've been doing ever since, blaming others. I blamed God and then I blamed Eve: 'The woman whom you gave to me, she gave me of the tree ...'

I was hiding from myself by blaming others. Well, do you blame me for it? 'Human kind cannot bear very much reality'. I certainly couldn't. That 'where are you?' still haunts me. Every time I hear it, I feel the guilt: all those evasions of responsibility, all those white lies and petty grievances, all that shutting of my ears to the cries of the world, all that closing of my eyes to the wonder of creation, all that hiding from the mystery of being, the hiding inside the security of certainty, the hiding inside the hiding, the hiding, the hiding, the story of my life, Adam's story.

## Eve's Story

It's strange really, but I knew right from the beginning that it was the right thing to do. Actually, I've never felt the need to apologise. I am rather proud of what I did, even though I've been so misunderstood.

Poor Adam, it took him ages to admit that he'd eaten the fruit. Not me. When God asked me what I'd done I said it straight, just a couple of words: 'the snake persuaded me – and I ate'. That was it. No excuses, no evasions, no unhealthy guilt. My conscience was clear. And it still is, in spite of all those stories they told about me.

You see, I just knew we had to do it. Don't ask me how I knew, it was instinctive I suppose. The fullness of our lives depended on us knowing what we were created to know. So my story is about consciousness; and conscience – the inner voice. I've learnt that it rarely lets me down.

So, at the beginning, I knew – intuitively – that it was up to me to take the initiative. Adam was so passive, so silent, so unable to make decisions. He found it hard to take responsibility and things *were* left to me. I took things on willingly: I had the energy, and the inspiration. I had the understanding.

No, please don't think I'm boasting The serpent recognised it all too. That's why he enjoyed my company, I think. It's true he teased me, flattered me, even flirted with me but he had a natural wisdom of his own and I respected that. And he recognised my wisdom and I appreciated that and enjoyed it. Adam couldn't really give me the mutuality my nature needed; which was a shame because I was created equal to him, his counterpart. The relationship was to be reciprocal, with each supporting and sustaining the other.

What makes me feel guilty now – though I know it's irrational – is that I think I valued my individuality more than he did his. I knew I was the culmination of God's creation, the climax of it all. Adam had no part in it. He was used, and I've always felt he secretly resented that. He was neither participant, nor consultant, not even a spectator to my coming-into-being. He had no control over my existence. I was independent of him: each of us owed our existence solely to God. What a mystery that was! The fragility of it all. What a divine moment that was – when I came into the world and ended androgeny.

When Adam spoke that first time he recognised himself for the first time as a sexual being Until that moment he was *Adam*, a human being. When he saw me he knew he was something else too, an *ish*, a male. He needed me for that.

He needed me for other things too, like helping him to see what was in front of his eyes. Like the Tree. Which was just waiting for us. Those beautiful, sumptuous, sweet-smelling figs, ripe and bursting on the boughs. That divine fruit. It was a delight just to look. Let alone the smell, the aroma, drifting across the garden at evening in the cool of the day, inviting us to look, to touch, to taste, to know: to know what that mysterious prohibition was all about. To know once and for all. To know once – and for *all*.

It was obvious it was meant for us, for our growth, our understanding. Adam cut out this knowledge. He denied what he could see and smell. He denied his wish to know. He said that we had to love God and be good and do what we were told. I felt that denied a lot. It denied his hatred of God, for instance. He certainly denied his anger at the one who had created this ever-present, ever-tempting possibility.

I don't really know what went on in Adam's heart, but I know that I loved and hated that God who planted this wonderful, desirable, forbidden Tree right where we had to see it, every day, morning and evening, when we lay down and when we rose up. It was unavoidable. And the love and the hate were unavoidable too. It felt healthy to recognise them both.

Inside myself I kept destroying that God on whom I was so dependent, and then full of remorse I would open my eyes, and look around, and recall where I was – with guilt, and then gratitude. I felt my loving feelings and my aggressive feelings were contained and containable, my passion to devour was not just destructive. Perhaps it was even desired.

So one day I decided to give God what God wanted, which was for us to eat and know and die. In spite of what was said. It was only by going against God that we would achieve the wisdom for which we were destined, for which we had been created. I knew about death already. I had seen the other trees, how they blossomed, bore fruit, the fruit rotted and fell, the trees withered and died – only to be reborn again.

The cycle of life included death: this was nature. It was second nature to me. The eternal succession of creation and destruction, the rise and the fall: it was out there and it was here in me. It was in my body, the flux of life, keeping the rhythm, keeping time

> The time of the seasons and the constellations
> The time of milking and the time of harvest
> The time of coupling of man and woman
> And that of beasts. Feet rising and falling.
> Eating and drinking. Dung and death.

I knew it all before I ate of the Tree. It's true: there was a wholeness then, an innocence. I forget how simple it all was, how undivided.

But we needed the other wisdom, the 'knowledge of good and evil' they called it, which is not about morality or sexuality – later projections onto our story they were. No, the knowledge of good and evil that we needed was our greatest divine gift: our consciousness, our ability to differentiate and discriminate.Just like God had done.Just like God wanted us to do. Had not creation itself, those wonderful seven days, those majestic seven stages, been all about discriminating? Darkness and light, heavens and earth, work and rest, male and female: God's creation was one prolonged adventure in discrimination. We had to partake of that too.

Death was the completion of God's creation. God needed us to bring that into the world. It was the one part of creation that waited upon us. I knew that.

So I ate. And gave to my man. It was my initiative, my decision. It would have happened without the snake. Our conversation may have speeded things up a little, but it had to happen – sooner or later.

I didn't consult with Adam. I didn't ask for his advice, or his permission. I was a free woman, more free in that act than I'd ever been
before. And there was no guilt.

Adam took it very badly. I felt sorry for him. He was ashamed,
like a little boy. I felt very protective towards him then and went
along with his attempts to cover up what had happened. I felt a bit
guilty about that I suppose. There was nothing to hide. I wasn't
really much of a help to him for a while. But if I'm honest – and this
bit is hard – I think that I despised him a little for what he did. He
was so passive, so bland. He ate because he was hungry. He didn't
savour the moment, hold that exquisite joy and pain of the birth of
the new. He hid inside his passivity and took on all the guilt.

He stole something from me when he did that. He made the guilt
unhealthy, neurotic. He wasn't strong enough to realise that there
had been a deliberate decision here, to eat, an ethical decision taken
to transcend the given prohibition, a decision taken in accordance
with the spirit which is the centre of our being.

I shouldn't despise that lack of understanding in him, but I can't
help it. He knew so much and yet so little that really counts. And yet
he named me well: *Chava* – Life. Although his naming me signified
a break in our mutuality, our equality, I love that name: *Chava*, the
mother of all life. For in it I recognise my power, and my potential,
my creativity and my possibility of giving life.

But I am also the mother of *all* life. So I know too my potential to
destroy. I know my depravity. I devour my own. I know my hatred;
and my hunger always for more. I know my greed: I am insatiable.
I am never satisfied. And the mother of all life knows too the pain of
birth, the dying of the day, the barrenness of night, the emptiness,
the hole, the black hole at the still centre

> Between midnight and dawn, when the past is all deception,
> The future futureless ...
> When time stops and time is never ending

The horror, the horror of it all. This too I know. This too I have
wrought. This too is my life: the story of Eve.


## The Facts: The Authorised Version and Its Correct
## Interpretation by a Surviving Witness

Ladies and Gentlemen, may I be permitted to interject a few words at
this moment? I humbly beg your forgiveness for interrupting such a
serious and important occasion, but what you have just been hearing –
and it pains me to have to say this, yet I have no choice but to forgo my

customary reticence and sensitivity in these matters – what you have just heard is the most deplorably subjective, emotive, ill-conceived collection of excuses that it has ever been my misfortune to listen to.

That mendacious, slanderous, weak little man. And that unforgivably inflated and self justifying woman! Do not be deceived, I beg you! Do not be beguiled by their cunningly constructed defences! The simple truth is that there is not a single honest word in anything you have yet heard. Believe me. I should know. I was there. I will tell you exactly how it was. The facts. This is my story. This is – pray forgive the small conceit -this is the serpent's tale.

The facts are these. They are indisputable, incontrovertible. Firstly Adam and Eve ate the fruit because of me. I was at the centre of the Garden and at the centre of the drama. I saw everything. I made it all happen. I was subtle, shrewd, sophisticated (in my own way), with a natural cunning all my own. In a word, I had style.

Without me nothing would ever have changed there. It was so boring, I can't tell you. But let me try. Just imagine it: there they were, the two of them, beautiful young lovers, not a care in the world, no desires, no needs, no shame. The poor dears, so innocent, so uncorrupted, so desirable. Especially when they cleaved to one another and became one flesh. It made me feel so ... excluded. But that's irrelevant: I was left out at the best of times. They ignored me completely. Me! Oh, I don't want you to think I minded, really, them not paying any attention to me. It didn't particularly concern me. I knew my place. I had my tree for company. Nobody could call me jealous.

So that's the picture: the two of them, innocent as the day they were born, and me, waiting, waiting to see, waiting to see what would happen, waiting to see when I could make something happen, waiting to be seen, waiting.

Second point. And remember I'm telling you how it was. The facts. Everything that happened was her fault. I've often taken the blame, but that is completely unfair, unjustified. All you have to do is read the story. She was the one who did it, not me. She was the one who responded to me: her first mistake. I just used my natural charm to beguile her with that naive little question which was so implausible she was just forced to tell me I was wrong. Stupid woman, she couldn't help herself, she just had to correct me.

I saw her eating something one day – I'm pretty sure it was a banana – so I said to her, in a casual opening-a-conversation-sort-of-way: 'Excuse me darling, didn't God say that you shouldn't eat any of the fruit around here?' Innocent question, wasn't it? Well, I held my breath, didn't know if she'd fall for it. She just looked at me at first, looked at me with that disdainful look I'd seen so often – not the

way I looked at her, believe me. Slowly, she finished her mouthful –
yes,it was a banana – swallowed, and then said, in that precise,
pedantic way of hers:

> Of the fruit of the trees of the garden we may eat
> But of the fruit of the tree in the midst of the garden
> God has said: You shall not eat of it, and you shall not
> touch it, lest you die.

Well, I knew I had her then. First she'd made the mistake of reply-
ing. I had her the moment she opened her mouth. And then that silly
mistake: You shall not touch it'. Perhaps she thought she was being
clever, interpreting the prohibition, adding to it to make it clearer for
a poor sub-species like me – she could be very condescending, you
know – but when she said that I couldn't believe my luck. Mistake
number two: elaborating on the facts, free associating, amplification
of the material.

I couldn't contain myself. I slid towards her: 'You won't die!' She
backed away of course – I don't know why I always have that effect
on people – and as she recoiled from me she tripped and, putting her
hand out to steady herself, she touched the Tree. The Forbidden
Tree. Such a delicate movement, even then, as she stumbled. Such
grace, even as she fell.

'See', I said – I was enjoying this – 'See, you haven't died just by
touching the tree. You won't die by eating from it either'. This was
brilliant, though I say so myself. Then I had my greatest inspiration.
I suddenly knew what she wanted, so I went on: 'God knows that on
the day you eat from the tree your eyes will be opened and you will
be like God, knowing good and evil'.

She had no answer to that, did she? I'd done my job. I'd slipped
inside her, subtly, surely, successfully. The rest you know. She ate.
He ate. They felt guilty. Whatever pathetic stories they tell you. They
felt guilty all right. Otherwise why did they hide? Like children
who've been naughty and daddy was going to be *very* angry.

And this is my third and final point. Even that depressed professor from Vienna got it right. Human beings are dependent, as children, on the external parental world: it protects them but can also
punish them. In adult life they create a God in the same image and
project onto Him all their childhood hopes and fears.

Even before God spoke to them, Adam and Eve were terrified,
guilt-ridden. And what did God do? It was so predictable. He punished them and threw them out. I rejoiced at that moment, exulting
in my power. I felt exhilarated. I had the Garden to myself again. It
was … Paradise.

And I like eating dust. Honestly.

## Completing the Circle: The Fourth Voice

So, now, it's my turn. At last. I'm glad – and relieved. I've been waiting a long time. I've had to learn to wait, to hold my silence. I who spoke and the world came into being have had to learn to speak only through my silence, my voice of soundless stillness.

In the beginning I thought it would all be more straightforward, the harmony of linear time and cyclical time, the spiralling progression of creation and rest: it was so beautiful a conception. I had such high hopes, for us all. I should have known better. I, especially, should have known better.

But I, like Adam, soon learnt to hide. I hid within my creation, waiting to be found. They learnt about hiding from me. I didn't blame them for that. I was disappointed in myself really, but I took it out on them. When Adam heard the question 'Where are you?' it was the question I was asking myself.

It was also his question to me, though he did not dare to voice it yet. Having eaten the fruit he slowly began to know this question I had planted in his soul.

When they ate the fruit I rejoiced, but could not let them know. My children had defeated me, and it was what I wanted, though I had not realised it. My omnipotent fantasy of total control had been the illusion it always is. And beyond the pain and disappointment of the loss of control, there was the relief Because that amount of power was frightening, and sharing the work, the responsibility for the world, was something I realised could help us both. Mutual dependence felt better than omnipotent control.

So I waited to be involved. My waiting is my hiding, my hiding my waiting I have been very disappointed though, not just by the failure to search for me, but more by the failure to search in the right way. But perhaps it was my fault. Perhaps those stories I told were too difficult. In the beginning I created stories, images, myths, pictures in words, for my children, like any parent might do, making it up as I went along, enjoying the telling, enjoying their enjoyment of my telling, my self-disclosure.

I spoke to their minds and souls spontaneously, through Torah, through stories, a great outpouring of creative energy. It was my gift. It was the way I felt we could meet most freely, most intimately, most naturally, through language and symbol and the mystery of multiplicity, the One and the many, the One within the many, layer upon layer of meaning, clues but not solutions, relishing the indeterminacy and uncertainty which is at the heart of our being.

But somehow it went wrong. When I thought I was revealing myself most openly, expressing the essential paradox of my being, always present and here and now, always absent because always more and different, you experienced this as my hiding from you. But I wasn't hiding. I was there. I am there. I will be there. That was my promise, and still is. On my life.

I think my biggest mistake was that I told the stories as if I was outside of them -the stories and the people. So they kept looking beyond themselves rather than within themselves. Of course I am beyond as well as within, transcendent as well as immanent. But that was the whole point. The paradox was the point. I felt that paradox was the most valuable spiritual possession I could give. I thought it would keep us close.

But they insisted on imposing a uniformity of meaning and possessing the one and only truth: a sure sign of weakness. When they lost their sense of paradox then all the systems and religions they constructed to remind themselves of who I was (and who they were) began to become inwardly impoverished, for only paradox comes anywhere near to comprehending the fullness of life: their life, my life – our life. Non-ambiguity and non-contradiction are one-sided. They are unsuitable for expressing the incomprehensible. They betray the essence.

I have been betrayed, but I blame myself. I am the guilty one. You see there is a place for honest guilt, for the recognition of shortcomings, for the failures to live up to who we know we could be. Guilt leads us towards consciousness and wholeness. It is part of our humanity, and part of our divinity. We are not omnipotent. We are who we are: incomplete, waiting hiding. Accepting our guilt we taste redemption.

But don't get me wrong. Again. I'm not talking about 'original sin'. It hurts me to say it but Augustine got it wrong. He seriously misread my story. I feel so sad to see how indelibly culture has been shaped by his projections onto my story sexual desire as sinful; Adam's sin corrupting all of nature and all humanity.

It's all wrong and we all know it. But I was powerless to prevent the perversion of my truth, as I always am. I had to allow him to misunderstand. He had free will. That was the point of the story – the essential freedom to choose. To choose between good and evil was to be a conscious choice. Only unconsciousness makes no differentiation between good and evil. Life needs the opposites, for without opposition there is no energy. Good and evil are simply the moral aspects of this natural polarity. The tension of opposites makes life possible: yin and yang. 'I form light and create darkness, I make peace/wholeness and create evil' – my prophet said it for me. (Isaiah 45:7).

I am what I am. I too started as undifferentiated being. Creating the world and *Adam,* male and female, was part of the evolution of my consciousness too. I was telling my story when I told the story of the garden. The differentiation between man and woman starts in the deep sleep, in an unconscious state. Our development is towards greater consciousness, the source of our freedom.

The gift of freedom: how easily it is abused. The horror is endless, unbearable. I am frightened by what I see: 'they take bribes, they rejoice at the arrival of rockets, they worship death – none of that is new. What is new is that they're not aware of any guilt, let alone sin'.

I admit it: I am more frightened than I have ever been, for a world without an awareness of sin is a world without a chance of redemption. So, if there is to be guilt, let it be the honest guilt, the true guilt, the tragic guilt, the necessary guilt, which emerges in the struggle with yourself to become yourself. Let it emerge out of your wrestling, a signpost on the journey to me.

It is true that I hide from you. But you know, even better than I, the extent to which you hide from yourself. 'Where are you?' I do not need you to become another Moses, another Mother Teresa. Something else is asked of you. And this revelation comes only if you really listen to what stirs your inmost being. Guilt emerges in your hiding from this knowledge. In the story the shame and the guilt and the harshness of my words to Adam and Eve is the burden and the *blessing* I bestow upon humankind.

So, yes, blessed is the guilt for it may lead you deeper into yourself It may even redeem you: from the evasions, the lies, the grievances, from the shutting of your ears to the cries of the world, from the closing of your eyes to the wonder of creation, from the hiding, from the mystery of being, the hiding inside the security of certainty, the hiding inside the hiding, the hiding – the story of our lives, you and me. The circle is closed. The Garden is empty. And 'the end is where we start from'.

## Notes and Bibliography

The following notes indicate the sources that are consciously evoked in my text.

*Adam's Story*
cf. Martin Buber, *Hasidism and Modern Man,* Humanities Press International, USA, 1958/1988, pp.122-28, for his amplification of the question of Genesis 3:9 'Where are you?' in the essay 'The Way of Man According To The Teachings of Hasidism'.

*Eve's Story*
cf. Phyllis Trible's revisionist essay 'Depatriarchalizing in Biblical Interpretation' in E. Koltun, ed., *The Jewish Woman,* Schocken, New York, pp. 217-40.

T.S.Eliot, *Four Quartets,* Faber & Faber, London . Excerpts are from 'East Coker' lines 42-46 and 'The Dry Salvages' lines 43-45.

*Completing The Circle: The Fourth Voice*
cf. C.G. Jung, *Psychological Reflections:* A New Anthology of his Writings 1905-1961, ed. Jacobi & Hull, Princeton/Bollingen Paperbacks,1973, pp. 245, 308, 357. Also Jung's Collected Works (RKP), Volume 11, para. 291.

The quotation beginning 'They take bribes ...' is from Heinrich Boll, *Women In a River Landscape,* Secker, 1989.

# NOTES ON THE CONTRIBUTORS

DAVID BIALE is the Director of the Center for Jewish Studies at Graduate Theological Union, Berkeley. He is the author of *Power and Powerlessness in Jewish History*, Schocken Books, New York 1987 and *Eros and the Jews*, BasicBooks, 1992.

RABBI LIONEL BLUE is a graduate of Leo Baeck College, former convenor of the *Beth Din* of the Reform Synagogues of Great Britain and a well-known broadcaster in the UK. His books include: *To Heaven with Scribes and Pharisees*, Darton, Longman & Todd, London, 1975 and *A Back Door to Heaven*, Darton, Longman and Todd, London, 1979.

DANIEL BOYARIN is the Taubman Professor of Talmudic Culture at the University of California. He is the author of *Intertextuality and the Reading of Midrash*, Indiana University Press, Bloomington and Indianapolis, 1990 and *Carnal Israel: Reading Sex in Talmudic Culture*, University of California Press, Berkeley & Los Angeles 1993.

RABBI HOWARD COOPER is a graduate of Leo Baeck College and a psychotherapist. His books include: *Soul Searching: Studies in Judaism and Psychotherapy*, SCM Press, London, 1988 and *A Sense of Belonging: Dilemmas of British Jewish Identity*, Weidenfeld & Nicolson, London, 1991 with Paul Morrison.

JOHN COOPER is a solicitor. He is the author of *Eat and Be Satisfied: A Social History of Jewish Food*, Jason Aronson Inc., North Vale, New Jersey/London 1993 and is currently completing *A History of Jewish Childhood*.

SARA COOPER is a psychoanalytical therapist in private practice. She teaches and supervises on counselling courses.

SHEILA ERNST is a psychotherapist and group analyst in private practice with the Group Analytic Network in North London. She worked at the Women's Therapy Centre in London for many years. She is co-author of *In Our Own Hands*, The Women's Press, London, 1981 with L. Goodison and co-editor of *Living with the Sphinx*, The Women's Press, London, 1987, with M. Maguire.

TIKVA FRYMER-KENSKY is the Director of the Department of Biblical Civilisation at the Reconstructionist Rabbinical College. She is the author of *In the Wake of the Goddesses: Women, Culture, and the Biblical Transformation of Pagan Myth*, Free Press, New York, 1992.

SANDER L. GILMAN is the Goldwin Smith Professor of Humane Studies at Cornell University and Professor of the History of Psychiatry at the Cornell Medical College. He is the author of more than twenty-seven books including *The Jews' Body*, Routledge, New York and London, 1991.

RABBI DANIEL LANDES holds the Roeters van Lennep Chair in Jewish Ethics and Values at Yeshiva University in Los Angeles and is Director of the National Education Project at the Simon Wiesenthal Center.

FRANCIS LANDY is lecturer in Bible at the Department of Religious Studies at the University of Alberta. His books include *Paradoxes of Paradise: Identity and Difference in the Song of Songs*, The Almond Press, Sheffield, 1983.

JONATHAN MAGONET is Principal of Leo Baeck College. He is the co-editor of *Forms of Prayer* (Vols. I, II, III,) the prayer books of the Reform Synagogues of Great Britain, and the author of *A Rabbi's Bible*, SCM Press, London, 1991, *Bible Lives*, SCM Press, London, 1992 and *A Rabbi Reads the Psalms*, SCM Press, London, 1994.

RABBI RODNEY MARINER is a graduate of Leo Baeck College, convenor of the *Beth Din* of the Reform Synagogues of Great Britain and Rabbi of Belsize Park Synagogue.

RABBI JULIA NEUBERGER is a graduate of Leo Baeck College where she teaches Introduction to Bible. She is Chancellor of the University of Ulster and chairs the Camden & Islington Community Health Services NHS Trust.

EDUARDO PITCHON is a psychoanalyst and founder of LINK Psychotherapy Centre.

HANNAH ROCKMAN is currently a clinical psychologist at the North Manchester General Hospital specialising in sexual and marital therapy.

RABBI ELIZABETH SARAH is a graduate of Leo Baeck College. Former Minister of the Buckhurst Hill Reform Synagogue she is currently the Director of Programmes Division of the Reform Synagogues of Great Britain.

RABBI SHEILA SHULMAN is a graduate of Leo Baeck College. She is the Rabbi of Beit Klal Yisrael (North Kensington Reform Synagogue) and she lectures on Jewish Thought at Leo Baeck College.

RABBI MARK SOLOMON is lecturer in Rabbinics at Leo Baeck College and Rabbi of West Central Liberal Synagogue.

DR SARA SVIRI is lecturer in Medieval Jewish History at the University College London.

RABBI DR ALAN UNTERMAN is minister of the Yeshurun Synagogue, Gatley, South of Manchester and lecturer in Comparative Religion at the University of Manchester. He is the author of *The Wisdom of the Jewish Mystics*, Sheldon Press, London 1976 and *A Dictionary of Jewish Lore and Legend*, London, 1991.

ARTHUR WASKOW is Director of the Shalom Center and author of *These Holy Sparks: The Rebirth of the Jewish People*, Harper and Row, San Francisco, 1982 and *God-wrestling*, Schocken Books, New York, 1978.

www.ingramcontent.com/pod-product-compliance
Lightning Source LLC
Chambersburg PA
CBHW060031030426
42334CB00019B/2267